"Scott Davis has put together the only how-to book that I've seen that provides a step-by-step program in building and leveraging your brand as a financial asset. It provides new insights into how your brand can drive your business."
  —Ed Farualo, vice president of marketing, CIGNA Insurance

"Managing a brand is like receiving a large inheritance, you have to leverage it with great care. I wish Davis had handed me this book before we started the Schwinn brand turnaround! It's an excellent read and sheds new light on the systematic approach to brand building."
  —Gregg R. Bagni, former senior vice president of marketing and product development, Schwinn Cycling & Fitness, Inc.

"Leading-edge brand management aligns the entire organization to deliver the brand promise and create powerful assets. Through concepts and stories, Scott brings the fundamentals of brand management to a higher level with the idea of brands as assets in a practical way."
  —Dean Adams, vice president of brand strategy, 3M

"Leaders have vision, brands have personalities, and Scott Davis captures both in this landmark book about brand asset management. Scott's keen eye and unfailingly correct marketer's instinct form a visionary book about nurturing brands into our global lexicon."
  —Joan Lewis, senior vice president of marketing and communications, Standard & Poor's

"In this era of mega-mergers, globalization and the Internet sustainable commercial success still boils down to effective brand management. Scott Davis does a remarkable job in helping the reader understand and formulate a winning brand strategy."
  —Dan Jaffee, president, Oil Dri Corporation of America

"The brand is very often the most underleveraged asset a company owns. Scott's approach to Brand Asset Management will enable companies to start to maximize the long-term growth of their company by fully realizing the level of profitability their brands offer."
  —Tim Yaggi, vice president of global brand management, Whirlpool Corporation

"Scott Davis has provided a succinct but powerful step-by-step explication of what makes a great brand tick. Packed with practical insights and vivid examples, anyone interested in building a brand or keeping theirs strong should read this cover-to-cover."
  —Kevin Lane Keller, author, *Strategic Brand Management*, and Osborn professor of marketing, Amos Tuck School of Busi

"A practical tool to help you think about your brand . . . and not just at budget time!"
    —Randy Iles, senior vice president of marketing, Pella Windows

"Scott's approach to Brand Asset Management helps Internet companies see the value of maintaining and growing a brand over time. Scott's book is one for the 21st century. As the Web becomes more crowded, and there is less and less that separates offerings, the brand will emerge as the primary point of difference. It will be the brand that drives traffic and business to successful companies' websites. *Brand Asset Management* paints a clear path on how to realize the growth that so many e-commerce companies seek."
    —Douglas Llewellyn, senior strategic marketing manager, CNET, Inc.

"Scott's holistic approach to Brand Asset Management successfully links together senior management and the future of the company with the brand. *Brand Asset Management* provides a cohesive and strategic plan aimed at driving the brand's future value as well as the overall performance of the company."
    —Dave Murphy, senior vice president of marketing and sales, *The Chicago Tribune*

"In an increasingly competitive and fragmented retail world, a consumer's ultimate choice of where to shop may come down to the brand and how well it fits with who they are and what they need. Scott Davis's approach to Brand Asset Management allows companies to clearly understand their point of difference and value and how to compete most effectively for both the consumer's share of mind and share of wallet."
    —Phil Schneider, senior vice president of sales and marketing, Pier One

"Promises and expectations. Customers of high-tech service providers need these desperately to anchor themselves in the midst of tremendous change in most every other aspect of their business. Service providers have so much to gain by embracing Brand Asset Management—and Scott Davis has just the tool to get it going!"
    —Mike Gearin, group leader in new product development, Cincinnati Bell Telephone

"Scott Davis's excellent book demonstrates his profound understanding of brand marketing and brand value enhancement. Even though we already own and manage the four leading (and only) 'power brands' in our business, we've found that Scott's book offers us a myriad of new tools, concepts, ideas, and systems to increase the value of these brand assets."
    —Chuck Berger, chief executive officer, Scott's Lawn and Turf

"No more can you give birth to a child, walk away, and call yourself a good parent than can you forge a brand, fail to manage the asset, and call yourself a good marketer. Scott Davis brilliantly shows you how to be an effective brand parent. Scott Davis is a modern day brand visionary. He proves the power of managing a brand as an asset. And teaches you how."
   —Barry Krause, president, Publicis & Hal Riney Advertising Agency

"Scott Davis takes the mystery and mumbo-jumbo out of building and maintaining a brand. A clear, concise, useable, and useful approach to branding in the 21st century. The BAM (Brand Asset Management) approach to brands and branding is a clear, concise, step-by-step approach to branding. Should be useful and usable for every organization."
   —Donald E. Schultz, author, *Integrated Marketing Communications,* and
      professor of integrated marketing, Northwestern University

"If you care about your brand—then this book is a must read. It creates new thoughts about driving the brand's importance. I was reminded about a number of steps that should be taken to care for and focus the brand on the customer perceptions. This material is particularly interesting to our organization and me, as we are moving other brands into our main brand—True Value— and this book is a guide on strategies and tactics."
   —Donald Hoye, chief executive officer, TruServ

"Scott Davis has hit a nerve with Brand Asset Management. His techniques will help companies more fully understand the potential of 'the brand' by helping them discover the true emotional benefit a brand provides. This discovery represents a level of 'consumer intimacy' that few businesses ever achieve. However, to fully develop this intimacy, a company must be true to the essence of the brand in everything that it does. If done well, the reward is loyalty—the greatest gift a consumer has to give. Like so many great ideas, Brand Asset Management is also a simple one. But don't for a minute take this simplicity for granted. I strongly recommend Davis's book."
   —Scott Lutz, vice president of new enterprises, General Mills, Inc.

"A great tool for established and new brands. Davis delivers key insights on defining, building, and leveraging a successful brand. With all the chatter about relationship management, it's important to remember the key to a good relationship is a strong brand identity and Davis outlines perfectly how to get there."
   —Debra Kennedy, director of marketing, Nokia

Brand Asset Management

Brand Asset Management

Driving Profitable Growth Through Your Brands

Scott M. Davis

Foreword by David A. Aaker

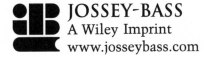
JOSSEY-BASS
A Wiley Imprint
www.josseybass.com

Published by Jossey-Bass
A Wiley Imprint
989 Market Street, San Francisco, CA 94103-1741   www.josseybass.com

Jossey-Bass books and products are available through most bookstores. To contact Jossey-Bass directly call our Customer Care Department within the U.S. at 800-956-7739, outside the U.S. at 317-572-3986 or fax 317-572-4002.

Jossey-Bass also publishes its books in a variety of electronic formats. Some content that appears in print may not be available in electronic books.

Library of Congress Cataloging-in-Publication Data

Davis, Scott M., 1964-
    Brand asset management : driving profitable growth through your brands
/ Scott M. Davis ; foreword by David A. Aaker.—[2nd ed.]
        p. cm.— (The Jossey-Bass business & management series)
    Includes index.
    ISBN 0-7879-6394-1 (pbk. : alk. paper)
    1. Brand name products. 2. Product management. 3. Brand name
products—United States. 4. Product management—United States. I.
Title. II. Series.
HD69.B7 D38 2002b
658.8'27—dc21   2002009865

FIRST EDITION
PB Printing 10 9 8 7 6 5 4 3 2 1

The Jossey-Bass
Business & Management Series

*To my parents, Ronald and Beverly Davis, who have
taught me so much about life, love, and happiness.
I only hope I can share half the wisdom with my
children that you have shared with me over the years.*

*To my wife, Debbie, who helps me live, love, and be
happy every day. You continue to make my heart feel
good, and I look forward to growing old together.*

*To my children, Ethan, Benjamin, and Emma.
You have shown me how far one can actually take
the concepts of living, loving, and happiness. You have
also shown me how far one's heart can possibly stretch.
I love the three of you more than I could ever possibly
express.*

Contents

Foreword

Scott Davis has provided thoughtful insights into the creation and management of brands in *BrandWeek* and other venues for many years. His background as an active brand consultant and an adjunct professor at the Kellogg School supports his flare for selecting important issues and providing perspectives that have substance and depth, and also marketplace relevance. In this book, he turns to Brand Asset Management which certainly should be at the heart of every company's longer-term growth strategy.

Conceptualizing brands as assets is a big idea. It can generate lasting shareholder value. And it can change the way brands are managed. But it is not easy.

Why will brands generate shareholder value? Brand power is the alternative to price competition. The story is all too familiar whether it be cars, cereals, computers, or consultancies. There is pressure on price from new entries, retail power, and from overcapacity. Competitors, especially the number 3 or 4 brands, sometimes in panic begin to provide a price proposition. As a result, consumers' focus on price and margins erodes and the whole industry turns hostile. A strong brand is the only alternative to destructive price competition. The customer loyalty needs to be based not on price but on points of differentiation, including brand personality, intangibles, emotional benefits, and self-expressive benefits.

We know that building brands pays off. There are countless anecdotes about brands such as Saturn, Apple, Harley, IBM, Budweiser, and Nike. But we do not have to be satisfied with anecdotes. Bob Jacobson of the University of Washington and I conducted two studies of the relationship of brand equity to stock return. One involved thirty-four firms such as Ford, Sears, Marriott, Coca-Cola, American Express, and Kodak where a single brand accounted for much of the firm's sales, and another involved nine high-tech brands such as Microsoft, Oracle, and Dell where brand building was often hypothesized to be of a lesser impact. We showed in both studies that actually brand equity's impact on stock return was only slightly weaker than that of reported earnings.

How does viewing brand as an asset change the ways brands are managed? First, it means that brands are to be managed at a much higher level in the organization. Brand image could be delegated to the tactical specialist, the "advertising department," or an agency. Brand equity, however, is in the purview of the CEO and CFO. They have seen vivid examples of brands being sold in the marketplace for billions. Charged with creating shareholder value, they recognize that building brands is one vehicle to do just that. Thus, top managers either become active brand builders or sponsor others in the organization who are.

Second, it means that brand management is strategic and thus the brand manager needs to be involved in creating the business strategy rather than being one of the implementers because the business strategy should be the prime driver of the brand strategy. Both business strategy and brand strategy should reflect the same strategic vision and corporate culture. In addition, the brand identity should not promise what the strategy cannot or will not deliver. There is nothing more futile, wasteful, and damaging than to develop a brand identity or vision implying a strategic imperative that will not get funded because it is not a business priority. An empty brand promise is worse than no promise at all.

Third, it means that the organization needs to be adapted to brand building. Structures, cultures, people, and systems need to be developed to promote and support brand building. There needs to be a person or group that will actively manage the brand. There needs to be a process that will ensure that a brand strategy is in place, that truly effective brand-building programs are developed, and that the use of brands in different contexts generates synergy and clarity rather than waste and confusion. All this will not happen by itself. There needs to be a commitment and a road map.

Fourth, measures of brand equity need to supplement the short-term measures that dominated in the past. These measures, commonly tracked over time, will tap the major dimensions of brand equity—awareness, loyalty, perceived quality, and associations, including dimensions such as personality, organizational characteristics, and symbols. The emphasis will be on tracking brand identity elements that distinguish and drive customer-brand relationships. This implies an in-depth understanding of the brand and the brand's relationship with its customers.

Why is it hard to conceptualize and manage brands as assets? Brand management is difficult. There are multiple brands, complex sub-brand structures, brand extensions, and global organizations all in the context of market complexities, competitive pressures, new media realities, channel dynamics, and global forces. There are few simple answers and approaches.

Further, short-term pressures on managers are intense and act as inhibitors or worse to effective brand building. The problem is that short-term measures such as sales, costs, or profits are easy to measure and will have a short-term impact on stock value. In contrast, any intangible asset whether it be people or information technology is virtually impossible to measure with comparable accuracy and reliability.

In *Brand Asset Management,* Scott provides help and guidance to those who would build brand assets and maximize their strategic and economic value. He introduces an eleven-step process that is a practical way to attract the creation of a brand strategy. Along the way, he provides a host of practical tips on how to create and manage brands. The Brand Value Pyramid encourages brand building to move beyond features to benefits and values. The BrandPicture set of concepts leads to a deep understanding of the brand's context. The House of Pricing shows readers how to leverage the premium pricing that is earned by strong brands. Scott goes the extra step by providing guidance on creating an organizational culture and measurement system to support the brand-building effort.

I envision *Brand Asset Management* becoming common nomenclature in the branding community. Your brand—and your company—will benefit from this book.

Orinda, California   DAVID A. AAKER
Vice Chairman, Prophet Brand Strategy
Professor Emeritus, Haas School of
Business, University of California
at Berkeley

Preface

When I originally wrote *Brand Asset Management* in 1999, the economy and the business world in general were booming. Dot-coms were still the rage. In fact, anything that had a technology "buzz" to it was destined for greatness, as the market was on a ride that seemed to have no end. At the time, some of the concepts in *Brand Asset Management* (which are long-term in nature) were being questioned, as many were in a "build it and they will come" mind-set with little attention paid to building or managing the brand.

Fast-forward three years, and the world is a different place. So many different events combined together have left customers confused, insecure, and a bit anxious about the world around them. These events have also left companies struggling as they try to figure out how to survive and ultimately thrive again in a zero-growth economy, with a level of scrutiny on their business practices like none seen before.

If anything positive has come out of these challenging times, it has to be the fact that so many of us are experiencing, personally and professionally, an awakening of some fundamental human values that have been asleep, perhaps, for too long. For many businesses, this awakening has forced a first-time exercise of assessing their own values and reasons for being, to better understand how to operate and compete more effectively in the future.

In the brand world this has translated into many companies focusing for the first time on defining what business they are in, determining how they can more effectively meet and exceed both customer and employee expectations, as well as waking up to a stronger desire than ever to become an authentic brand—one that is true to its core values, day in and day out, employee by employee.

Brand Asset Management has always been about doing just that: defining, managing, and measuring your brand in as thoughtful and authentic a way as possible, to drive out the most value and profits from your brand.

While not all the examples in *Brand Asset Management* tell a good story today (for instance, K-Mart, pets.com, eToys, and TheStreet.com), the principles nonetheless continue to be right on target and more relevant than ever:

- Successfully building a brand has to start with senior management defining what role the brand will play in helping the company reach its longer-term goals and objectives.
- Determining where your brand will have the highest likelihood of success, long-term, requires an extremely accurate snapshot, or BrandPicture, of where your brand is today.
- The future positioning and personality you choose for your brand and the bridge plan between today and tomorrow should provide the brand lens required to clearly make "on-brand" strategic decisions in the future—from the right new products and services to introduce, to the right messages to communicate, to the right channel strategy to adopt.
- Without the right metrics in place, which go beyond the traditional measures of awareness and recall, there is no possible way a company can confidently maximize its brand's chances for long-term success.
- Aligning your organizational structure and culture to better match what you are trying to accomplish as a company and as a brand will not be optional in the future.
- Finally, until you realize that your brand is the greatest untapped asset within your organization and needs to be thought of and managed as such, then there is a high likelihood that it will be mismanaged, underleveraged, underappreciated, and ultimately undervalued.

To my surprise, *Brand Asset Management* (which is now in five languages and its third hard-cover printing) hit a nerve around the world. I continue to get e-mails daily, thanking me for putting together such a straightforward and useful book.

Fortunately, since I wrote this book, I have had the pleasure of working directly with Dave Aaker, who is arguably the strongest brand in the brand-consulting world. We are colleagues at Prophet, the firm we work in together. Through my relationship with Dave and the rest of the Prophet team, my thinking and work on managing the brand as an asset has continued to be stretched and deepened.

As a result, I have come strongly to believe that the next "big brand thing" can only be about one topic: once companies fully appreciate the asset value of their brand and the principles within *Brand Asset Management,* then the next logical place to focus on is the effective deployment of the brand across every possible "touch-point" the brand has with its customers, stakeholders, and employees—from the first interaction with the brand, to making the sale, to building a loyalty-based relationship, post-sale.

I talk about this as a company's need to effectively and holistically manage its brand-customer relationship across every brand touchpoint that exists. The new brand mantra has to be: Every time a customer, stakeholder, or employee interacts with your brand, it is another opportunity to either reinforce what your brand stands for or denigrate it—the choice is yours. Those companies that both understand and embrace this philosophy, I believe, will ultimately win the battle of the brand and the battle for share of mind and wallet.

My new book, which comes out in Fall 2002 and is coauthored with Michael Dunn, is called *Building the Brand-Driven Business: Operationalize Your Brand to Drive Profitable Growth* and serves as a nice companion to *Brand Asset Management. Building the Brand-Driven Business* is constructed around bringing your brand and its implicit and explicit promises and messages to life, inside and outside the organization, through the greatest ambassadors your brand has: your employees. *Brand Asset Management* focuses on how to get clarity on what your brand does and does not stand for and how that answer should inform all of your major strategic decisions. I hope you enjoy the book.

Glencoe, Illinois   SCOTT DAVIS
July 2002

Acknowledgments

Anyone who has ever written a business book knows that it is usually the culmination of many people's efforts over many years. This book is the result of many client projects, client interviews, best practices studies, and countless hours of developing intellectual equity. So many thanks are owed.

To my friend Carl Bochmann, who served as my BAM mentor for several years. Carl has continued to encourage me, challenge me, push me and, importantly, has helped to remind me every January 6 how far BAM has come and how far it has to go. Thank you, Carl.

To Tom Kuczmarski, my good friend, who taught me how to not only become a good consultant but a better person. Your encouragement for more than twelve years has helped this book become a reality.

To the team that helped drive BAM forward over the years, including Darrell Douglass, Curt Wang, Jeff Swaddling, Erika Seamon, and Tom Shapiro—all part of the early team—and Cynthia Opie, Corinne Chocolaad, Dan Morrison, David Roberts, and Rick Strezo—all part of the more recent BAMers.

To Jeff Smith and Karen Daniels in particular, who are owed special thanks for their help in bringing BAM to life, both internally and externally, over the past few years. In addition, my other partners, Art Middlebrooks and Michael Petromilli, consistently lent their support and helped pick up the slack when I was in "deep writing mode."

Another special thanks to Tammy Hicks, who helped to keep me organized and sane, if that's possible, throughout the book-writing process. Eva Malecki lent her marketing brilliance, and Michelle Villgomez, Rich Hagle, and Alan Venable lent their editing skills to the manuscript, as has Carl Bochmann.

To my many BAM business clients and friends who added their wisdom to this book, including Vicky Shire, Harriet Gold, Dave Murphy, Anne Greer, Bob Roemer, David Friedman, Brad VanAuken, Brad Larsen, Jerry Dow, Amy Kelm, Cindy Bishop, Gregg Bagni, Scott Snyder, Barry Krause, Jay Luttrell, and Jean Leon Bouchenoire.

To my parents, who gave me constant support and encouragement during the process and read the manuscript often. To my wife, Debbie, who really took the brunt of this book effort by going solo in taking care of our three-year-old twin sons, Ethan and Benjamin, and our baby, Emma. And, by the way, those nights spent protecting the boys from monsters in the hallway and hiding in the basement paid off.

Finally, a special thank you to Cedric Crocker and the gang at Jossey-Bass, who truly made this writing effort a pleasure and who represent the epitome of professional publishing.

S.M.D.

Brand Asset Management

Introduction

Does Brand Asset Management^{SM} Strategy Matter?

Brands are among a company's most valuable assets, and smart companies today realize that capitalizing on their brands is important. Doing so can help them achieve their growth objectives more quickly and more profitably.

These companies know that brands are more than just products and services. They know that brands are also what the company does and, more importantly, what the company is. Usually brands are why a company exists, not the other way around.

But most companies are not maximizing their potential financial returns because they are not maximizing the power of their brands. With proper brand management, for instance, your company's sales of $100 million today can be increased by $30–50 million in five years. However, this will happen if and only if you take advantage of the most important growth weapon at your disposal: your brand.

What Is a Brand?

A brand is an intangible but critical component of what a company stands for. A consumer generally does not have a relationship with a product or a service, but he or she may have a relationship with a brand. In part, a brand is a set of promises. It implies trust, consistency, and a defined set of expectations. The strongest brands in the world own a place in the consumer's mind, and when they are mentioned almost everyone thinks of the same things. 3M invokes innovation, Hallmark stands for caring, FedEx means guaranteed delivery. Conversely, certain words connect you back to certain brands. Family entertainment conjures up Disney. Personal service suggests Nordstrom's. Irreverence represents Virgin, and individual performance most often will connect you back to Nike.

A brand differentiates products and services that appear similar in features, attributes, and possibly even benefits. Is Tide that much better than Surf? Is Starbucks that much better than Caribou Coffee? Is Sony that much better than JVC? Probably not.

What makes leading brands better is the PATH they travel in the human mind? PATH is an acronym for promise, acceptance, trust, and hope. This PATH is intangible and can be emotional. It strikes at the core of who we are as humans. Can you actually buy promise, acceptance, trust, and hope? Well, yes. A strong brand makes these intangibles tangible in the consumer's mind. Weak brands do not.

A Mercedes buyer may indeed be getting a well-engineered, durable, and reliable automobile, but is probably also paying for German engineering, prestige, and a statement that he or she has "made it."

Similarly, buyers of Nike shoes may also be after better athletic performance; FedEx users buy reassurance that whatever they send will get there on time; John Deere purchasers believe it's the best piece of machinery around; and Volvo buyers assume they are buying greater safety.

A brand is about confidence and security. On an average day consumers are exposed to six thousand advertisements and, each year, to more than twenty-five thousand new products. In such a world, brands take away the confusion. Brands help consumers cut through the proliferation of choices available in every product and service category.

The most common misperceptions managers have about brands have to do with the variety of marketing tools and tactics we are all familiar with. We may think any or all of the following are appropriate definitions of a brand:

- A brand is a tagline like "We bring good things to life."
- A brand is a symbol like that Nike swoosh.
- A brand is a shape like that Absolut bottle or that Coke bottle.
- A brand is a spokesperson like Bill Cosby for Jell-O.

- A brand is a sound like Intel's familiar four notes.
- A brand is an actual product or service—Kleenex tissue or Xerox copies or a Sony Walkman.

Sure, all these help bring the brand to life and into consumers' streams of consciousness, but in reality they are simply well-executed marketing and selling tactics.

Who Owns the Brand?

The brand is marketing's responsibility, right? But what about the customer's bill (that's the finance department's purview) or the customer who has a question (customer service) or the customer whose opinion is valued (market research) or the customer who has to have someone contact them (sales)? The customer's knowledge and perception of the brand will be formed by every manager's and employee's actions, behaviors, activities, and contacts. Indeed, the brand is owned and should be managed by every employee in the organization.

This means the brand must be enhanced and guarded at every point where the organization touches the customer, regardless of industry and regardless of company. These touchpoints build the consumer's perceptions about the brand, good or bad.

The Benefits of Effective Brand Management

Let's look at brand strength from two perspectives: customer actions and company strategies. Without doubt, customers perceive the importance of a strong brand:

- 72 percent of customers say they will pay a 20 percent premium for their brand of choice, relative to the closest competitive brand. 50 percent of customers will pay a 25 percent premium. 40 percent of customers will pay up to a 30 percent premium.
- 25 percent of customers state that price does not matter if they are buying a brand that owns their loyalty.
- Over 70 percent of customers want to use a brand to guide their purchase decision and over 50 percent of purchases are actually brand driven.

- Peer recommendation influences almost 30 percent of all purchases made today, so a good experience by one customer with your brand may influence another's purchase decision.
- More than 50 percent of consumers believe a strong brand allows for more successful new product introductions and they are more willing to try a new product from a preferred brand because of the implied endorsement.

How might your company benefit by having a strong brand? Consider the following points:

- *Loyalty drives repeat business.* It is estimated that the lifetime value of a customer of one of P&G's brands is several thousand dollars. For Coke, it is even higher. For automobile companies, it can be several hundred thousand dollars. Every additional year you keep a customer loyal to your brand, the future profits derived from that customer will be considerably higher. A recent study by Bob Pasikoff, president of Brand Keys, shows that an increase in customer loyalty of only 5 percent can lift lifetime profits per customer by as much as 100 percent. It also suggested that an increase in customer loyalty of just 2 percent is equivalent to a 10 percent cost reduction in certain sectors.
- *Brand-based price premiums allow for higher margins.* Strong brands allow for higher price points and higher margins. Starbucks represents the ultimate example of a strong brand driving a price premium (such as $1.60 for a medium coffee), resulting in higher margins. Starbucks stock has soared 700 percent in the last five years. Similarly, the Lincoln Navigator delivers a far higher margin than the Ford Expedition, which shares the same popular SUV platform.
- *Strong brands lend immediate credibility to new product introductions.* A well-established brand can provide instant credibility for a new product. Gillette's Mach 3 became number one in personal shavers within a month of its introduction. Charles Schwab's Internet brokerage business is rated at the top of the class even though it didn't exist a few years ago. And users line up to get the latest version of Microsoft Windows well before it goes on sale.

- *Strong brands allow for greater shareholder and stakeholder returns.* There is a positive, demonstrable relationship between strong brands and returns to shareholders. Yahoo! and General Electric continue to be among the most powerful brands in their respective categories and among those with the highest returns for shareholders.
- *Strong brands embody a clear, valued, and sustainable point of differentiation relative to the competition.* No one can touch FedEx's claim of overnight delivery. Similarly, a recent study showed that 66 percent of executives will not buy personal computers for their company if they do not run on Intel chips.
- *Strong brands mandate clarity in internal focus and brand execution.* A strong brand generally means that all employees understand what the brand stands for and what they need to do to uphold its reputation or promise. Southwest Airlines and Herb Kelleher, in particular, have had total clarity in strategic direction for years because internally everyone knows what the brand stands for and how that should "come to life" with customers.
- *The more loyal the customer base and the stronger the brand, the more likely customers will be forgiving if a company makes a mistake.* For instance, the strike at Saturn in 1998 had little impact on Saturn's loyalty or sales. Indeed, Saturn's new $20,000 LS model is expected to eclipse sales of its entry-level car.
- *Brand strength is a lever for attracting the best employees and keeping satisfied employees.* A recent *Wall Street Journal* article mentioned the fifteen companies with the best reputation and satisfaction ratings. In order they are Johnson & Johnson, Coca-Cola, Hewlett-Packard, Intel, Ben & Jerry's, Wal-Mart, Xerox, Home Depot, Gateway, Disney, Dell, General Electric, Lucent, Anheuser-Busch, and Microsoft. Pretty powerful brands and pretty powerful companies. Companies that have strong brands and loyal customers tend to have employees who take pride in their jobs and feel good about themselves.
- *70 percent of customers want to use a brand to guide their purchase decision.* Given a choice customers do not want to go through the mentally exhausting and unsure process of trying a new brand. They do not want to have to work their way through

the proliferation of new products and services offered to them in any given category every year. Brands are the shorthand that customers use to guide their all important purchase decisions. And, given a choice, they will stay loyal to a brand for a long time. Figure 1 shows what drives consumer loyalty to a brand.

Note that the word "retention" has not been used yet, nor will it be later. Customer retention is not the same as customer loyalty. Midwest Airlines may retain me as a customer if it is the only one that gets me to Sheboygan, but if three airlines go there and I always use Midwest anyway, that is loyalty. Loyalty implies choice—a very important distinction.

Consider the following companies and brands: Campbell's, Coca-Cola, Eveready, Ford, Gillette, Heinz, Kellogg's, Colgate, Goodyear, Kodak, Ivory, and Wrigley. What do they have in common? All were leaders in their categories in the 1920s and still are seventy-five years later. But consider these: Evian, SnackWell's, Healthy Choice, Starbucks, Saturn, Yahoo!, and Netscape. As you have probably guessed, these are all much newer brands that nevertheless quickly became the most powerful in their categories and have garnered incredible loyalty in a short time.

The bottom line is that you do control your company's destiny, and brand is one of the primary drivers. This book explains how to manage your brands so they can lead every major revenue- and profit-generating strategy your company undertakes.

Figure 1. What Keeps Consumers Loyal to a Brand

Consumer Brand Loyalty Drivers

Tier 1
• Brand provides high quality (70%)
• Brand consistently performs (61%)

Tier 2
• Brand is what they are familiar with (33%)
• Brand offers a good value/price (30%)
• Brand fits personality (26%)
• Brand effectively solves problem (26%)

A New Approach to Managing Brands

To unleash the power of a brand, don't think of it as just another marketing tactic along with direct mail and brochures. It's not just a marketing issue; brand management has to report all the way to the top of an organization and has to involve every functional area. Nestle, Coke, IBM, Polo Ralph Lauren, and many others all have brand reporting directly to the number one or number two person in charge. Company size does not matter. It's the mindset of the company that matters.

Brand, next to people, is the most important asset your company owns. Yes, it is intangible. No, it is not on the balance sheet, as it is in the United Kingdom, Hong Kong, and Australia (in the United States, brand is generally considered part of the value of goodwill). And no, it is not easy to place a financial value on a brand. However, to ultimately manage brand as a profit driver, you have to rethink your management approach.

Brands as Assets

There are a few simple ways to think about your brand as an asset, but they generally prove the point rather than define it. *Financial World* and *Interbrand*, for example, have placed a value of $47 billion on the Coca-Cola brand name. And *Fortune* magazine stated that if Coke lost everything except for "the formula" and its brand name, it could walk into any bank in the world and get a $100 billion loan to start the company from scratch without many questions.

Similarly, Carl Icahn recently paid over $40 million for the rights to the brand name PanAm in the hopes of resurrecting the company and the brand name sometime in the future. And when Rolls Royce was sold in 1998, Volkswagen bought all of the tangible assets (plants and machinery) for over a billion dollars and BMW bought the rights to the brand name for $66 million. Many analysts believe BMW received the better deal.

How then do you define a brand as an asset and how can an organization start to recognize the strategic and, more importantly, the financial rewards a brand can offer to a company?

Thinking About Brands as Assets

When I explain this concept, as I have to thousands of business executives and graduate students, I often use a real estate analogy. Imagine that Jane and Jim each bought a condominium rental property at the same time. They both purchased a hard asset with an assigned value to it; each paid $100,000. They bought the exact same floor plan in a large complex. Their intentions are similar. They want to rent the condominium to receive a monthly income. They hope to increase the rent every year to increase their earnings. And they hope to sell it one day for a profit.

This is where the similarities stop. Jane decided early on that she wanted to build a rental property business and create her own brand. So she decided to try to maximize her property value and return potential in the hope of growing her portfolio of properties and her brand. She didn't have a lot of money to start. But what she did have she invested in that condo. She renovated it, putting in hardwood floors, adding an extra bathroom, and wiring in a Bose speaker system and a security system. She invested an additional $8,000 in the property, bringing her total investment costs to $108,000.

Jane bought ads in local papers and described her property on the Internet. In addition, she approached businesses that may have employees relocating soon and hired the top real estate broker in the area to represent her. To advertise and hire the broker Jane spent an additional $2,000, but the broker adds prestige to the property through sophisticated marketing approaches, reduces the potential for lost rental time, and may increase Jane's rental price. Jane's total investment costs now total $110,000.

Jim, however, decided not to invest any additional money in his condo, feeling that he will make the most money if he keeps costs as low as possible. He decided to try and rent the unit himself, posting a sign in front of the building alongside four other signs advertising similar rentals.

Within a week, Jane rented her condo for $1,000 a month and signed a three-year lease with her happy tenant. Jim couldn't find a renter for four months because of the competitive market for similar condos. The tenant he finds pays him $750 a month on a month-to-month lease.

Fast forward three years. What has happened to each of our condo owners? Jane has accumulated earnings of $12,000 in year one, $13,000 in year two, and $15,000 in year three, a total of $40,000. Jim had earnings of $6,000 in year one (remember, it took him four months to find a renter), $7,500 in year two, and $7,500 in year three; he never had a full year of rent, as he consistently lost renters and had to find new ones. Consequently, Jim's total earnings over the three years were $21,000.

As a result of her success, Jane was able to invest in a second rental property at the end of year two, with a down payment of $30,000 on a $125,000 property. She invested the same $10,000 in her second rental property on upgrades and a broker. Fortunately, Jane was able to find a renter immediately and had an income of $15,000 on her second home in the first year.

At the end of three years, Jane's first home was appraised at $150,000 and her second home had appreciated to $140,000, a total of $290,000. Also, Jane had begun to get a reputation of providing top-notch condos with both brokers and renters. More importantly, Jane's Rental Properties started to take off as a valid business concept and a respected brand.

Jim's unimproved condo is appraised at $125,000. His annual income potential is $12,000. To sum up Jane and Jim's situations after three years:

	Jane	*Jim*
Total Assets	$290,000	$125,000
Net Worth	$210,000	$125,000
Year Three Annual Income	$36,000	$12,000
Number of Homes Owned	2	1
Reputation	Very Positive	Neutral

Jane and Jim bought the same asset at the same time but took very different approaches to managing and growing it. Their goals were similar at the beginning; how far they have come toward achieving them is very different.

Lessons Learned for Brand Asset Management (BAM)

What can we learn from this real estate example as it applies to Brand Asset Management?

- Brands have a hard value like real estate does, which can be appraised and have a financial worth assigned to it.
- If managed well and invested in consistently, your brand should appreciate over time and you should be able to charge a price premium relative to close competitors.
- Image and perception help drive value; without an image there is no perception.
- Your brand should be looked at as a long-term asset, but also as a vehicle for driving earnings on a regular basis.
- Long-term perspectives will only help to drive that value; anything done for short-term reasons will probably only denigrate the value of the brand.
- The brand has to be managed by its owners (such as senior management) or decisions may be suboptimized. Jane took control of her brand, invested in it, and grew its overall asset value. Jim did not.
- Successful brands provide a platform for future products and allow entry into related areas. They provide the fuel to reinvest in the brand or invest in complementary areas.

The Need for a Dramatic Strategic Shift

Strong brands drive overall value, income, profitability, and long-term growth. If you believe this, you probably agree it is worth investing in a new approach to maximize your brand's value. No longer should you be satisfied being one of the many "Jims" in the business world today.

It's time for a revolution. Brand Asset Management is a balanced investment approach for building the meaning of the brand, communicating it internally and externally, and leveraging it to increase brand profitability, brand asset value, and brand returns over time. Indeed, it forces us to shift from traditional brand management plans toward a comprehensive Brand Asset Management Strategy. Each shift away from past approaches takes you a step further to maximizing the value of your brand. A few of these shifts from the traditional approach of managing your brand to managing your brand as an asset are highlighted in Table 1 and will be discussed in depth throughout the book.

Getting to this new approach is tough; staying there may be even tougher. Witness Nike. For years it had been the technology and performance leader, setting the standard for the highest quality in athletic shoes. It showed the world how a Nike shoe was born on college tracks and tested with young athletes, aimed at making them better athletes. It was a true success. However, in the mid-1990s Nike seemed to have changed its approach and appeared to be resting on its past image and status. Performance became secondary. Poor labor practices tainted its reputation, and professional athletes seemed only to wear Nikes when paid to do so. The stock market and consumers had a hard time holding Nike up to the level of standards it had set years before.

In other words, Nike forgot what made it Nike: producing the best shoes with the best technology that allow athletes to perform

Table 1. The Shift from Traditional Brand Asset Management

Traditional Brand Management		Brand Asset Management Strategy
Brand management	→	Brand asset management strategy
Brand managers	→	Brand champions and ambassadors
Retention	→	Deep loyalty
One-time transactions	→	Lifetime relationships
Customer satisfaction	→	Customer commitment
Product-driven revenues	→	Brand-driven revenues
Three-month focus	→	Three-year focus
Market share gains	→	Stock price gains
Marketing manages the brand	→	All functional areas manage the brand
Awareness and recall metrics	→	Sophisticated brand metrics
Brand is driven internally	→	Brand is driven externally

at their highest level. Other companies took advantage of this and increased their market share. Adidas, for example, now touts itself as the brand with the best technology and performance—Nike's old positioning. Nike will come back, but it took for granted its most powerful asset, the Nike brand.

Why Brand Asset Management Has Not Taken Hold

There is, in general, resistance to projects that will not affect the bottom line for three to five years or more. Most companies shift employees around so often that they cannot see the fruits of longer-term efforts; in addition, they have too many short-term expectations, see too few reasons to take a risk, and are saddled with reward systems and career paths that are not designed around the brand and focused on the longer term.

Also, companies tend to promote their brand managers into other areas of the organization every eighteen to twenty-four months to further their careers. Senior management does not give brand managers an incentive to think long term about brand management or brand strategy, so they naturally think only about the best way to make an impact in the short run.

Many companies, whether primarily financially or operationally driven, have few employees who understand what the brand stands for. Such companies lack customer "intimacy" and underappreciate how the brand can ultimately help a company accomplish longer-term goals. By definition, these companies are more susceptible to consumer brand switching (see Figure 2).

But Dell gets it. Ralph Lauren gets it. The Gap gets it. Starbucks gets it. John Deere gets it and Yahoo! gets it. The brand is your drawing card. Your brand is not something to be buried in the marketing silo and handed over to a freshly minted MBA to manage over the next eighteen months. Your brand should be managed at the highest levels within and throughout the organization, and your brand can help you to maximize your organization's overall growth potential and profit returns.

Wall Street is increasingly aware of the power of brands and is now declaring the brand to be one of the top five factors taken into account when making a stock recommendation (the other factors

Figure 2. Why Would a Consumer Leave a Brand?

Brand Switching Triggers

1. Brand failed to deliver its promise (52%)

2. Brand was not available (52%)

3. Brand no longer met needs (42%)

4. Another brand was recommended (41%)

What do you see from these points? The point is that you control your own destiny. There are no mysterious forces outside of your control that build a strong brand.

are senior management team, track record, five-year growth plan, and the market they compete in).

This book is called *Brand Asset Management* because it is truly about managing your brand as an asset. A brand has tangible and intangible value that is owned equally by customers and management. Whether it is managed as such is another story.

Having taught Brand Asset Management courses all over the world, I have gleaned a few truths about it that seem to be universal:

- Brand Asset Management is not just the next reengineering or TQM. It is a long-term strategy and mindset similar to innovation, not just a flavor of the month.
- Many companies recognize its importance but do not know how to get started.
- Many organizations still tie managing the brand to having the right advertising agency instead of the right internal management team.
- Many businesses today recognize that there is an inextricable connection between the success of the brand and the success of the organization. However, most do not know how to start

managing their brand as an asset. This is not surprising, as it has not become a common business mindset yet. Organizational functional silos can not implement broad-based brand strategies if they are not taught or encouraged to. In fact, research shows that over 70 percent of companies today believe they are not managing their brands well.

In a nutshell, this book is about helping companies better understand how to manage their brands as assets. But it's not about searching for the silver bullet—the best name or logo, the coolest service or product, or anything on the Internet. This book is about a mindset shift. Obviously a long-term commitment is required for this mindset shift to take hold and for the approach I describe in this book to work.

This book provides a roadmap to start to achieve Brand Asset Management excellence. It provides some new approaches and leverages successful approaches already established in many companies. And it demands that the brand be looked at holistically, encompassing every functional area within the organization.

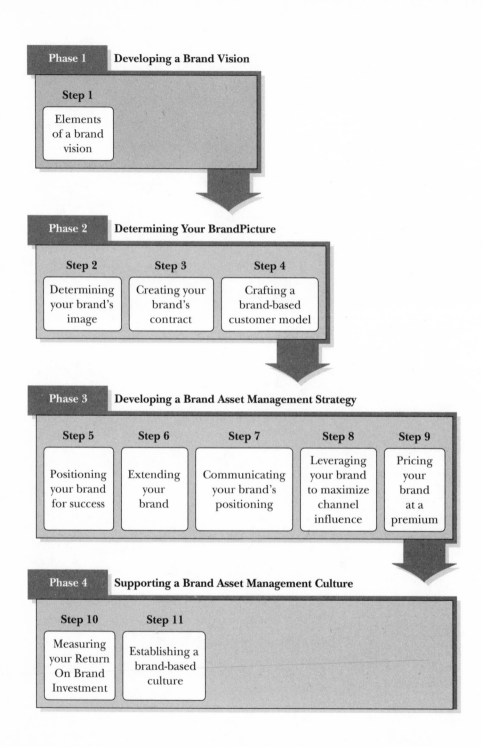

An Overview of Brand Asset Management

Brand Asset Management is a proven process for managing brands as assets in order to maximize their value. This chapter explains the basic BAM approach and how you can use it to improve your company's profits.

The process involves four phases and eleven steps. The chart on the facing page demonstrates this; the same chart appears on the facing page of each succeeding chapter to indicate where you are in the process as you follow the advice in this book. This chapter outlines the phases and steps, and the remaining chapters discuss the steps one at a time. Also in this chapter, key terms are briefly defined that are discussed in detail later.

Phase One: Developing a Brand Vision

First, define the strategic and financial goals and objectives that your brand should help achieve:

- How well does your Brand Vision link to the corporate vision? If it is not linked, can Brand Asset Management form that linkage?
- What financial growth gap are you trying to fill? How many dollars can brand management add to the bottom line?
- Does senior management agree on the goals and objectives for the brand? Will the brand be viewed as an asset or simply as a marketing tool?

Step One helps answer these questions.

Step One: Elements of a Brand Vision

The Brand Vision simply and clearly states what the branding effort must do to help meet corporate goals. Without this, the money spent on brand work is likely to be cut or eliminated along with other discretionary spending if the company has an off quarter or year.

A successful Brand Vision commits senior management and the rest of the organization to consistent brand investments and points out a clear path to how the brand's success will be gauged. A Brand Vision also helps determine what portion of the growth gap (the difference between revenues and earnings today and desired revenues and earnings three to five years from now) the brand is responsible for.

Developing a Brand Vision is the only step driven entirely by internal management interviews and discussions. The intent is for senior management to clearly articulate what its expectations are for what the brand can help the business achieve over the next three to five years. Thus the vision should include a statement of what the brand stands for, its intended audience, the brand's benefits, and the financial and strategic goals for the brand. Your Brand Vision should be directly linked to your corporate strategy and corporate vision.

The vision also defines the best brand-based strategies to pursue. For example, it clarifies whether you should recreate the brand through a new positioning, increase the value perception of the brand through a premium pricing strategy, leverage new products to drive future growth, develop other strategies or a combination of strategies. (A number of strategies are outlined in Phase Three, and ways to implement them are covered in Phase Four.)

A Brand Vision could be as simple as the following one for a leading eye care company:

> Around the world, our eye care brand will stand for leadership in visual care. Consumers and the professional channel will recognize us as the industry leader in visual care solutions, including the best service, follow-up, expertise, and product innovation. Our brand will help us to fill one-third of our stated financial growth gap through price premiums, better relationships with the channel, and close-in brand extensions.

The key to a successful Brand Vision is to discuss the implications behind every word in the vision. As Vicky Shire, vice president of marketing at Nicor, Inc., says, "Without the Brand Vision you might go off in many different directions, without knowing which one is the right one. The Brand Vision enables you to execute the brand strategy and, ultimately, may be a way to achieve the corporate vision."

Phase Two: Determining Your BrandPicture^{SM}

The purpose in this phase is to understand customer perceptions and perspectives about your brand relative to the competition and opportunities for growth. This phase asks the following questions:

- Among current and target customers, what does our brand really stand for today? What are its strengths and weaknesses? How does our brand compare to competitive brands?
- How consistent is our brand's image across various customer segments?
- What image do we want our brand to have in the future? What is the desired contract? How will we bridge the gap between today and tomorrow?
- How do our customers make brand-based choices? What are their top purchase criteria? How does our brand stack up to those criteria and to the competition?
- What unmet customer needs and wants could our brand fill over time?

Steps Two through Four help answer these questions.

Step Two: Determining Your Brand's Image

To complete a BrandPicture first requires developing a full understanding of your brand's image in the minds of past, present, and future customers. Like a person, your brand can be described in adjectives, adverbs, and phrases. The more positive they are, the stronger your brand image and the more leverage you most likely will have in growing the brand.

This step introduces the Brand Value Pyramid^{SM}, which illustrates the power of moving your brand's associations beyond features and attributes to benefits and values. The lower your brand lies on the pyramid, the less differentiated it is and the more likely that it can compete only on cost. Brands at the top of the pyramid—Mercedes, Polo Ralph Lauren, John Deere, Nordstrom's—all charge and get premium prices.

Brand image includes your brand's benefit associations and "persona." In other words, it gets at the benefits customers associate with your brand and the human characteristics or personality traits they see in it. Identifying your brand image gives you a good idea of what your brand stands for in the marketplace and what value consumers have placed on it.

For instance, the persona of the John Deere brand, if described as a person, might incorporate the following: hard working, rugged, Midwestern, great value, dependable, family-oriented, male, college educated, money-saving, wholesome, trusting, likes to wear green. Each of these descriptors helps describe the personality of John Deere, and one can quickly get a feeling as to whether or not this is a "person" whose values and characteristics a customer would want to associate with.

For your company, listing these descriptors vis-à-vis your key competitors helps when determining what market segments you want to target and the positioning you want to adopt.

Step Three: Creating Your Brand's Contract

A Brand Contract lists customer perceptions of all the current promises your brand makes, both positive and negative, as well as the promises it should make going forward to maximize customer satisfaction and happiness. For instance, McDonald's brand contract includes promises of fast food, friendly service, value prices, clean bathrooms, consistency around the world, fun for kids, and the like. In the future, McDonald's may consider a promise such as "food on your terms," implying custom preparation or delivery.

A good Brand Contract is honest. For instance, Motel 6's contract with customers includes rooms that are clean and well maintained, low prices, and good service, but probably not the nicest of furniture or the biggest of bathrooms. That's just what Motel 6 is and what it promises.

Conversely, United Airline's "Rising" campaign is a broken Brand Contract based on empty promises. That campaign, launched in August 1997, implied a contract of better, more customer-friendly service, bigger seats, wider overhead bins, fewer sold-out flights, and preferential treatment of its best customers. United basically promised to fix the problems most business travelers face regardless of airline. But recent airline customer service ratings show that United is at its lowest ebb ever. In October 1999 United moved away from "Rising" and is in search of a new "promise." Similarly, Holiday Inn's "No Surprises" campaign was considered a failure when guests found lots of surprises, such as long lines and rooms that were not ready for occupancy or already occupied by another guest.

When you make customers a promise, you have no more than eighteen months to follow through before total credibility is lost.

Step Four: Crafting a Brand-Based Customer Model

This is the final part of Phase Two's BrandPicture. Crafting a customer model forces you to truly think about the behaviors and beliefs of the customers who are buying your goods or services.

The customer model provides an understanding of how consumers think and act and why and how they make purchase decisions. It speaks to opportunities and barriers for brand growth. Importantly, the model helps you understand the specific purchase criteria a customer considers, in ranked order, when making a purchase decision.

In addition, the model uncovers consumer beliefs about your brand, the category, and the competition. Here again, perception is reality. If you are in the ceiling tile business and customers still believe asbestos poses the same threat it did thirty years ago, you are going to have to help them understand today's safe ceiling tile. You may know what's best, but you must deal with customer beliefs anyway.

Dell's approach is among the best. As the personal computer market continues to grow and the industry's customer model becomes more and more important, Dell's direct-to-consumer sales approach, which has been in place since the company's inception and is 100 percent driven by customer needs, continues to be a major selling benefit for new customers. Dell's consistent focus on how customers want to buy a personal computer (that is, on their terms, not the manufacturer's) will help the company keep its lion's share of an expanding market.

Phase Three: Developing a Brand Asset Management Strategy

The purpose in this phase is to determine the right brand-based strategies for achieving the goals and objectives stated in the Brand Vision and in the market-based perceptions and perspectives from the BrandPicture. The four steps in this phase (Steps Five through Eight) help you answer these questions:

- What brand-based strategies should we use to meet the growth goals outlined in our Brand Vision?
- What is the right positioning for our brand? Is the positioning unique, credible, valued, sustainable, and aligned with internal and external perceptions?
- How extendible is our brand? What are its boundaries? What screens should we leverage to make smart extendibility decisions? What new product opportunities exist for our brand?
- What channel strategy will support our goals and objectives for the brand? What is the best way to influence the channel with our brand?
- Can we price our brand at a premium based on its strengths compared to the competition's? How much of a premium? How else can we use our brand to improve our profits?
- What communication tactics will strengthen our brand and maximize its asset value? Where is the power in the selling process?
- Once that power is gained, how can we maintain and further take advantage of it?
- How can we maximize our power base through branding efforts?

Step Five: Positioning Your Brand For Success

A strong brand position means having a unique, credible, sustainable, fitting, and valued place in customers' minds. It revolves around a benefit set that helps your product or service stand apart from the competition.

In this step, the goal is to determine the right positioning for your brand over the next three to five years, which will ultimately help you shape your overall strategy going forward.

Unfortunately, taglines and creative ad copy are often thought of as substitutes for positioning. This is dangerous; it places positioning as important only to marketing when it is critical to every function. Imagine if Nordstrom's had rude salespeople, low-quality clothes, hard-to-understand billing, and lots of sales—but a really good ad slogan. This would seriously undercut its positioning as the best service provider of any retailer.

Once you know how you want to position the brand, it becomes fairly evident which innovations you should focus on, what pricing strategy makes the most sense, how best to leverage distribution channels, and how you should communicate brand benefits to your target audience.

Saturn is the best and most holistic example of a positioning that works. Saturn is "your" car company. For everything consumers dislike about traditional car dealerships, Saturn stands for the opposite—no haggling, minimal choices, customer friendly, good value. For Saturn's target market, first-time or female buyers who often are more intimidated by the experience than others, Saturn helps take the stress out of buying a car. Saturn is currently trying to extend its positioning to current customers who want to trade up to its $20,000 car or to new customers that want to embrace the Saturn "experience."

Sometimes a brand's position puts boundaries on the strategies a company can successfully pursue. Volvo and safety are synonymous, but in the summer of 1995 Volvo tried to reposition itself away from safety and toward performance. Instead of owning a benefit, Volvo was trying to increase sales by competing for the same performance-driven buyer who was also considering Lexus, BMW, and Mercedes. As Figure 3 shows, the market did not buy it

Figure 3. Volvo's Revenues by Year

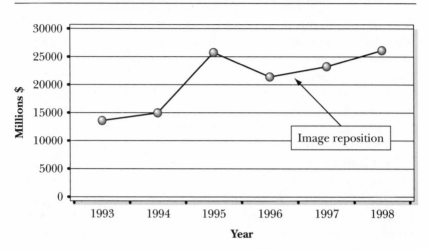

and sales plummeted in 1996. Volvo was sold to Ford in 1999 for less than many thought it should have.

Today, Volvo has repositioned its brand back to safety and has, in fact, combined safety and performance in its communications, highlighted by its tagline: "Protect Your Body. Ignite Your Soul."

Step Six: Extending Your Brand

Once your positioning is well defined, you can start to think about the boundaries of your brand and how far they might be stretched. Here you start to see the potential of your brand and decide whether it will allow you to reach the growth goals established within the Brand Vision.

It is tempting to stretch your brand as far as possible, but Step Six encourages you to look for those areas that will have the highest impact on your bottom line, help to fulfill the Brand Vision, and leverage key findings resulting from your BrandPicture.

In general, good brand extensions, such as Gillette extending its original men's razor line into one for women, stay true to the brand and help fill conservative revenue or earnings goals. Other examples include regular strength Tylenol extending into extra-strength Tylenol and Blockbuster's recent guarantee of "going home happy" with the promise of new videos in stock.

More expansive brand extensions can help achieve more dramatic growth. One example is Apple's iMac, which extended Apple from its traditional older user base to a younger market with a more moderate budget.

Another expansive brand extension is The Gap's Baby Gap. Traditionally, stores owned by The Gap competed only in the teen and adult clothing segments. The new extension allows The Gap to compete in the infant and toddler segments as well.

So brand extensions support and stretch the brand as it is positioned today and relative to the growth goals established in the Brand Vision. Good brand extensions should also help you expand into new categories or new markets—such as Caterpillar getting into fashionable shoes.

Step Seven: Communicating Your Brand's Positioning

Brand-based communication is like positioning: critical and often misunderstood. Many companies assume that branding and advertising are the same; if they get a good ad agency they expect good results. But brand-based communication is about determining the right mix of communication vehicles to maximize your potential for achieving the goals established in the Brand Vision.

There are eight brand-based communication vehicles (each discussed later in the book):

1. Advertising (television, radio, print, billboards)
2. Internet
3. Public relations
4. Trade and sales promotions
5. Consumer promotions (point of purchase, coupons, refunds, contests)
6. Direct marketing (catalogues, mailings, fax, e-mail)
7. Event marketing
8. Internal employee communications

The communications challenge lies in determining the right mix of these to use.

All communications are ultimately aimed at achieving specific and measurable goals. They target an audience that is desirable and accessible, build the overall value of the brand by securing and reinforcing the preferred positioning, and address the benefits that fit customer-stated needs and wants.

Step Eight: Leveraging Your Brand to Maximize Channel Influence

You can enhance your position in the channel by maximizing the strength of the brand. The stronger your brand, the greater your chance of being able to direct the channel instead of it directing you. Although Wal-Mart and Home Depot have shifted the fundamental balance of power between stores and brands, the Internet and direct marketing have more than offset the power of these superstores by allowing companies to have more control over the distribution of their products and services.

Martha Stewart is a great example of a brand that is pulling consumers into the channel that she uses, and it is as much a driver of K-Mart's renewed success as any other factor.

Step Nine: Pricing Your Brand at a Premium

The ability to charge a premium for your brand over that of the competition is critically important to driving the brand's asset value. It is also relatively easy to leverage and an opportunity there for the taking. Your BrandPicture should help you determine whether your brand allows you to charge a premium price.

A model called the House of Pricing helps you determine how best to equate your brand's value with the price you charge. As mentioned, Starbucks is the epitome of premium pricing; it has not only branded a commodity but taken the lead in pricing that commodity. Some automobile manufacturers also are great examples. Not many people know that the Lexus and the Toyota Camry have the same engine, even though the latter is priced as much as $10,000 less.

This step also discusses the eight ways that leveraging your brand as an asset can help you drop dollars to the bottom line by either allowing you to charge a premium price or to lower associated brand costs (acquisition costs):

1. Price your brand at a premium relative to the competition
2. Launch new products more cheaply than the competition
3. Recoup development costs sooner
4. Lower acquisition costs for new customers
5. Establish loyal customers who continue to pay a premium
6. Use premium pricing to exert greater control over your channel
7. Use a strong brand to seek out cobranding and licensing opportunities
8. Leverage the strong brand across many target segments to own the category without diluting the value of the brand

Phase Four: Supporting a Brand Asset Management Culture

The purpose of the two steps in this phase (Steps Ten and Eleven) is to determine how to get your organization to rally around the brand as an asset and make sure the strategies you recommend are implemented and measured. The two steps address these questions:

- How should we set up our organization to maximize brand success? How do we review and reward those involved with managing the brand as an asset?
- What metrics should we use to evaluate our brand's performance? What decisions should those metrics help us to make?
- How do we most effectively train and educate employees about our Brand Asset Management strategy?
- How do we get senior management to stay actively involved, supportive, and committed to our efforts?

Step Ten: Measuring Your Return On Brand Investment (ROBI)^{SM}

For years, the only two brand-related metrics that were leveraged consistently across companies were awareness and recall. If your ad received high scores on either of these measures, the brand was deemed a success. However, even companies with 100 percent awareness and recall, such as Rubbermaid, sometimes suffer stock price and market share erosion. This should point us in a new direction.

Critical areas not being measured widely include conversion of awareness to purchase, understanding of positioning, and placing a financial value on the brand. These are new metrics that companies are beginning to adopt.

It is important to only use metrics that are truly meaningful to your brand-related activities. Your first question should be: What decisions will this metric help me make? Thus you can begin to determine which metrics you need versus those that might simply be nice to have.

Proverbial wisdom is true: you cannot manage what you cannot measure. One criterion for the right metrics is that they are meaningful and repeatable over time (so as to make comparisons). Also, more metrics are not necessarily better metrics. The challenge is finding the right set of metrics to ultimately help you achieve your Brand Vision.

Step Ten specifically discusses eighteen brand metric approaches, ranging from the eight I generally use with my clients (I call these the ROBI Eight—Return On Brand Investment) to the simple "Top Box" metric 3M uses (the percentage of current customers who say they are very satisfied as well as very willing to repurchase *and* very willing to recommend).

Step Eleven: Establishing a Brand-Based Culture

More often than not, this is an area in which companies fall short. But without a pervasive brand-based culture companies limit what they can hope to accomplish with the brand. A strong brand culture affects the roles of every functional area, of senior management, of internal communications, and of the reward and measurement systems.

Hallmark is one of the very few companies I have seen that has truly adopted a brand asset culture. Step Eleven explains how to start building a brand-based culture and what the expectations should be.

A Few Brand Definitions

A few definitions are worth reviewing at this point. Some of these terms are defined again later, with examples.

BAM—the acronym for Brand Asset Management.

Brand—an intangible but critical component an organization "owns" that represents a contract with the customer, relative to the level of quality and value delivered tied to a product or service. A customer cannot have a relationship with a product or a service, but may with a brand.

A brand is a set of consistent promises. It implies trust, consistency, and a defined set of expectations. A brand helps customers feel more confident about their purchase decision. A brand is an asset and, next to your people, no asset is more important. It is a long-term proposition—a strong brand stays consistent with what it means for a long time, often decades.

David Friedman, marketing vice president at U.S. Cellular, defines the brand as "the promise of what our company stands for and what we deliver to our customers. At U.S. Cellular, we define our brand as a way of doing business."

Brand Asset Management—a balanced investment approach for building the meaning of the brand, communicating it internally and externally, and leveraging it to increase brand profitability, brand asset value, and brand returns over time.

Corporate Branding—a composite of all the experiences, encounters, and perceptions a customer has with a company. It implies that all internal and external communications are aimed at presenting a single, unified message. Corporate branding strives to build trust in the company, not in a particular product or service. G.E. and Yahoo! have great corporate brands that embrace practically every product or service their respective brands endorse. Sony may be the ultimate corporate endorser with Sony DVD, Trinitron, Walkman, PlayStation, My First Sony, and others. Marriott is another impressive corporate brand, incorporating Marriott Conference Centers, Marriott Vacation Club, Mariott Marquis, Marriott's Residence Inn, Courtyard by Marriott, Fairfield Inn by Marriott, Spring Hill Suites by Marriott, Renaissance by Marriott, and Town Place Suites by Marriott.

Brad VanAuken, former director of brand management and marketing at Hallmark, states that "companies are moving away from the old P&G model where people manage individual brands to much more of a corporate branding mindset. The corporate brand is leveraged across more and more products and services. This implies a movement from having the brand be a function of a division toward having the brand be the driver for the entire organization."

Product Branding—branding in which the product or service is synonymous with the brand. Product branding allows the consumer to fit product perceptions and brand image into one and strives to build trust in the brand. Look at P&G's list of product brands:

1. Laundry and cleaning: Bounce, Cheer, Cascade, Comet, Era, Dawn, Joy, Tide
2. Health care: Ivory, Crest
3. Beauty care: Cover Girl, Ivory, Head & Shoulders
4. Food and beverage: Pringles, Folgers
5. Paper: Pampers, Luvs, Always

Most consumers have no idea that each of these brands is produced by P&G, and that is intentional.

The advantages and disadvantages of product branding are almost the reverse of those for corporate branding. Advantages include the ability to take risks more often, the ability to have a wider variety of products and services that may have no connection to one another under one umbrella, and less fear of failure. In addition, product branding allows an organization more opportunity to control shelf space or a place in the customer's mind. Tide, Cheer, and Era, for example—all P&G brands—account for two-thirds of most retailers' laundry detergent offerings and shelf space. Similarly, The Gap also owns Banana Republic and Old Navy, which allows it to "own the consumer" at several price points and across several styles.

The disadvantages of product branding include lack of economies of scale, lack of endorsements and instant credibility, and, especially for new brands, the need to start from ground zero in educating the customer about your brand.

Brand Positioning—the place in consumers' minds that you want to own. Specifically, it is the benefit that you want them to think of when they think of your brand. It has to be externally driven and relevant. It has to be differentiated from the competition and, most importantly, it has to be valued.

A good positioning is a single idea to be communicated to your customers. A good positioning is a credible promise of value, delivered in ways that distinguish your brand from that of your competitors. A good positioning is a concise statement that summarizes your brand's promise to its customers.

Note: The words *product* and *service* are often used interchangeably in this book, as are the words *customer* and *consumer.* Specific points about business-to-business branding versus consumer branding will be pointed out where applicable or necessary. Importantly, the majority of the concepts discussed in this book apply to every type of business—large and small, public and private, and product- versus service-focused.

Developing a Brand Vision

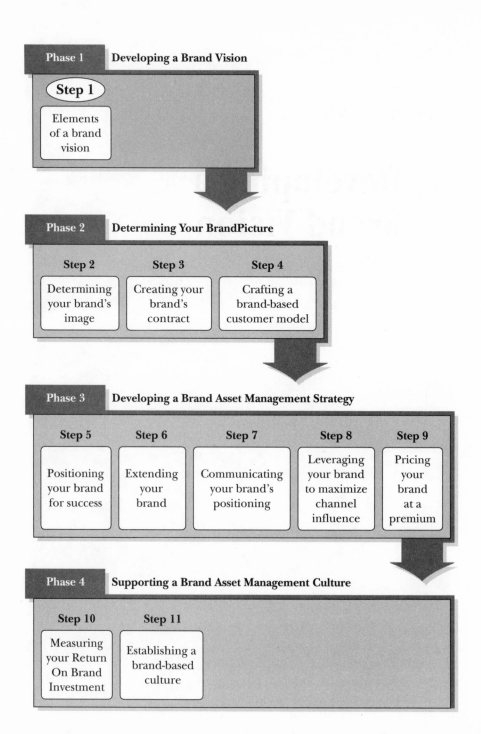

Elements of a Brand Vision

When Lou Gerstner first started at IBM back in the early 1990s (when IBM was in fairly serious trouble), he told Wall Street analysts, "The last thing we need right now is another vision."

This may be your first reaction as well, but a Brand Vision is the most important statement your company can make about its future growth and direction. A good Brand Vision gives clear direction about what role the brand should play in helping a company achieve its longer-term strategic and financial growth goals.

To help distinguish Brand Vision from other corporate statements, let's quickly review the function of corporate mission, value, and vision statements. A corporate vision statement defines what a company is all about, what its purpose is, what customers it serves, and what unique benefits it provides. It is generally written to provide a rallying cry and to signal where the company is spending its energies and why. A corporate mission statement should be written for employees first, stakeholders and shareholders second, and others (Wall Street, industry analysts, and the like) last. It should not be rewritten more than every three to five years, because the odds of completing a meaningful mission in any less time is not very high.

The corporate values statement articulates the shared values an organization wants its employees to embrace as they conduct day-to-day business. Words like integrity, trust, respect, value, quality, and teamwork are mentioned in many corporate values statements. A good values statement dictates how a company wants to run its business as well as how the company wants others to perceive it. A well-executed corporate values statement generally results in high employee satisfaction, which often correlates to strong market performance.

Corporate vision statements broadly help define and prioritize the specific financial and market-based strategies a company should execute in order to reach its overall goals and objectives. Having a corporate vision is a prerequisite to creating a brand vision.

I recently finished leading a team in conducting a major study titled *Brand Asset Management for the 21st Century.* More than seventy companies were involved, representing several hundreds of billions of dollars in revenues, with the goal of trying to better understand the best practices of those who are leveraging and treating their brand as an asset. The best were defined as those whose brands were number one in profitability in their category and either number one or number two in total market share.

One shocking finding was that more than half the companies said they had no long-term strategy or corporate vision in place. If they were to try to create a brand vision now, their work would likely turn into a corporate vision project instead. This is a common pitfall for organizations that attempt to spearhead branding efforts in the absence of a corporate strategy.

Why Is a Brand Vision Needed?

Why is a Brand Vision needed in addition to the three other statements? Primarily because many companies today do not treat their brand as an asset, nor do they believe it has the power to much affect the revenue and profit streams outlined in the corporate vision. Often they still view the brand as a tool or a tactic or a "marketing thing" that is best left to ad agencies to figure out.

Unless a company can focus on and reach consensus about what the brand can or should do for it, the company will most likely continue to shift brand strategies or cut brand investments altogether in the next cost-cutting campaign.

A Brand Vision should help to define how the company plans to leverage its brand or brands in order to reach its corporate vision, uphold its corporate values, and achieve its stated corporate mission. Ideally, the Brand Vision should be derived at the same time as the corporate mission, corporate values, and corporate vision are crafted. As the illustration across from the first page of this chapter shows, a Brand Vision is the starting point for setting a Brand Asset Management strategy.

The Purposes of a Brand Vision

As a guide to leveraging the company's brands, a Brand Vision serves three purposes. First, it forces senior management to reach consensus on longer-term growth objectives and stake out where that growth could and should come from. This helps to get away from the traditional approach of placing a dollar figure *only* on growth ("we will double the business in five years"), and moves the company beyond by declaring what role the brand will play in reaching its growth objectives.

Second, a Brand Vision guides research. One of the most powerful and accurate ways of considering growth options is to conduct research with current and potential users. This helps a company learn how far its brand can extend geographically and what new products or services the brand might offer in the future in light of its current reputation, credibility, value provided, and the like.

Third, a Brand Vision ultimately mandates telling all stakeholders about the company's vision for the brand. It serves as a commitment to where the company is heading and what role the brand will play in helping it get there.

Without committing to a goal for the brand and without reaching some consensus and clarity on your related intentions for the brand, it will be easy to dismiss conducting research on the brand. In projects I have worked on, senior managers have often reacted to the idea of conducting brand research with questions such as: What do they know about our business? How can you expect customers to drive our business strategy? We have gotten by just fine without brand feedback from customers; why is it so important now?

Case Study: A Utility Tries to Set a Brand Vision

Twelve senior managers of one of the top utilities in the country met to talk about the future of their company. They believed they had a strong brand, but the company was only known for supplying gas.

Their growth objective, at 10 percent annually for the next five years, was fairly aggressive. Their traditional growth rate had been 2–3 percent annually, as utility growth is primarily dictated by housing and building starts.

They decided a first step would be to create a Brand Vision so they could better understand how their brand could be leveraged to help achieve this growth. The vision might also lead them to a research plan so that they could talk to the right customers, ask the right questions, and see just how extendible and strong their brand was.

They thought the task of creating a Brand Vision would be fairly straight-forward. However, there were a few problems. First, they had never had to think strategically about their brand because they had a captive market (deregulation had not taken affect yet). Second, having little familiarity with brand issues, the assumption going in was that the brand would not help in achieving longer-term goals and objectives. Third, no one was sure why they should tinker with a well-established organization that had consistently met expectations and goals. Fourth, no one had succeeded at branding in utilities—how could they?

But these executives had enough foresight to know that if they were going to compete in the future and not become just another pipe company, they would have to start to view their brand differently. To do that, they knew they would have to develop a Brand Vision as the starting point for developing the brand to help achieve their aggressive new growth goals.

More importantly, they knew a Brand Vision would help them start to address questions they never asked before, including these:

- What are the customer-perceived strengths and weaknesses of our company and our brand?
- How credible would we be in offering electricity and other value-added services?
- What price premiums could we charge, if any?
- How far out of our present territory could our brand take us?

You may wonder, why not wait until after conducting market research to answer some of these questions? Why force senior management to answer them now when the truth generally resides in the marketplace?

The reason is that without agreement on where the company ultimately wants to leverage its brand, it is very difficult to start prioritizing brand-driven growth opportunities. It is even hard to figure out whom to conduct research with.

Relative to its growth goals, the utility's senior managers were split right down the middle. Half believed they should expand to a five-state region, and the other half favored focusing on getting more revenue from current customers. Half believed they should offer value-added services such as cable television and home security systems, and the other half favored offering only gas and electricity.

The key to creating a brand vision is to aim not for total consensus but for a coming together of perspectives. There is no sense in trying to get extremists to come over to the other side. But without some agreement on brand goals and roles it becomes very difficult to know where to even start in developing a Brand Asset Management Strategy.

Here are two Brand Vision statements as they appear in the companies' respective Web sites:

3Com's Brand Vision

To connect more people and organizations to information in more innovative, simple, and reliable ways than any other networking company in the world . . . 300 million customers worldwide rely on us to connect with the customized, personalized information they need at home, at work, and on the move.

IBM's Brand Vision

At IBM, we strive to lead in the creation, development, and manufacturing of the industry's most advanced information technologies, including computer systems, software, networking systems, storage devices, and microelectronics. We translate these advanced technologies into value for our customers through professional solutions and services businesses throughout the world.

A good Brand Vision has four components: a statement of the overall goal of the brand, the target market the brand will pursue, the points of differentiation the brand will strive for, and the overall financial goals for which the brand will be accountable. Here is a typical Brand Vision and the one the utility discussed earlier used to differentiate itself from the competition and achieve the strategic goals management had agreed on:

Within a five-state region, our utility will strive to become the market leader in providing both residential and commercial customers with a comprehensive portfolio of energy and energy-related products and services. We will strive to have our customers think of both our brand and our employees synonymously with the highest levels of service, trust, responsiveness, caring, and education. We will build long-term relationships with our current and potential customer base by consistently providing high quality products and services. Our brand-related efforts will help us achieve half of our stated growth goals over the next three to five years, which accounts for approximately $400 million in revenues.

This Brand Vision had a number of implications:

- The utility will serve a five-state region within three to five years versus the third of one state it serves now.
- It will offer gas, electricity, and other value-added services (such as furnace cleaning) instead of just gas.
- Where necessary, the utility will have to rely on education, training, and some major shifts in the mindset of employees and senior management.
- Market leadership means the utility will have to go up against competitors it has never faced in the past and that provide products and services that the utility currently does not provide and may not be credible in offering today.
- Long-term relationships imply that the utility will strive for high loyalty measures and additional sales to current customers—two areas it has not had to focus on in the past.
- The utility will definitely count on the brand, for the first time, to help achieve its financial goals.

The utility ended up going through the entire Brand Asset Management process and, from all accounts, the BAM effort was deemed an incredible success. Awareness and satisfaction levels rose to all-time highs.

It is estimated that a high percentage of customers of competitor utilities, both gas and electric, will switch to the utility once deregulation takes hold, as a result of its branding efforts. And its stock price jumped 25 percent in the last year. Not bad for a company that started developing a brand asset management strategy only eighteen months earlier.

Building a Brand Vision: A Four-Part Approach

Let's assume you do have a corporate mission, corporate values, and a corporate vision in place. This means corporate-wide financial goals have been set—revenue growth, profit growth, market capitalization, stock price appreciation, and the like. Broad strategic goals have also been set. These generally fall into four areas: geographic goals, market and customer goals, specific growth initiatives, and customer satisfaction goals. With these in place, you are ready to start creating your Brand Vision.

A well-crafted Brand Vision can be set in less than a month. There are four parts to this step (see box).

Part One: Conduct Senior Management Interviews

Senior managers should be interviewed one-on-one to better understand their intentions for the brand. I recommend having discussions with the entire senior management team, including the

---

Defining a Brand Vision

What Is It?
- A clear articulation of the strategic, financial, and brand goals that management has created for the brand
- A first step to strategic screens as to where the brand can and cannot go

How Is It Used?
Provides a vision that forces management to articulate what they want the brand to "do" for the organization over the next five years, relative to brand value, revenue, and profit contributions

Key Inputs
- Management interviews
- Team analysis
- Strategic documents
- Past brand research

A Four-Part Vision Approach
- Part one: Conduct senior management interviews
- Part two: Create a financial growth gap
- Part three: Collect additional data and create a Brand Vision starter
- Part four: Meet with senior management to create a Brand Vision

A Brand Vision has been set.

---

chairman, CEO or president, CFO, all senior vice presidents, and other key influencers. Ask questions such as those in the following box:

Brand Vision Interview Guide for Senior Management

- In the future, what markets, business lines, and channels do we want to compete in? How does this differ from today?

- What are the strategic and financial objectives for our organization? What role do you believe the brand will play in helping to achieve those objectives?

- What does our brand stand for today? Strengths? Weaknesses? How about relative to the competition?

- What should the brand stand for tomorrow to help us achieve our corporate goals?

- What level of resources are we putting into our strategies tied to the brand? How will we know if our branding efforts have been successful or not?

- Will we be able to achieve the stated objectives as we currently define the business today (with the brands we currently have in place) or do we need to redefine our business?

- What should the role of senior management be relative to Brand Asset Management? Are there any companies out there today that you would hold up as a model for successfully managing and leveraging a brand?

Sending an advance memo stating the purpose of the interview and the key topics you intend to cover will increase the success of most interviews. You will most likely be surprised by the amount of interest and candor you receive from senior managers, as well as the diversity of their answers.

Once all interviews are conducted, it's time for rigorous analysis to reach key findings and conclusions. This analysis will be used in Part Four of this step.

Part Two: Determine a Financial Growth Gap

Once you understand what the growth gap is, you will have more insight into what financial role the brand should play in filling it. Here's how to craft your company's growth gap:

1. Determine what your revenues are today. Let's say it's $100 million.
2. Determine what would happen to that $100 million over the next five years if no dollars were invested in growing those revenues. Let's assume that because of competitive pressures and shifting marketplace needs, your $100 million in revenues today may decrease 5 percent annually, resulting in less than $80 million in revenues in five years.
3. Determine your company's five-year revenue goal. Let's say it's to double business to around $200 million, or to experience 15 percent annual growth.
4. Determine your company's five-year growth gap by subtracting $80 million from your $200 million goal to give you a growth gap of about $120 million.

Figure 1.1 shows an example in which the expected annual growth rate is 8 percent but if nothing changes the growth rate will be minus 3.5 percent.

Now the question becomes how to fill that growth gap. Options may include increasing prices, increasing distribution, pursuing new markets, introducing new products, or making strategic acquisitions. Another option is to build and leverage your brand more successfully. There may be overlap in these strategies, but clearly pointing out a revenue goal tied to the brand will force your organization to think more strategically about how best to leverage the brand.

Reaching consensus on a financial goal for the brand moves management and the organization one step closer to treating and managing the brand as an asset. Without such a goal, a company may not try to increase revenues through price premiums, further sales to loyal customers, or word-of-mouth and brand-driven referrals.

Ideally, your Brand Vision interviews will help you determine how much agreement senior management has tied to the financial goals as well as to the brand's strategic roles.

Figure 1.1. Sample Revenue Growth Gap

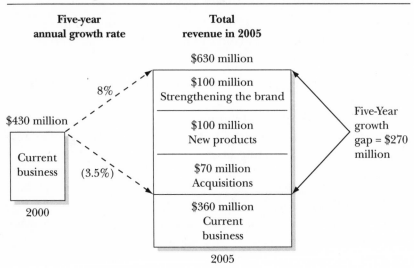

Part Three: Collect Additional Data and Create a Brand Vision Starter

Internal goal setting is critical to setting a strong Brand Vision, but setting goals in a vacuum can be dangerous. Therefore, also collect some external data on where your industry is heading and what competitors are doing, look at market research studies conducted in the last few years, and review past strategic plans. This will provide additional information that should increase your confidence in setting a Brand Vision.

With regard to the competition, take an in-depth look at your company's top two competitors and one up-and-comer (someone seen as a strong competitor in two or three years). This will help you better understand where your competitors are heading, what their strengths and weaknesses are, and what your best opportunities are. This data will be augmented later when you determine your BrandPicture.

Having analyzed management's perspectives and collected additional information, you should be in a good position to craft a high-level report on what the Brand Vision could be and the rationale behind it. At first you may not feel comfortable putting a stake in the ground this way, but at this point no one else is more qualified to do it than you.

Part Four: Meet with Senior Management to Create a Brand Vision

Your objectives for this Brand Vision meeting should be to report interview findings, facts, and conclusions; reach consensus or at least a coming together of disparate views; and actually leave the meeting with a starter Brand Vision. Preferably it will build upon a draft you write prior to the meeting.

This type of meeting can be contentious, confrontational, even scary. However, if senior managers commissioned the project, agreed to the interviews, and took the time to get back together as a team, you will know they are seeking a productive Brand Vision discussion.

Preparation is key. It will boost your confidence and you'll have the answers to some of management's questions, which is the purpose of meeting. Bring backup data for anything you are presenting. Presell your presentation to a few attendees and get their perspectives so that you will have a few champions or "friendlies" in this meeting. Send out any prereadings along with an agenda.

Because it is difficult to get a group of leaders together, be as prepared and confident as you ever have been. For example, if someone asks, "How does this align with our current strategic plan?" you should be able to answer the question before they can finish asking.

My experience with such meetings is that, similar to the interviews you conducted earlier, you will have great success if you are focused on the one thing that is important to everyone: growing the company.

The desired end is to reach agreement on the Brand Vision and your brand's specific roles and goals. Another result will be clear direction on what you need to learn to determine your BrandPicture. Coming out of Step One, you should have a clear indication of the customers you need to talk with, the questions you need to ask, the competitors you should focus on, and the extendibility options you should look at.

Before moving on to Step Two, consider one more Brand Vision example mentioned also in Chapter Two.

Case Study: Visual Care Company

A leading visual care organization developed the following Brand Vision statement:

> Around the world, our eye care brand will stand for leadership in visual care. Consumers and the professional channels will recognize us as the leader in visual care solutions, including the best service, follow-up, expertise, and product innovation in the industry. Our brand will help us to fill one-third of our stated financial growth gap through price premiums, better relationships with the channel, and close-in brand extensions.

What are the implications of this vision?

- "Around the world" defines this company as playing in the international market as well as serving its current U.S. markets.
- "Visual care" means that the brand and the company will be valued by consumers as an organization that listens to customer needs, supplies great before, during, and after service and that provides expert-based recommendations.
- Desired customers include past, present, potential, and lost customers, influencers of those making the decision to purchase, and nonusing individuals.
- "Professional channels" refers to doctors, optometrists, primary care physicians, and the like.
- "Visual care solutions" suggests that this brand can go beyond glasses into other closely related product lines.
- "Best service" means courteous, respectful, and friendly people who are knowledgeable and medically qualified. It also implies no hard selling.
- "Best follow-up" means that this company is striving for long-term relationships.
- "Best product innovation" implies that it needs to be leading edge in its product and service thinking and approach.
- The financial numbers are self-evident.

This level of specificity provided the company with a clear understanding of where management wanted to go, who its target market would be, what might be found in the Brand Contract (discussed in Step Three), and a good understanding of the research plan that needs to be developed.

This company wanted to triple its $100 million business within the next three to five years in a highly fragmented and competitive industry. My guess is that it will succeed because of the degree of senior management commitment and focus and because of the clarity of this Brand Vision.

Summary

The benefits of having a strong, well-thought-out Brand Vision are many:

- It forces you to determine just where you want the brand to be after three to five years.
- It prompts discussion about questions that most likely have never been discussed before (What is a brand? What is *our* brand? How will our brand help us grow?).
- It helps management drive toward consensus on longer-term goals and objectives, and it helps top management know they have articulated their growth goals well.
- It helps you determine what type of research will need to be done with your customers and who that research pool should include.
- It gives you permission to start developing a Brand Asset Management strategy within your organization.

Most importantly, a good Brand Vision tells you and others whether the organization believes the company, its brand, and the future are totally linked or not. There is no step within the BAM process that is more important than this first step.

The next step is to go to the marketplace and determine your BrandPicture.

Determining
Your BrandPicture

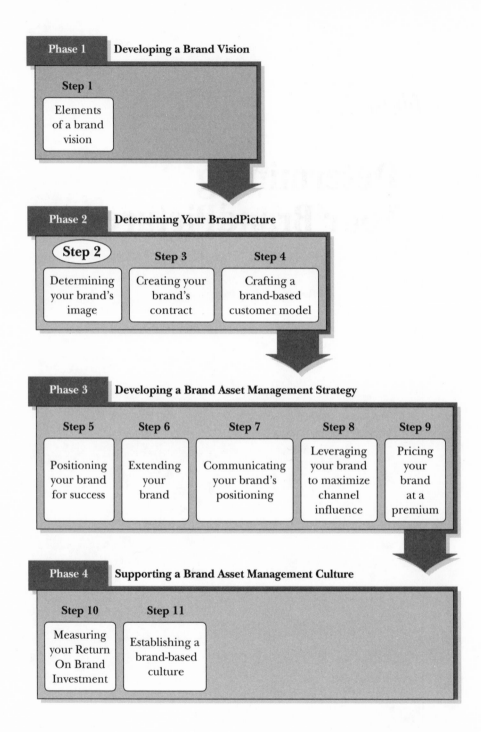

Determining Your Brand's Image

The BrandPicture lays the foundation for building and leveraging your brand and for Brand Asset Management to take hold at your company. A well-crafted BrandPicture will guide your company to develop the right strategies and achieve the Brand Vision discussed in Step One. Without the BrandPicture, you may make decisions about your brand that do not fully leverage your strengths or that actually damage your brand over time.

Your BrandPicture is externally driven, reflects your brand's image from your customers' perspective, and looks at the promises the brand makes to customers. It also helps you determine how your brand stacks up to the competition, how purchase decisions are made in your category, and where your brand might be extended. The BrandPicture is basically a snapshot of your brand today.

Determining your BrandPicture involves three tasks: understanding your brand's image, understanding the contract your brand has with its customers, and deriving a customer model that gets at perceptions and perspectives of your brand and the category. This chapter discusses the first of the three (see the illustration facing this page).

Brand image has two components: the associations customers ascribe to the brand and the brand's "persona" (see Figure 2.1). Brand associations help you understand the benefits your brand delivers to customers and the role it plays in their lives. Brand persona is a description of the brand in terms of human characteristics; this also helps you better understand the brand's strengths and weaknesses as well as the best ways to position it.

Figure 2.1. Two Components of Brand Image

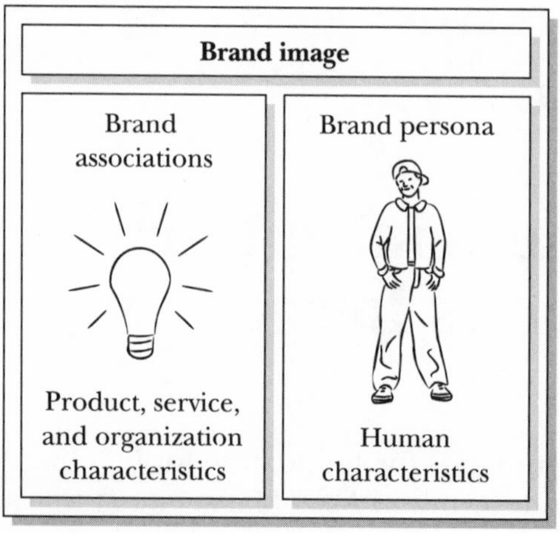

Brand Associations

Brand associations are part of a laddering approach that allows you to determine the power of the benefits your brand offers and, ultimately, how valued your brand is. Laddering has been used by advertising agencies for years to develop creative ads; now it is being used to help determine long-term brand strategies.

Features and attributes of a product or service are undifferentiated unless they translate into a higher order of perceived benefits to the customer. Similarly, benefits are relatively weak unless they link to the customer's central values and beliefs.

For instance, Ralph Lauren has laddered up to the highest point of brand value in consumers' minds. Many designers offer a variety of high-quality, durable, classic-looking clothes, but few of them can say their clothes allow customers to make a statement. Wearing Polo Ralph Lauren clothes (Polo Sport, Polo Jeans, and other lines), however, is like driving a Lexus in its appeal to social status. Lauren apparel becomes part of who the customer is by striking an emotional chord with that customer and having beliefs and values that he or she finds desirable.

Ralph Lauren helps its customers feel better about themselves, more confident and secure—even more fulfilled and more happy.

These emotional values help the Ralph Lauren brand transcend other brands. Although attributes and benefits can be replicated by a competitor, emotional values are virtually untouchable. This is why the Lauren brand is so powerful and why it transcends even its closest competitors.

Any brand that reaches this level of association and value with consumers is at the *brand pinnacle*—the place where every brand should strive to be. Regardless of industry, if you have a brand you have the opportunity to reach the pinnacle within your category.

The Brand Value Pyramid

The Brand Value Pyramid (Figure 2.2) best demonstrates the power of brand associations. The further up the pyramid you go, the more powerful your brand and the harder it is for competitors to usurp your position and strengths.

The pinnacle of the Brand Value Pyramid is as good as it gets, nearly an unassailable position. The concept of the Brand Value Pyramid is often the missing link for companies trying to better

Figure 2.2. Brand Value Pyramid

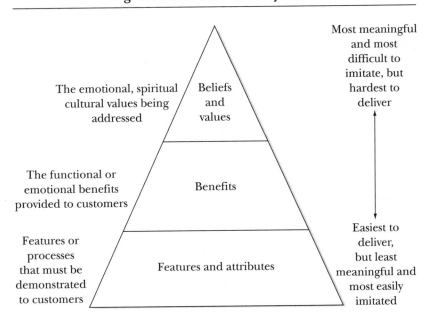

understand and leverage their brands for maximum strength. At the pinnacle of Ralph Lauren's Brand Value Pyramid, I believe, is self-esteem and self-worth. By being associated with Ralph Lauren, consumers feel better and more secure about themselves (see Figure 2.3).

Other brands have also reached the pinnacle of the Brand Value Pyramid. Among them are Saturn, Nordstrom's, American Express, Disney, Hallmark, Ben & Jerry's, Federal Express, Intel, G.E., John Deere, and Caterpillar. AOL, Yahoo!, and the Southern Company are getting there.

Brands at the top of the Brand Value Pyramid enjoy incredible customer loyalty, an ability to charge price premiums, and an ability to sell new products and services through the brand's endorsement power. Also, word-of-mouth referrals—maybe the ultimate sign of brand value—become the norm. In the end, this all translates to bottom-line growth and increases the asset value of the brand. In short, features—unlike values, in general—can be duplicated and should only serve to bring your benefits and values to life. This is a position to own, nurture, and cherish.

Case Study: Sears

For several years, Sears had tried to find its value in the minds of its customers. After years of struggling, it finally learned that customers thought of it as a supplier of appliances and durables. They had forgotten that Sears is also a major purveyor of apparel and other soft goods.

The repositioning of Sears to the "softer side" helped it focus on what it wanted to be associated with in customers' minds and also helped it realize that its forays into real estate, insurance, and credit would probably dilute the positioning it strived for. Although struggling a bit now, for several years in the 1990s Sears did find itself back on top of the Brand Value Pyramid.

Case Study: Evian

Evian is a brand that was at the pinnacle but lost its position. In the early 1990s Evian owned a unique set of brand associations: bottled water as a convenient, healthy, and natural way to quench your thirst. These associations went beyond benefits and became values, which allowed Evian to temporarily get to the pinnacle of the Brand Value Pyramid. The values associated with Evian included "helps me feel better about myself," "helps me cleanse my body," and "helps me be the healthiest I can be."

Figure 2.3. Ralph Lauren's Brand Value Pyramid

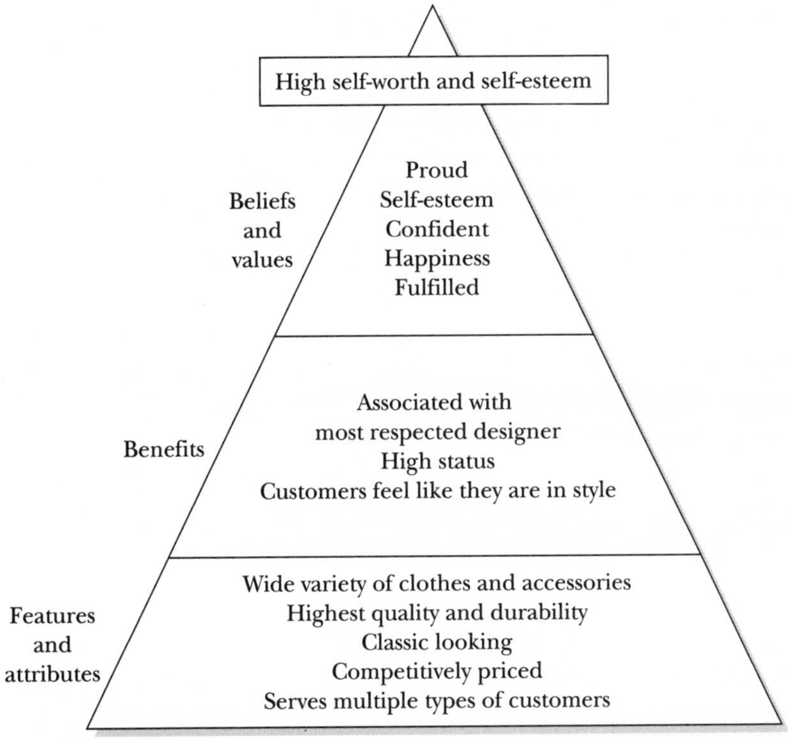

Not anymore. What previously were values and benefits are now simply attributes and thus are just the price of entry into the natural water industry. Crystal Geyser, Aquafina, Poland Springs, and others own the same attributes that were Evian's exclusively a few years ago (except when Evian owned them, they were values). Coke's bottled water, Dasani, threatens to shift the entire category to one that is based primarily on price and distribution—the lowest level of the Brand Value Pyramid—and will most likely pave the way for many of the brands just mentioned to disappear within the next few years.

Determining Your Attributes, Benefits, and Values

Start by following a rule that is applicable to all three parts of the BrandPicture: conduct research on competitive brands at the same time you conduct research on your own.

If your customer research does not compare your brand to competing brands, competitors may be able to claim the same benefits and associations as you. This may result in a strategy that has no sustainability because a competitor can readily duplicate it.

As mentioned earlier, when researching competitors try to include your two primary competitors and one up-and-comer who is new to the industry or product category. The up-and-comer may be a new company or an established one, but in either case it is a potential source of competitive trouble; you need to understand what level of benefits it could achieve and, as best as possible, where it is with its branding efforts.

For instance, Motorola may consider its top two competitors to be Ericsson and Nokia. An up-and-comer that it should investigate is Lucent Technologies, which is starting to steal market share, owns Bell Labs, and has started to create an aura of doing everything right—the darling of Wall Street and of those on the cutting edge.

Customer segmentation research is another important part of determining your brand's associations. Segmentation can be considered, researched, and analyzed in a number of ways, such as by demographics, psychographics, geography (zip codes), or needs. I recommend needs-based segmentation because it allows you to focus on customers' needs and wants and most closely aligns you with strategies that are likely to succeed.

Within the population you want to target, talk to numerous types of customers:

- Current customers
- Customers of competitive brands
- Former customers (who now use competitive brands)
- Potential customers (those who are about to make a decision to buy in your category)
- New customers (those who are using your brand for the first time)
- Your competition's new customers (those using a competitor's brand for the first time)
- Loyal customers (those who have been using your brand for a long time)
- Disgruntled users (customers you are in danger of losing soon)

For instance, in the veal industry, lost customers, or forgotten users, are attractive segments to pursue. These are individuals who grew up eating veal but as adults have not been buying it or ordering it in restaurants. The industry question is whether these "ex-users" can be brought back into the fold and again look to veal as a staple in the family diet.

In the telecommunications industry, a popular market segment is "Fortune 500 Wannabes." These are smaller organizations that think they can become much larger and want to start acting bigger now—companies that are proactive about the future. America Online was not always as big as it is today.

Regardless of the industry you are in, it is important to include other category influencers in your research. These may include industry experts, channel members such as brokers, distributors, and retailers, as well as (when possible) competitors. These additional interviews add value to your research, make your findings more robust, and force you to look at the big picture.

Once you understand who to conduct the research with, take those customers and influencers through a series of questions and exercises that will help you determine the level of associations that they declare your brand owns:

Brand Association Questions

- When I say the name of our brand, what is the first thing that comes to mind? Why?
- What are the strengths and weaknesses of our brand?
- What factors have contributed to your perceptions of these strengths and weaknesses?
- What brands did you consider before you bought our brand?
- What are your perceptions of the other brands you considered (strengths and weaknesses, attributes)?
- Why did you choose our brand?
- Has our brand met your needs and expectations?
- What benefits has our brand provided you? Does it meet your expectations?
- Describe the experience you had with our brand before you made the purchase . . . as you used the product . . . after you used it.

- Describe exactly what you bought when you purchased our product or service (benefits, hopes, and the like).
- When describing our brand to another potential buyer or a friend, how would you describe it?
- Why would you recommend our brand to another person (or why wouldn't you)?
- Does one brand make you feel differently about yourself (or reflect differently on you) than another?
- Describe the staff and service providers and how they interacted with you. How did they make you feel?

As you can tell, these questions are aimed primarily at finding out the benefits and associations a current customer has received as a result of having purchased your brand. This set of questions, although not comprehensive, is fairly typical of the questions you need to ask the segments you are researching. Of course, the questions would have to change if you are talking with competitors' users or nonusers.

The ultimate goal is understanding where your brand is on the Brand Value Pyramid. You must use the data you collect to draw conclusions and find patterns of associations that you can ascribe to your brand and competing brands. The point of this analysis is to discern whether your customers believe you have achieved the highest level of associations—beliefs and values. If the answer is yes, what will it take for you to maintain that position? If the answer is no, there are three questions to answer: Why is another brand at the top? Why is your brand not at the top? What can you do to help your brand move up the Brand Value Pyramid?

There are three keys to success in using brand associations and the Brand Value Pyramid:

1. Understand that there is an incremental movement up the Brand Value Pyramid—each layer you move up is dependent on fully achieving the previous layer.
2. Look for alignment across attributes, benefits, and values—the best brands have aligned associations, each fitting together and supportive of one another.
3. Make sure that this alignment is meaningful to your customers and difficult for competitors to imitate.

Here are a few more brand value pyramid examples.

Case Study: John Deere

The John Deere brand has reached the highest level of associations and rests on the top of the Brand Value Pyramid (see Figure 2.4). Customers state that at the attribute level, John Deere provides the highest-quality, reliable, and dependable products, all helping to address their diverse needs. Just at the attribute level, John Deere is a powerful brand.

Talking to users and nonusers shows that John Deere has ascended up the Brand Value Pyramid by providing its customers with many benefits: dependability, the best-cut lawns available, high resale value, and great service support (customers know if there are problems, John Deere is there to back up its products).

Because customers receive such benefits, John Deere has reached the highest level of value. Customers know that they have bought the best, think

Figure 2.4. John Deere's Brand Value Pyramid

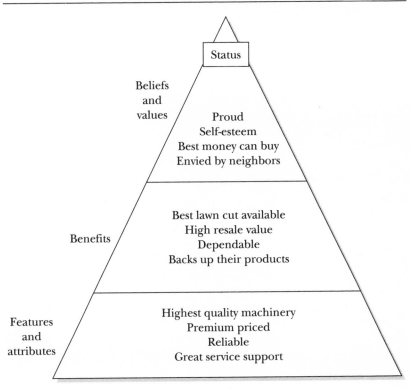

that they have status that their nonowner neighbors do not, and feel good about themselves because they are associated with the best that money can buy. Deere's recent commercial of a father receiving a John Deere hat and a set of keys to his new tractor from his family typifies these values.

Case Study: Saturn

Saturn has risen to the highest level of the Brand Value Pyramid (see Figure 2.5) because it has touched a customer value that no other car manufacturer has. It created an automobile that is as much about service as about the quality of the car itself. Buying a Saturn is a unique experience.

At the attribute level, Saturn promises high-quality cars, fair prices, committed and noncommissioned employees, and an appreciation of the

Figure 2.5. Saturn's Brand Value Pyramid

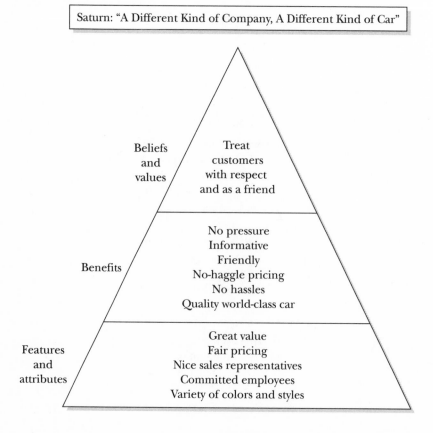

Saturn: "A Different Kind of Company, A Different Kind of Car"

Beliefs and values — Treat customers with respect and as a friend

Benefits — No pressure / Informative / Friendly / No-haggle pricing / No hassles / Quality world-class car

Features and attributes — Great value / Fair pricing / Nice sales representatives / Committed employees / Variety of colors and styles anxiety of a first-time or female car buyer. At the benefit level, Saturn provides customers with a friendly, no-hassle experience filled with information, education, no haggling, and no pressure. This has all helped translate to the highest level of value for customers, whom Saturn treats with respect and as a friend. Saturn has reached the pinnacle of the Brand Value Pyramid.

It will be interesting to watch as Saturn tries to stay at the highest level of the Brand Value Pyramid as it comes out with higher-end cars at higher prices. Will Saturn be able to capture the next level of car owners, those looking to trade up to an SUV or a sedan? In addition, the 1998 strike at Saturn may have tarnished its aura; how will it repair the damage? Saturn is still owned by General Motors; will GM allow it to stay entrepreneurial and customer focused?

Case Study: Dove Soap

Barry Krause, president of Publicis & Hal Riney, believes that all attributes of a given product or service are able to ladder up and be translated into human benefits: "Look at Dove soap. They talked about one-quarter cleansing cream. They laddered up to talk about the benefit of softer skin. They laddered softer skin into the benefit of being more attractive. They laddered this up to an ultimate human value—which is love. Love is on the top of everyone's emotional benefits list."

Case Study: Snackwells

Nabisco built Snackwells' value on low fat (and average taste) to meet a growing trend. Unfortunately, the trend has shifted to food that is overall healthier and good for you. Some would also say that decadence is back. Snackwells did not stay up to date and adapt their brand away from low-fat toward good-for-you; as a result, revenues have decreased from their incredible case sales of the early to mid-1990s, and Nabisco is having a hard time finding Snackwells' value again.

Case Study: Virgin

Virgin and its founder Richard Branson has tried to start at the top of the Brand Value Pyramid. Branson claims that customers who, like himself, want to be associated with an irreverent icon will want to be associated with Virgin. As you can imagine, not too many brands start at the top and fill in the layers below. I believe he will be hard pressed to make this work, at least in the United States.

Case Study: Planet Hollywood

Similarly, Planet Hollywood, whose stock recently dropped to 83 cents from a high of $24 a few years ago, thought the entertainment value of its restaurants would be enough to take it to the top of the Brand Value Pyramid. To get there, though, the food and service have to be good and the experience has to be exciting and differentiated. None of this ever took hold.

Rather, the focus appeared to be on customers' desires to be linked to "the stars." Not a bad way to get them to try Planet Hollywood once, but not great for repeat business or word-of-mouth recommendations. Planet Hollywood recently filed for Chapter 11 and is closing down several of its restaurants.

Again, you have to work your way up the Brand Value Pyramid, earn each level, and strive to reach that emotional or spiritual value connection with customers at the pinnacle. This connection is powerful; it helps customers avoid going through a lengthy process every time a purchase is made and it allows a company that owns the brand the opportunity to experience all the brand benefits mentioned in the first chapter of this book.

One last point about brand associations: over time, values can become benefits and benefits can become attributes. This is especially true of the high-technology world. Intel's benefit of highest-speed processing used to provide top-of-the-pinnacle value as it allowed us to work as fast and efficiently as possible. Now Intel is challenged by the competition to the point where speed is part of the price of entry to the microprocessor chip world.

Brand Persona

Brand associations and the Brand Value Pyramid are half of your brand image. Brand persona is the other half. Independently, the halves provide little value. Together they provide you a deep understanding of your brand's image, its strengths and weaknesses, and its points of differentiation. A well-understood brand image ultimately leads to a positioning that is valued, unique, credible, and sustainable.

Brand persona is the set of human characteristics that consumers associate with the brand, such as personality, appearance, values, likes and dislikes, gender, size, shape, ethnicity, intelligence, socioeconomic class, and education. These bring the brand to life and allow consumers to describe it to others as they would a friend.

Similarly, consumers decide whether they want to be associated with a brand in much the same way and for the same reasons that they want to associate with some people and not others. Personas can be translated into selling propositions when they are attractive. If a persona is unattractive, however, it's necessary to fix the brand so that customers do want to be associated with it.

Oprah Winfrey, for example, is a person that many people want to be associated with. Her persona is warm, giving, empathetic, human, and nice. She has a good sense of humor, represents multiple interests, and is willing to try new things. She acts like a good friend to television viewers, and she shops at stores where we shop (such as Filene's Basement). She loves dogs, is always publicly fighting her weight, and is a Midwesterner with high values. These characteristics make her a strong person that we want to be associated with. Oprah is actually a very strong brand. As a result, she has been able to leverage her persona into every entertainment medium—from television to her own magazine—and continues to be one of the most admired people in America.

Consider John Deere again. In classes I have taught, students described its persona with words and phrases such as the following: hard working; rugged; Midwesterner; great values; dependable; family oriented; male; college educated; someone who saves a lot of money; wholesome; trusting; likes to wear green. This list describes a person you would very likely seek out as a friend and want as a neighbor—someone you can connect with and trust.

Thus you see the type of value the John Deere brand has, the strong potential it has to connect with its customers, the dollar value customers may associate with John Deere, and the likelihood of customers wanting to be involved with it.

My branding classes were also easily able to describe the Ralph Lauren persona: classy; stylish; comfortable; family oriented; rugged; cool; male and female; graduate school; all-American; in good shape; fun; strong family values. This makes it obvious why this brand has crossed so many boundaries and categories, from paints to furniture to men's and women's fashions to baby clothes. From both the Deere and Lauren personas you can imagine how they translate into communications, new offerings, higher prices, and the like.

Brand Persona Questions

How do you find out your brand's persona? Ask questions that complement those you asked to uncover brand associations. Some typical questions might include the following:

- Why do you consider brand X to be better than others?
- What are the strengths and weaknesses of brand X? How about relative to the competition?
- If you saw a person using brand X, what would you know about him or her (age, gender, personality, education, income level)?
- If brand X were a car, what kind of car would it be and why? (Cars typically used for this question are Chevy, Lexus, Saturn, Mercedes, and Volvo.)
- If brand X were one of the following places, which would it be and why? (Typical cities or geographical areas used here are Silicon Valley [cutting edge], New York [cosmopolitan], Paris [fashionable], Omaha [traditional].)
- If brand X were a department store, what store would it be and why? (Typical stores used here are Nordstrom's [high service], Sears [traditional], Wal-Mart [price focused], Niemann Marcus [higher-end].)
- What kind of animal best describes this brand? (A jaguar would be fast and nimble, a turtle would be slow and deliberate.)

Some of these questions may seem silly at first, but they are good ways to uncover characteristics of your brand that you probably never knew existed. The bottom line is that powerful brands have easily identifiable characteristics.

David Aaker, in *Building Strong Brands,* identified five human characteristics to which he claims 93 percent of all brands aspire:

Sincerity (Campbell's, Hallmark, Kodak)—down-to-earth, honest, wholesome

Excitement (Porsche, Absolut)—daring, spirited, imaginative, up-to-date

Competence (AMEX, CNN, IBM)—reliable, intelligent, successful

Sophistication (Lexus, Mercedes, Revlon)—upper class, charming

Ruggedness (Levi's, Marlboro)—outdoorsy, tough.

This is a great starter list, but as with humans there are many ways to describe a brand and some characteristics are more obvious than others. But all characteristics should be used together to most comprehensively build a brand's persona. Some characteristics may lead to the right approach to position a brand; others may serve as points of differentiation and ways to sell your brand to different targets.

Comparing Competing Brand Personas

As mentioned earlier, this type of research must be conducted relative to key competitors. Done in a vacuum, brand persona research leaves you with some good information about yourself but very little about the opportunities available to you.

For example, consider the way participants in the BAM courses I teach describe FedEx and its perceived closest delivery competitors:

FedEx	*U.S. Post Office*	*UPS*
Male or female	Male	Male
Young	Older	Middle-aged
Athletic	Grumpy	Evolving
Friendly	Not reliable	Inconsistent
Prompt	Low technology	Friendly
Dependable	Unsophisticated	Brown uniforms
Energetic	Overweight	Unionized
High technology	Complacent	Okay service
Problem solvers	Slow	Professional
Motivated	Rigid	International
Professional	Problem makers	Problem solvers

As an "up-and-comer," Exact Express, the new offering from Yellow Freight, may also be able to challenge FedEx's position. It offers seven-day deliveries, same-day deliveries, and a 100 percent satisfaction guarantee. These benefits certainly make Exact Express an interesting new choice in the overnight delivery competitive set.

As this book goes to press, UPS has launched a new ad and brand campaign that may shift the dynamics in this competitive market yet again. The campaign says, "At UPS, we deliver more than boxes. We deliver ideas on how to bring your products to market faster, more efficiently. Customized solutions from inventory financing to managing your call centers to reengineering your global supply chain. Of course, if you need a 2,000-pound orca whale delivered overnight, we can handle that too."

The descriptions of UPS, Exact Express, and the U.S. Post Office should help FedEx see where it stacks up, falls short, and is most vulnerable. Equally important, the comparison should help FedEx see where it has the most opportunity to grow.

Case Study: A Midwest Hospital Persona

A Midwest hospital was seeking to compete more aggressively against its major competitor. By deriving brand personas for both, my company came up with many interesting characteristics:

Client Hospital	Competitor Hospital
Female or male	Male
Dresses casually	Wears a blue suit
Middle-upper aged	Middle-aged
Middle class	Upper middle class
Clean but not polished	Professional
Older feeling	Contemporary
Warm, a friend	Cold
Caring	Superficial
Not money hungry	Expensive but worth it
Best available in Midwest	Best available in the country
Experience	Expertise

There were obvious differences in personas between these two hospitals. Our client was an older, "been-there-since-you-were-a-kid," Catholic, trusted hospital. The competitor was more about state-of-the-art equipment, top-flight doctors, and the best money could buy. We assumed that patients would choose the hospital that they believed would give them the best possible treatment. There might be lingering loyalty to our older hospital, but in the end sickness and health know no loyalty.

With this Brand Persona exercise, our client realized it needed to integrate its reputation for caring with new expertise that could be developed over time. It became obvious that caring, nurturing, and empathy cannot be bought by a competitor. However, our client could start to build expertise by recruiting doctors from the best schools and hiring them away from established hospitals, and by investing in the latest technology.

The hospital eventually became known as the "caring experts"—a persona and positioning that is both valuable and unique. The end results speak for themselves: market share is up dramatically and the image of the hospital has improved tremendously relative to the competing hospital.

Often a picture is the best way to describe a brand persona. If you do believe that a persona is representative of a human being, you should be able to create a picture of that person. Figure 2.6 illustrates the personas of four different brands in a services industry my company has done work for. You can immediately see the differences and the strengths and weaknesses of each.

Figure 2.6. Four Competitors' Personas

Company 1	Company 2	Company 3	Company 4
50–60 years old	Late 40s	40–50 years old	35–50 years old
Male	Male	Male	Male
Community college education	High school education	Graduate education	Ph.D.
Attire a little dated	Not professionally dressed	Professional attire	Medical attire, stethoscope
Friendly and caring	Auctioneer mentality, anything for a sale	Technical, experienced	Clean-cut

Shifting Brand Images over Time

Can a brand's persona be changed? If so, how great and how credible can the change be? I believe a brand can change just as a person is able to change. However, Woody Allen is not going to become an operatic soprano tomorrow, and Cindy Crawford is not going to be ugly next week. It is all about degree of change. The easiest changes are incremental and are begun well in advance of the need.

Often crisis is a catalyst to refocus or dramatically change a brand's persona. K-Mart, for example, came close to Chapter 11 bankruptcy a few years ago. But it has recently come back strong and is probably one of four major retailers that will survive over the next five years. K-Mart realized that its "blue-light special" image had been lost to Wal-Mart, that a slew of new stores like Target had come on strong, and that old stalwarts like Sears were not going away.

The shift in K-Mart's persona has gone way beyond the name change from K-Mart to Big K. Its old and new personas probably look like this:

The Old K-Mart Persona	*The New K-Mart Persona*
Older	Younger, hip, and modern
Dilapidated	Well-designed stores, attractive
Blue-light specials	Great values and brands
Unorganized/unkempt	Organized into stores within the store
Poor service	High levels of customer service
Lower to middle class	All classes
Competes with Woolworth's (such as Target)	Competes with many retailers

To compete more effectively, K-Mart decided to shift its focus to name brands (such as Martha Stewart), redesign its stores, bring in respected spokespersons (such as Rosie O'Donnell), leverage a new name (Big K), and develop and execute a major advertising and public relations push to relaunch the new K-Mart. The result is that K-Mart is back and performing very well.

Other companies have had mixed success. Quaker Oats, for example, changed the image of its oatmeal over a few years from a hot meal on a cold day to a healthy part of daily life. It never lost the former association, but added the latter. But another former Quaker product fared less well. When Quaker bought Snapple, it thought it had acquired the perfect complement to Gatorade. Snapple was cool, hip, and an up-and-coming drink that relied on its quirky image, its spokesperson Cathy, and its all-natural ingredients. But it took Quaker only a year to undo most of the good that Snapple's previous owner created. Quaker was obsessed with using the Gatorade channel to also sell Snapple, as opposed to continuing to build and enhance the Snapple persona that had been developed over time. Within a couple of years, Quaker sold Snapple to Triarc for a big loss. Triarc has since refocused on Snapple's strengths and has helped Snapple regain the persona that made it so strong to start with.

Case Study: The Chicago Tribune

The *Chicago Tribune* is in the process of changing its brand persona. For more than a century and a half, the *Tribune* has led the local newspaper scene thanks to its focus on editorial integrity and coverage that was both broad and deep. But in all that time, it never consciously pursued a particular brand position, leaving itself to be positioned by the nature of its content or the perceived profile of the people putting it together. Recently, the onset of the Internet, the explosion of media choices, the decline of time people devote to reading newspapers, and a trend of softening circulation forced senior management to rethink the *Tribune's* image and content offering.

The *Tribune* went through the BAM process we have been describing. It learned a lot about the newspaper's relative strengths and weaknesses, how readers described the *Tribune's* associations and persona, and, most of all, what readers wanted from it.

The *Chicago Tribune* uncovered a generally held image of its persona as conservative, middle to upper class, male-oriented, and even aloof, and recognized this would not help it thrive in the future. It needed to shift its image to change the marketplace's perceptions and the *Tribune's* potential for even greater readership market share gains.

Readers wanted a newspaper that spoke to their needs. They wanted a paper that was personally relevant to their lives. They wanted a more balanced approach to reporting and to get to know the columnists they spent so much time reading. They wanted new sections of the paper, such as Family and Home & Garden. They wanted enhanced business coverage and better organized local, regional, and national news.

Within six months of the BAM process, readers got all this and more and the *Tribune*'s image, circulation, and advertising dollars have all improved fairly dramatically.

Dave Murphy, the *Tribune*'s senior vice president of sales and marketing, says, "We discovered that when all areas of our organization participated meaningfully and genuinely in a process that made us more intimate with our customers, we learned and put to effective use information that we couldn't have gotten any other way. Today at the newspaper we are consistently asking, Is this what customers want? and, How can we improve their relationship with us? This BAM process helped us truly see our potential for long-term growth and how we can get there."

Summary

Brand associations and the brand persona are the sources of a brand's image. Identifying both elements clearly can help your company make dramatic changes that will enhance your brand's image and its performance in the marketplace. Understanding your brand's image allows you to better control its destiny. This requires that you look outside to determine what you have to do to compete more effectively.

By understanding your brand's image, your company can better choose strategies to either take advantage of the image or fix it. A well-developed brand image may lead to action steps such as increasing the brand's importance to desired target segments, increasing the value that customers ascribe to a brand, better capturing customers through skillful laddering, and the like.

Step Three deals with brand contracts. That discussion will help you better understand the makeup of the brand, including the promises the brand makes and the expectations customers have when they think about one brand relative to another.

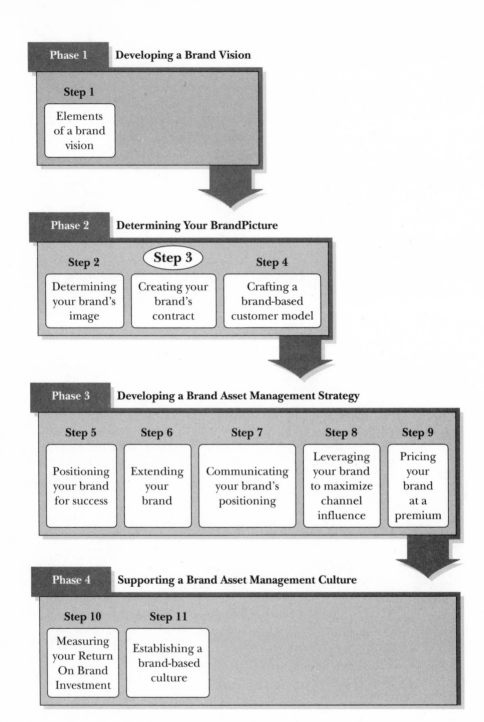

Creating Your Brand's Contract

A Brand Contract is a list of all promises the brand makes to customers. Such a contract is executed internally, but it is defined and validated externally by the marketplace. Brand Contracts can and should change over time. New promises can be added, other promises can be updated, and irrelevant promises can be deleted.

A Brand Contract is a critical piece of the BrandPicture (see the illustration on the facing page) because it helps to further define marketplace perceptions and expectations and forces managers to be honest with themselves. In addition to positive promises to customers, a Brand Contract can contain negative promises or attributes. It is important to build on the strong brand promises and mitigate the negative ones.

For example, one of our clients had a reputation for putting customers calling for information on hold for what seemed an eternity (as defined by the marketplace). Whether the client believed it or not, this had become a "promise" that customers had come to expect.

To develop a successful Brand Contract, a company has to first understand its brand's current set of promises as defined by the marketplace. Next, it must determine if this contract is the one it perceived the brand to have. Then it has to take action to either improve the Brand Contract or strengthen the positive promises already in place.

Critical to the success of a Brand Contract is that, before the contract is made and its positive promises publicly stated, your organization determines how best to make them a reality. For example, the client just mentioned addressed the on-hold problem by outsourcing its incoming calls to a call center. The call center would immediately answer the phone and either find someone to talk to the customer within thirty seconds or give a time when a company representative would call back. Thus "on hold" was no longer perceived to be a negative promise or expectation.

Developing a Brand Contract should be aligned with the brand image research from Step Two and be derived directly from it (see Figure 3.1).

The Importance of Upholding Contracts

In a recent *Wall Street Journal* article, a writer told of his experiences with AT&T's One Rate service. He talked about the brochure and its promises: No more roaming charges. No more peak hour extra charges. One low rate, such as a thousand minutes for $119. If you cannot get a signal, AT&T promises to find a carrier that can. AT&T claims you will like the service so much that you will use your cellular phone to make all your long distance calls, both from home and on the road.

These wonderful promises (all laid out clearly in the brochure) definitely hit cellular phone users' hot buttons. The future is here and One Rate is it.

Figure 3.1. The Brand Image and Customer Expectations

Brand image		Brand contract
Brand associations	Brand persona	• Consists of the product, service, and experience expectations set forth by the brand. • The expectations can be good and bad. • It starts by saying, "Our brand promises to. . . ."
Product, service, and organization characteristics	Human characteristics	

But the writer went on to talk about his frustrations with the One Rate plan. The service was inconsistent and did not work in certain areas within some of the biggest cities in the country. Many times his calls came to a "screeching halt" because the person he called could no longer hear him or because calls were cut off altogether. He was disappointed in the service and frustrated because the promise he thought the brand was making was being broken.

The implications of this for AT&T go beyond one customer's dissatisfaction with One Rate. The AT&T brand is on other products and services—telephones, cable television, and long distance service, among others, and a bad experience with one product or service tied to your brand will have direct implications on the acceptance and credibility of all other related product and service offerings.

Implicit Brand Contracts

A Brand Contract has to be market driven. That is, it must reflect what customers really think and what the company is really prepared to do. By looking at a company's current performance, we can see the contract that the company implicitly offers today and what it must do to improve the contract in the future. The Brand Contract is a set of promises that you believe will keep current customers satisfied even as it attracts a new clientele.

Here is the implicit Brand Contract that Starbucks would probably develop, based on its current performance, if it went through this process of writing a contract.

Starbucks' Implicit Brand Contract

Starbucks promises to do the following:
1. Provide the highest quality coffee available on the market today
2. Offer customers a wide variety of coffee options as well as complementary food and beverage items
3. Have an atmosphere that is warm, friendly, homelike, and appropriate for having a conversation with a good friend or reading a book
4. Recognize that visiting Starbucks is as much about the *experience* of drinking coffee as it is about the coffee itself

5. Have employees who are friendly, courteous, outgoing, help-ful, knowledgeable, and quick to fill customer orders
6. Provide customers the same experience at any one of the several thousand Starbucks worldwide
7. Stay current with the times (such as by using the Internet), meet customer needs (offer lunch), and help customers create the Starbucks experience on their terms (at the airport, in the office, or through retail distribution in the home)
8. Provide customers with an environmentally friendly establishment
9. Educate customers on the different types of coffee offered

A few ways that Starbucks currently supports such a contract include hiring people who have an outgoing personality; educating consumers through brochures and literature about the different types of coffee; continuing to offer new products that add to the experience (such as compact discs); and providing the same type of employee training regardless of location.

As another example, the evolution of Kinko's implicit Brand Contract over the last fifteen years has been interesting to follow. In the beginning, Kinko's strategy and positioning revolved primarily around serving the needs of university students, with Kinko's locations at or near most major universities.

A Kinko's Brand Contract back then would probably have included the following:

Kinko's "Old" Implicit Brand Contract

Kinko's promises to do the following:

1. Provide customers with friendly service
2. Be open twenty-four hours a day
3. Have convenient, sensible locations
4. Have knowledgeable employees working at each store who can help students and others troubleshoot any problems
5. Have a computer station waiting for customers who need one
6. Provide a variety of services, from copying to binding to producing business cards

From a customer perspective, Kinko's contract probably also included a few negative promises such as these:

7. Charge premium prices for every piece of paper sold
8. Have long lines at the cash register and to get on a computer
9. Have some poorly trained employees

Later Kinko's reached out to the at-home and small business communities. Consequently, it encountered many challenges as it tried to expand and develop a deeper and more meaningful contract with its customers. Kinko's had to migrate from its position as a college campus copy shop to one as a small business partner. To do that, it had to upgrade its implicit Brand Contract to meet the growing needs of smaller businesses as they become more sophisticated.

Why? First, competitors such as Mailboxes, Etc. have come into the market and tried to replicate Kinko's unique points of differentiation. Therefore, Kinko's must be concerned with keeping its current core business intact.

Second, many customers have become more sophisticated than Kinko's employees. This was not the case ten years ago, but expectations of service and expertise are much higher than they used to be. Third, as Kinko's has grown the service provided by employees has declined and become less consistent.

Kinko's also faces another problem. Strong franchises gain their strength by having customers experience the same level of service and satisfaction at any of their establishments regardless of location, and a good Brand Contract must reflect this. This may not be the case for Kinko's anymore.

For instance, there are two Kinko's within a few blocks of each other near my office in downtown Chicago. One of them I would trust with any client presentation; the other I would not.

Four Principles for Developing a Brand Contract

So how does one get started in developing a Brand Contract? Fortunately, your Brand Contract can be derived from the same research that you conduct in determining your brand's image. Again, be sure to conduct this research relative to a few key competitors so that you can make comparisons between your brand and theirs. Beyond that, if you keep four guiding principles in mind the process should be straightforward.

1. Understand the Brand Contract from Your Customers' Perspective

The research questions you should ask when developing your Brand Contract complement those you ask when determining your brand's image. These questions can include the following:

- In making a purchase in this category, what were the benefits you expected to receive?
- What are the most important aspects of service that a provider must be sure to offer?
- Did Brand X meet your benefit expectations? Why? Why not?
- What promises does Brand X make? Positive promises? Negative promises? What impact do these promises have on your perceptions of the brand?
- How did you arrive at your perceptions of promises?
- Do other brands make different promises or set different expectations than Brand X?
- Once you purchased Brand X, how well did the actual brand experience match with your expectations?
- What could have been done differently to make your purchase and brand experience an even better one?
- How well did Brand X match up to the promises you expected before the purchase, during use of the actual product or service, and afterward?
- When you think about Brand X, what other promises could you imagine it making?

The key to making this process work is to have it be driven by customers and key purchase influencers, not internal managers. You need to expect negative promises and not think about this exercise defensively. Think of it as a critical path to maximizing long-term brand satisfaction.

Your Brand Contract can and should shift over time and most likely will have nuances that vary with the customer set. For example, if you own a utility or a telecommunication brand the contract will be very different for commercial versus residential customers (see Figure 3.2).

Figure 3.2. A Utility's Brand Contract

All utility customers will require Brand Contract promises such as the following:

- Deliver gas and electricity reliably.
- Price the commodity fairly.
- Respond to emergencies swiftly.
- Promote safety and make sure that the commodity is being delivered in the safest way possible.
- Have a strong focus on providing customers with the highest level of service attainable.
- Simplify the billing so customers can understand the bill.

Businesses require a Brand Contract including:

- Provide additional related products and services that will help my company save more money.
- Help me manage my overhead by planning to maximize my energy efficiency.
- Assign a customer service or sales representative that will be there when I need them.
- Conduct an energy audit on a regular basis to help me better understand my energy issues.

Homeowners require a Brand Contract including:

- Combine my electric and gas bills.
- Provide me with a variety of payment plans.
- Do not let me suffer through an automation maze when I call with a simple question.

2. Translate the Brand Contract into Standards

The critical translation from promises to standards helps you determine whether you have in place what it takes to make the brand promise come true.

When Fred Smith and his senior management team transformed the brand identity of Federal Express to that of FedEx a few years ago, they had two primary objectives. First, they wanted to increase their brand's commitment to the delivery and services promises that the company had perfected over the years; second, they wanted to update the look of the company with a new logo and colors.

To introduce this initiative to FedEx employees, as the story goes, Smith and his team rented out a large part of a Memphis Airport hangar and had all the employees attend a special meeting there one morning. The hangar was packed with curious employees. In dramatic fashion, the management team started the meeting by showing employees the old Federal Express airplane and told them to say goodbye to it forever. As it drove off, the new FedEx airplane entered with its new logo, new colors, and fresh and innovative look.

After the unveiling, the management team talked about the promises FedEx makes to its customers every day and how those promises differentiate FedEx from its competition and keep it number one in customer satisfaction and loyalty. Management went on to explain that the redesign symbolized the company's commitment to continuous improvement and to meeting the demanding high-quality service needs of its loyal and expanding customer base.

Employees went back to their offices motivated and with renewed vigor. Upon arrival back at headquarters, they discovered that everything had been changed to reflect the new brand. From the signage outside to the business cards and stationery on each desk to the screen saver on everyone's computer, everything that had been Federal Express that morning was now FedEx.

The implicit message of this quick conversion was that FedEx is in a business in which speed and timeliness mean everything to customers. FedEx's ability to keep its promises to customers ("your package will be there by 10:30 tomorrow morning"), and even delight customers by delivering a package earlier than expected, has been key to keeping the business so successful. FedEx has one of the strongest Brand Contracts I have seen.

Importantly, a promise means action. A promise of overnight delivery means developing a flawless distribution and transportation infrastructure for a business that promises action "when it absolutely, positively has to be there overnight."

The McDonald's Brand Contract promises customers that they will get the same experience in each and every McDonald's restaurant. That means that owners and franchisees have to abide by a common set of guidelines, quality controls, and standards. This allows McDonald's to uphold its promise globally. Indeed, McDonald's promise of having the best french fries led it to invest in new fryer technology that made their fries taste even better.

IBM Consulting's Brand Contract

In the early to mid-1990s, "Solutions for a Small Planet" was born out of an effort to reconnect all of IBM under one positioning umbrella. It allowed for the (apparently) seamless introduction of IBM's e-business, which today is the fastest growing part of the company. Lou Gerstner, CEO at the time, helped IBM recognize that it is in a service business as much as a product business (in fact, one-third of revenues today comes from services) and that new service offerings would only help to build the IBM brand.

IBM Consulting was being tested as one of many new service offerings, aimed at helping IBM expand and become recognized as a global solution provider. Part of the project my company conducted was aimed at helping IBM Consulting define the promises it would have to make in the marketplace to be successful.

Many inside IBM believed the marketplace would not find IBM to be credible in offering consulting services; one early internal hypothesis was that the consulting services business should be called Watson & Associates (after founder Thomas Watson) to separate "Big Blue" from the new offering. The marketplace rejected Watson & Associates because it believed the power of the IBM brand was too strong to not leverage in any new service offering.

Many executives and CIOs in outside firms thought IBM Consulting could be a great success because of the inherent expertise. However, this part of the marketplace believed that IBM Consulting would need to make and keep several brand promises to be credible, including these:

- Any recommendation made by the IBM Consulting Group will include two non-IBM recommendations or solutions to establish objectivity. (Many executives wondered if IBM would use the Consulting Group to sell more hardware and software; some said that the first time IBM Consulting recommended an IBM-only solution as the only solution would be the last time they would use IBM Consulting.)
- IBM will invest in methodologies for its consultants to employ on engagements.
- IBM will hire some new people from proven and established consulting firms for the Consulting Group. (The marketplace also needed evidence that retraining of current IBM employees, now to be called consultants, was taking place.)
- The IBM Consulting Group will prove that the value it provides is above and beyond the free advice customers had been receiving for years.
- IBM will learn how to market its consulting skills to new buyers. (Potential clients generally learn about consulting firms through seminars, speeches, articles, books, and word of mouth.)

The IBM Consulting Group activated its Brand Contract through many new initiatives. First, it hired numerous outsiders from other consulting firms to lead projects and bring the credibility needed to launch this successfully. Second, it brought in an outsider from one of the top consulting firms in the world to run the business because the consulting business model was very different from that of the hardware business model.

Third, it spent months developing unique methodologies. Fourth, it hired my company to train over 3,000 consultants worldwide on core consulting skills and to share findings from our global branding project. Fifth, it set up new career tracks and compensation packages that more closely align with the consulting industry, as opposed to traditional IBM career tracks. And sixth, it spent a lot of time marketing its new offering and expertise in the way the market demanded.

The IBM Consulting Group operationalized its Brand Contract, received the right amount of funding and support from senior management, realigned the organization to more closely focus on the unique consulting needs of different customer segments, and fulfilled the brand promises the marketplace had articulated. As a result, the IBM Consulting Group is now one of the top consulting firms in the world and its brand is synonymous with extremely high-quality consulting and many satisfied clients.

To summarize the second guiding principle: you must be able to translate promises into action. You may have to make changes in your infrastructure, invest in operations, and allow time for training. Customers must perceive that your promises are backed by the right level of support. When you say you are the best in service, you have to know how to define service from a customer perspective and then know how to implement it and measure yourself relative to customer satisfaction levels. Figure 3.3 shows an example of how brand associations translate into a Brand Contract and the need to operationalize these promises.

3. Fulfill the "Good" Promises of Your Brand Contract or Risk Damaging the Brand

This principle is intuitive, but does deserve some attention. Starbucks' promises are in place every day. It is important that customers' experiences are similar and satisfying each time they visit a Starbucks. Such consistency leads to loyal customers. When Starbucks announced a price increase in 1999, it had minimal impact on sales and the brand overall because, as mentioned in Chapter One, powerful brands are able to overcome negative news more readily. Similarly, when Starbucks comes out with a new product, like frappuccino a few years ago, there is instant acceptance because the company has credibility and people assume that the quality of the product will be high before they even try it.

But as Starbucks increases its outlets and distribution channels, it risks losing control over the promises of its Brand Contract. I consistently hear complaints about the taste of Starbucks coffee on United Airlines. It's probably better than coffee on any other airline, but because it's Starbucks the expectations are inherently higher.

Figure 3.3. Moving from Brand Associations to a Brand Contract at a Major Newspaper

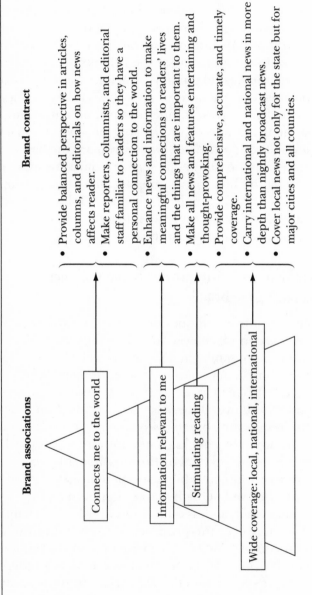

Brand associations

Brand contract

- Provide balanced perspective in articles, columns, and editorials on how news affects reader.
- Make reporters, columnists, and editorial staff familiar to readers so they have a personal connection to the world.
- Enhance news and information to make meaningful connections to readers' lives and the things that are important to them.
- Make all news and features entertaining and thought-provoking.
- Provide comprehensive, accurate, and timely coverage.
- Carry international and national news in more depth than nightly broadcast news.
- Cover local news not only for the state but for major cities and all counties.

Connects me to the world

Information relevant to me

Stimulating reading

Wide coverage: local, national, international

Countless companies do not treat their brand and its contract as seriously as they should. For instance, Avon may be taking a risk by opening up a spa in Manhattan because it undermines the foundation of what the company was built upon: one-on-one relationships with each customer in her home, not in Avon's "home."

As mentioned earlier, Volvo's move from safety to performance a few years ago was not consistent with its Brand Contract, which resulted in a downturn in sales. And can ATA become an airline for business professionals after years of the jingle, "With ATA, you're on vacation"?

When my company helps develop a Brand Contract, we always ask the client to think about a few contract stipulations that do not exist today but that they would like to see in the future. This forces an organization to think about the future and connect back to the Brand Vision. Obviously, future promises need to be worked on today if they are to come to life in a few years.

4. Uncover and Address the "Bad" Promises of the Brand

TCI, one of the largest cable providers in the country and a recent acquisition by AT&T, underwent a major overhaul of its identity and services a few years ago. The TCI brand had so many negative connotations that the company had to do something for fear of losing its business to the satellite industry.

Three of the worst brand promises customers articulated about TCI were these:

- You will wait a long time to get from TCI's impersonal telephone automation system to a human being.
- You will have to miss a day of work if you need to have a service call; you never know when a service person will show up.
- Someone will have to come out to your home to fix any problem you have with your cable.

TCI improved its Brand Contract by directly addressing these three issues, as well as a few others that had less of an impact on the brand. TCI now answers phone calls on the first ring, has technicians that can generally solve your problem over the phone, and is able to narrow the window of time for a service call down to a couple of hours.

Summary

The Brand Contract concept is simple: understand the promises your brand makes, identify those that are important to your customers, and identify the promises that your brand can make, as well as shortcomings or areas for improvement. Then develop a contract that states all of this. The result will be a customer-driven, operationally achievable contract and a valuable brand in the marketplace.

Developing a Brand Contract is Step Three in the brand asset management process and the second part of Phase 2, developing a BrandPicture. Once a Brand Contract is established, we can move on to defining a brand-based model of the customer, which is the subject of Step Four.

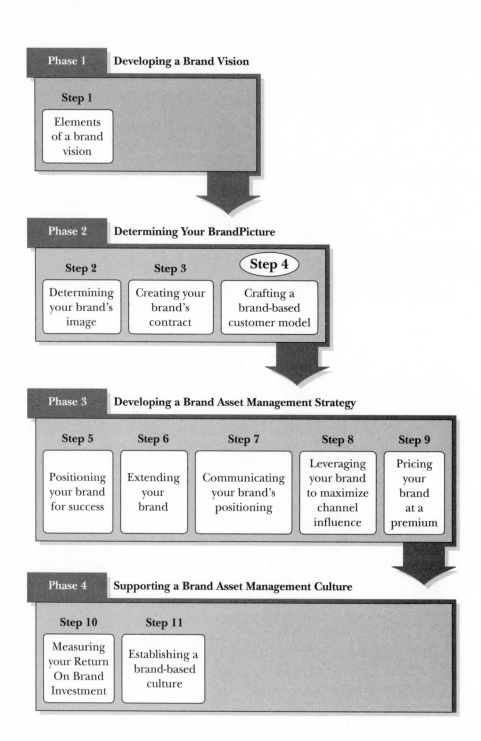

Crafting a Brand-Based Customer Model

Developing a customer model is the third and final part of the BrandPicture (see the illustration on the facing page). The intent here is to provide a comprehensive understanding of customer beliefs and behaviors that bear on the brand, the product or service, the category, and the competitors. The customer model considers former, present, and potential customers and encompasses the range of beliefs and behaviors that such customers hold, not just the prevalent opinion.

Consider the following tale of a company that knew its customers well . . . and then lost touch with them.

Case Study: The Schwinn Story

Schwinn: an American icon, the world's finest. Remember the Collegiate, the Varsity, the Stingray? Schwinn was among the elite brands for several decades. Years ago everyone knew about Schwinn, what it stood for, and the high quality of its bicycles.

But in 1992, Schwinn filed for Chapter 11 and almost went away for good. What happened?

In its early days, around a hundred years ago, Schwinn stood for the finest mode of transportation money could buy. It was a high-prestige brand that captured the nation's attention before the car was invented and took over the transportation market. Back then, a Schwinn cost $127—more than some early cars.

Fast-forward to the 1940s and 1950s, when another generation knelt before the Schwinn dynasty. The brand was still prestigious, but as a leisure item rather than a mode of transportation. Schwinn repositioned accordingly and marketed its "dream machines" primarily to boys and their fathers.

In the 1960s Schwinn repositioned its brand again and marketed to families, bringing women and girls into the mix. This brought unprecedented success; Schwinn was the top brand and, by 1970, was manufacturing a million bicycles a year. At the time, Schwinn was better known than Coca-Cola and owned the all-American image.

In the 1970s Schwinn added exercise bicycles to its line in response to the fitness trend, but continued to upgrade its ten-speed bikes, the most popular bike then. It remained the market leader.

In the early 1980s, however, Schwinn started to lose focus on both its brand and the market. Dirt bikes and mountain bikes were starting to take off, but Schwinn management believed these were just passing fads and that the company's brand would be degraded if it sold such products. Long-faithful dealers were not happy and began carrying and recommending other brands. Soon strong competitors with strong brand names, such as Huffy and Trek, became forces to be reckoned with.

Stubbornly, Schwinn held onto its past even as a new generation was growing up that had never heard of the company. The Collegiate and Varsity were becoming relics as mountain bikes started to take control of the industry.

As Schwinn kept its focus on ten-speeds, it quickly lost its prestige, and although awareness remained high, consumers' associations with it turned negative. Schwinn had become "uncool" and—even more damaging—irrelevant.

In other words, Schwinn lost control of its image and its Brand Contract became meaningless. It no longer knew who its customers were, how they were segmented, or whether it could serve them credibly. Even if Schwinn had known which segments of the market to pursue, it did not know what mattered to them, what their purchase criteria were, or how to compete against the upstarts who now owned the market. An American icon was dying.

The happy ending, however, is that during the 1990s Schwinn adopted several bold survival strategies and redefined its brand in terms of marketplace needs and wants. It jumped on the mountain bike trend before it was too late and today is number one in the category, having overtaken Trek's former lead. The company reinvented itself, led by stars such as vice president of marketing Greg Bagni, and has recaptured the four F's—fun, family, fitness, and function.

Schwinn has become the anti-Schwinn. It now sponsors and advertises during the Gravity Games and X-Games, and many popular stunt riders use Schwinn gear. The brand's new associations with irreverence and cool have allowed Schwinn to return to the top of the Brand Value Pyramid. And its contract promises the highest-quality, most durable bicycle around. Its brand image, Brand Contract, and target audience have dramatically changed, and Schwinn is once again an American icon.

A Customer Model Answers Three Questions

Developing a customer model is done to provide answers to three important questions relative to the brand:

1. How do customers choose one brand over another when making a purchase?
2. How does your brand stack up against competing brands?
3. What opportunities exist for brand growth and expansion?

Finding the answers enables a company to better position and extend its brand and to exert greater influence on the purchase decision, thus leveraging the power of the brand more completely. Table 4.1 shows an energy customer's model framework.

The answers also provide insights for future management of the brand, including a better understanding of consumers' perceptions of individual brands and brand categories. For instance,

Table 4.1. Energy Customer Model Framework

Purchase process	*Competitor brands*	*Needs and wants*
Diagnostic process	Beliefs about incumbent brands	Beliefs about danger
Purchase drivers and criteria		Beliefs about environmental impact
	Criteria for measuring competition	
Purchase process		Beliefs about gas vs. electric
	Knowledge of competitive changes under deregulation	
Rating purchase criteria		Beliefs about effects of deregulation
Management's ratings of purchase criteria		Core service expectations
		Specific needs and wants

many travelers believe that when making hotel reservations they are talking to the hotel they will be staying at. Most often this is not the case.

Learning how your brand stacks up against competitor brands is also very useful. More often than not, my company's clients undervalue their brand's strengths and overvalue competitor brand strengths.

Question 1: How Do Customers Choose a Brand?

Addressing this one question should help your company focus its brand building on whatever it takes to convince a customer to buy your brand instead of a competitor's, regardless of the category. This involves answering three further questions:

- What kind of purchase process and purchase criteria do customers use?
- How do they rate your brand, as opposed to competitors' brands, by those criteria?
- Who at the customer decides to make brand-based purchases? Who else influences the decisions? Which criteria are important to each?

Finding Out Your Customer's Purchase Criteria

Regardless of industry, customers usually use purchase criteria such as price, value, consistency, convenience, innovativeness, length of time in business, customer service, personal relationships, relationship strength, relationship length, dependability, payment and credit policies, past experiences, peer recommendation, advertising, benefits received, location, and availability.

Most customers do *not* cite brand as a top criterion, probably because the brand assumes a lot of the factors just listed, such as dependability, consistency, and length of time in business. When we surveyed customers across categories, they cited nine criteria most often. In order, they are the following:

1. High quality and reliability
2. Consistent performance

3. Familiarity
4. Availability and convenience
5. Price-value relationship
6. Fit with customer personality
7. Ability to solve a customer problem
8. Customer service
9. Advertising

Implicit in this list is another characteristic: trust—which is often synonymous with the definition of the brand. The essence of a good brand is that people trust it. Trust implies that customers know exactly what they are going to get when they make the purchase, and that it is on terms they are comfortable with. It may also imply experience with the brand. Especially on the top three purchase criteria—high quality and reliability, consistent performance, and familiarity—trust cuts across each.

Rating Brand-Based Purchase Criteria

Once you have determined the broad list of customer purchase decision-making criteria, the next step is to ask both your and competitors' customers how your brand is performing relative to them.

To do this, ask customers to rank the alternatives on a scale of 1 to 5. This forces customers to think through the criteria relatively as opposed to absolutely, and to differentiate between brands.

At the end of this process, you will know how your brand stacks up against the competition. It will also tell you where to focus attention to improve your brand's performance and, ultimately, strengthen the impact the brand has on the overall purchase decision.

For example, Table 4.2 compares brand purchase criteria for a major retail catalogue brand whose top two competitors are Sears and Wal-Mart. The criteria are listed in descending order of importance.

The catalogue retailer has scores of 4 or 5 on four of the seven attributes. It has the advantage of a major Internet retail business, which gave it a higher convenience score than Wal-Mart and Sears, who have not established major Internet service yet (although both have recently announced their respective Internet strategies).

Table 4.2. Most Important Purchase Criteria for Key Brands

Purchase Criterion	Catalogue Brand	Wal-Mart Brand	Sears Brand
Price	2	5	3
Accessibility/convenience	5	3	3
Brands available	4	3	2
Customer service	2	2	4
Payment and credit policies	5	4	3
Product selection	5	3	4
Past experience with retailer	2	3	4

Note: 5 = excellent, 1 = poor

The catalogue company's strategy is to charge higher prices but grant easy credit to customers. Its theory is that the resulting high volume will lead to high profits even if easy credit creates some bad debts. In the future, though, if service stays poor the company may find it more difficult to justify higher prices, regardless of easy credit.

The biggest advantage the catalogue firm has is the diversity of products it sells and the number of name brands it provides. Coupling that with a stronger push on its Internet business, if the latter is promoted well, could offset the pricing handicap.

This example shows how the purchase process and criteria are tied to the brand. The stronger a brand is compared to its competition, and relative to the most important purchase criteria, the better the chance that the brand can drive sales and influence the purchase decision.

Learning customer purchase criteria should clearly point out the areas companies should start to invest in and focus on as they attempt to strengthen their brands. In addition, it is important to ask your own management to conduct the same type of ranking and assessment of your brand versus that of the competition as if they were customers. This serves two purposes. First, it forces senior management to think like a customer. Second, and more importantly, it allows senior management to identify gaps between the market's perceptions of strengths and weaknesses and theirs.

Find Out Who Makes the Purchase Decision

It's also important to recognize the different roles that decision makers and decision influencers have in choosing one brand over another.

Smart brand managers think about everyone involved in the brand decision. They understand who the players are and try to figure out how to sell their brand to each. For instance, most people bring another person with them to choose a new car. The credit card you use is probably the same one your spouse uses, and whatever computer is in your office is probably the same one in the office next door.

Beltone, the leading manufacturer of hearing aids in the world, knows that many factors inhibit the sale of a hearing aid, including the stigma of wearing one, vanity, denial of having a problem, and denial of getting older. In overcoming these inhibitors, the number one enabler to selling a hearing aid may be a spouse, child, or close friend. Many potential purchasers would rather buy the hearing aid than hear one more complaint from a loved one. Beltone knows, therefore, that to be successful it must position and sell its brand to both the potential buyer and the loved one.

Similarly, in the business-to-business world there are numerous influencers but usually only one decision maker. IBM recognizes that to sell mainframes or personal computers to an organization, it must sell equally to the day-to-day PC users as well as to the CIO and the head of purchasing.

Hallmark unabashedly markets to the recipients as well as the buyers of its cards. It tries to convince the purchaser that the first thing the recipient will do is turn it over to see if it is a Hallmark. Marketing or truth? Regardless, Hallmark's strategy shows that it is one of the best at managing its brand as an asset.

Integrating the key purchase criteria exercise with the decision-making process enables you to better understand how you can manage your brand to maximize its potential to influence a sale in your category.

Question 2: How Does Your Brand Stack Up Against the Competition?

This second step in creating a customer model involves answering these questions:

- What brands do customers think compete with our brand?
- What do our customers believe about the competing brands in our category?
- What are the strengths and weaknesses of competitive brands? How does our brand compare on specific values and benefits?

Identify Your Competitors

Developing your Brand Contract and image requires considering only your top two or three competitors, but for the customer model you need to be aware of all competitors and understand how you are differentiated from them in ways that are truly important to your customers.

This competitive assessment requires you to look at competitors and competitive brands from the customer's point of view. Customers may define your competitive set much differently than you would. Whether a customer cites a direct or indirect competitor or a branded or nonbranded competitor, it is in your best interest to think about your competitor set in the same way your customers do.

In the Schwinn example, for instance, the competitive sets for transportation, children's recreation, adult exercise, and outdoor sport are very different.

Nontraditional Competitors

If you are in the shipping business and assume FedEx, DHL, UPS, and the Post Office are your most important competitors, talk to your customers. They may mention, for example, e-mail. In other categories, nontraditional competitors might include these:

- For automobile manufacturers and dealers: AutoNation and Buy.com
- For Xerox: Kinko's outsourcing copier service
- For Endust, Pledge, Bounty, and Hoover: maid services
- For the San Diego Zoo: Disneyland and Sea World

Don't forget the simpler alternatives to your offering. Note, for example, that Coca-Cola says its number one competitor is tap water, not Pepsi.

Compare Your Brand to Competing Brands

The failure to understand one's competition is ultimately the failure to know one's customers: who they are, how they think, and how the brand can be adapted to meet their needs. Once you understand that your brand faces both traditional and nontraditional competitors, you can study the benefits they provide, their strengths and weaknesses, and their future directions.

Figures 4.1 and 4.2 are competition matrices that show how a brand can be compared to competitor brands. Your brand image, Brand Contract, and the purchase criteria allow you to map your company's brand against others. As the figures show, you can map the competition from a number of different perspectives. The maps enable you to envision the strategies and approaches needed to maximize your brand's potential. Competitor mapping helps when you are trying to do the following:

- Prioritize segments to pursue
- Determine how best to position your brand relative to competitive brands

Figure 4.1. Financial Services Competitor Map

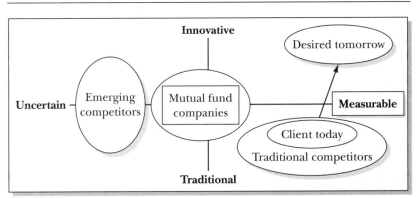

- Determine the right messages to convey considering the competition, your chosen positioning, and the segments you will pursue

Question 3: What Opportunities Exist for Brand Growth and Expansion?

Careful analysis of the customer model uncovers potential opportunities for growth in the category and extendibility for your brand. Brand extendibility and innovation are discussed in detail in Step Six, but developing and analyzing the customer model is the foundation for growth. The customer model addresses the following questions:

- What are customers' beliefs about our brand category? What opportunities for extendibility or growth exist as a result?
- What unmet customer needs and wants might we address? (Include those that your brand or your competitors are already trying to address but without apparent success.)

Answering these questions jump-starts the effort to determine the boundaries of your brand. This in turn allows you to offer a solution through your brand, thus improving its image, enhancing the Brand Contract, and further increasing the brand's value.

As you may know, customers cannot necessarily give you the next hot idea because they don't think about solutions. However, it is fairly easy for a customer to articulate their problems, needs, wants, and desires. Then it's your job to develop solutions that meet their needs and that are consistent with your Brand Vision and BrandPicture. Figure 4.3 shows high-need areas that were not being met within the home cleaning category.

Examples of Opportunity Areas

Saturn addressed a massive need that was not met by former car dealers and manufacturers. The problems and frustrations of first-time car buyers, women buyers in particular, were tied to the fear of being taken, misunderstanding the differences between cars,

Figure 4.2. Telecommunications Competitor Map

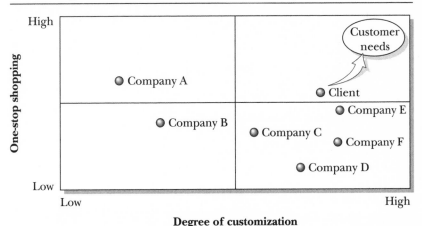

and concerns about haggling, credit terms, and the cost of new cars. Saturn was created to address these problem areas by inventing "a different car, a different car company."

eToys also meets a need that no one had satisfactorily addressed before. Parents no longer have the time to shop in crowded stores with long lines and kids on their arms wanting everything they see. eToys helps. It is convenient; it offers all the toys and books available at Toys 'R' Us through the Web. No parking lots, no lines, no pressure from kids seeing a storeful of new toys.

Similarly, for consumers who don't have the time to go grocery shopping Peapod lets them do it on-line. This successful service even allows consumers to choose the desired color of their bananas and have their groceries delivered to their home for a premium.

Cincinnati Bell Telephone (CBT) knew the Internet opportunity was growing and lucrative and wanted to figure out a profitable way to enter the category by leveraging its strong brand equity. In talking with small and at-home business owners, CBT learned that one of this segment's greatest frustrations was not being able to use the phone and the Internet at the same time over the same phone line. So CBT developed Internet Call Manager, which allows small business owners to decide if they want to take an incoming call or not. This device uses a caller ID, which displays

Figure 4.3. Home Cleaning Consumers' Desired Benefits

	Antiques, fine furniture	Old wood floors	Wood furniture	Kitchen cabinets	Combination furniture	Electronics	New wood floors	Formica
Protection	Brand A	Brand C	Brand B Brand F			X		
Moisturize	Brand B	X	Brand B	Brand B	Brand B	X	X	X
Deep clean	Brand A	Brand A	Brand A	Brand A	Brand A Brand E	X	Brand A	Brand E
Shine		Brand C	Brand F	X	Brand E Brand F	X		
Light dirt removal		Brand A	Brand D Brand F	Brand A	Brand E Brand F	Brand D	Brand A	Brand E
Dust removal		Brand D	Brand D Brand F	X	Brand E Brand F	Brand D	Brand D	X

Product benefits (Infrequent behaviors ↔ Frequent behaviors)

Surfaces

Delicate ←——→ Durable

X = No need

the name of the caller on the screen. To take the call, the recipient can pause the Internet without logging off. This new offering extended CBT's brand equity, helped it become a player in the Internet world, and was a big financial success.

Extending brand equity can be tricky, and timing can be everything. For example, I think Apple's Newton (a predecessor of today's Palm Pilot) failed because the market was not ready for electronic scheduling, which meant abandoning the comfortable habits of the written calendar and phone book. There was a great need for time management tools at the time (mid-1980s), but the wireless, electronic world was just starting to take hold and the Internet was years from being ready for use by the average consumer. Still, Apple hoped that "early adopters" would buy Newton and reach out to other nearby segments. But although the Apple brand was built on providing leading-edge technology, the deeply ingrained habits of customers could not be changed quickly enough to support the Newton.

Taking Advantage of Customer Beliefs

To take advantage of customer beliefs, you have to know those beliefs so you can figure out how to address the needs that stem from them. This is true even if the belief is wrong.

For example, some people wondering about utility deregulation think that new pipes will have to be run into their home if they decide to switch gas suppliers (not true). Others believe that the central station that monitors your home security system must be nearby, explaining the quick response when your burglar alarm is set off (also not true; most central stations are located in just a few states, physically remote from most customers). Some think dust only travels up and down, not sideways, which is why there is no dust on walls (untrue again; there is just as much dust on walls as anywhere else in a house).

All these misconceptions have been addressed by various brands. Utilities in California recently spent $100 million to educate gas and electric users about deregulation because their customers were most vulnerable to sales pitches from out-of-state suppliers preying on customers' ignorance. These utilities took the position that if they honestly explained how this works and took a leadership position in education, they would slow the exodus of customers.

Ameritech's recent foray into the home security industry has been a success in large part because it is local and already in most homes in the Midwest. Pledge's Grab-Its and P&G's Swiffer both address the many directions dust travels. All of these brands took advantage of the opportunity to address customer perceptions, right or wrong, and to gain loyalty as a result.

Don't Lose Sight of Your Customer Model

Once a customer model is established, keep it in view. As discussed earlier, remember the Snackwell brand, the all-powerful low-fat or no-fat brand in the early 1990s? Nabisco stayed the course too long with its target market, did not transition to healthy snacks as much of the industry did, and has paid the price: today the Snackwell's brand is practically irrelevant.

Holiday Inn almost became extinct because it lagged behind the industry's move to install officelike amenities in rooms. Crown books lost its edge when discounting became the industry norm at retail stores as well as on line. Where did Levi's customers go? How about 7–Up's customers? How did Volkswagen's customers come back so easily? A well-crafted, consistently updated customer model allows you to answer these questions and others.

Summary

A customer model helps you determine how others think about your category and the brands that compete in it. It forces you to get smart about your customers and what is important to them as it relates to your brand. It tells you what customers need and want, how they make a purchase decision, and where they rank your brand relative to the competition.

In addition, a customer model forces you to accept that customers' perceptions unchallenged are fact—unless you provide information that shows them otherwise. This is how you can use information to further drive your brand's growth. Also, a customer model helps you determine what customers think about your brand and the category it competes in, what is important to those customers, and what customers actually do because of their understandings and beliefs.

As for the BrandPicture, it is the primary input basis for a successful Brand Asset Management Strategy. The BrandPicture's three components—brand image, Brand Contract, and customer model—lay the foundation for better knowing how to position your brand, grow it through new products and extensions, communicate it, premium price it, and maximize your channel position.

With Phase One—the Brand Vision—well articulated and Phase Two—the BrandPicture—well crafted, it is time to turn to Phase Three and start by developing your brand positioning, which, in turn, drives the rest of your Brand Asset Management strategies.

Developing a Brand Asset Management Strategy

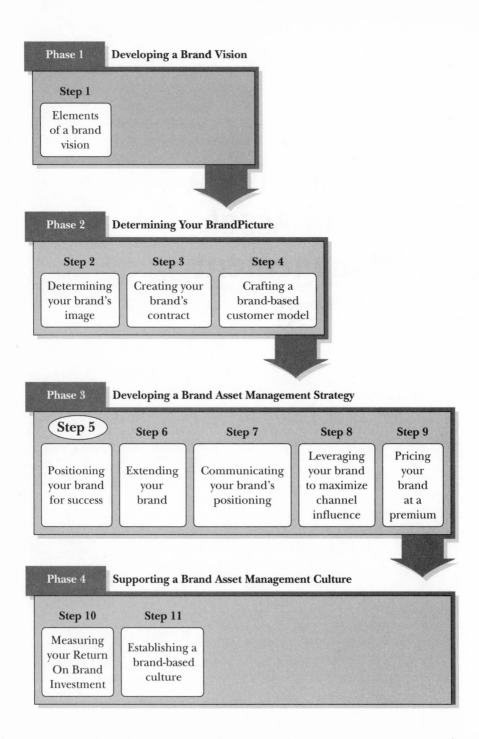

Positioning Your Brand for Success

Determining the right positioning for your brand is the transition point between Phase Two, determining your BrandPicture, and Phase Three, developing your Brand Asset Management strategies (see the illustration facing this page).

A strong brand position means the brand has a unique, credible, sustainable, and valued place in customers' minds. It revolves around a benefit that helps your product or service stand apart from the competition. Good positioning gives you the direction required to focus the organization and focus your strategic efforts.

A brand's positioning is the place in consumers' minds that you want your brand to own—the benefit you want them to think of when they think of your brand. It has to be externally driven and relevant. It has to be differentiated from the competition and, most importantly, it has to be valued. A good positioning is a single idea to be communicated to your customers. Some companies have a brand positioning that is easily understood and can be articulated by most everyone, such as the following:

Disney	=	Family Fun Entertainment
Nordstrom's	=	Highest Level of Retail Service
Saturn	=	Your Car Company
FedEx	=	Guaranteed Overnight Delivery
Wal-Mart	=	Low Prices and Good Values
Hallmark	=	Caring Shared
McDonald's	=	Food and Fun

Nike   =   Performance

Lucent and 3M =   Innovation

These companies reap several benefits. First, they tend to be the leaders in their category, industry, or niche. Second, they usually can consistently and credibly leverage their strong brands into other areas of growth. Hallmark's cobranded relationship with Microsoft, which allows card senders to design their greeting card on line, has been a major success. Similarly, Nordstrom's recently announced selling shoes on line; it is one of few retailers that can succeed in what appears to be a challenging category.

Third, at least within the United States almost everyone knows of these companies. If a purchase is to be made in their respective categories, these well-positioned brands will always make their way into the final decision set.

A good positioning is a credible promise of value delivered in ways that distinguish your brand from others. It is a concise statement that summarizes your brand's commitment, or promise, to customers.

Your brand's positioning is also your company's primary driver of internal and external growth, as well as the determinant of key operational strategies that bring your positioning to life.

Three Components of Well-Constructed Positioning

A well-crafted brand positioning has three primary components:

---

1. A definition of the target market you wish to pursue
2. A definition of the business your company is in or the industry or category it competes in
3. A statement of your point of difference and key benefits

The language of a well-crafted positioning usually takes this general form:

To (target market), Brand X is the (definition of business) that provides you with (stated point of difference/key benefit).

For example, "To computer manufacturers, Intel is the chip maker that provides the fastest and most reliable microprocessors available." Or, "To homemakers, Tide is the detergent that gets their clothes the whitest and brightest."

To define each component of positioning more completely, several questions need to be answered for each:

Target Segment Questions

- Would the customers we seek recognize themselves as part of this target market?
- Is the target market both identifiable and reachable?
- Is it clear why this target market would be interested in our point of difference?
- If we have not served this target market before, why do we want to serve them now?

Definition of Business Questions

- What is the category, industry, or business we compete in?
- How has this changed over time?
- Is the business we are in internally-driven or externally-driven?
- Will the marketplace value and believe our participation in this business?

Point of Difference Questions

- Is the key benefit important to our customer?
- Can we deliver the benefit?
- Can we own this point of difference over time?
- Is this point of difference sustainable over our competition and their directions?
- Regarding brand associations, does our point of difference have to do with either the middle tier of the Brand Value Pyramid (the benefit level) or top tier of the Brand Value Pyramid (the value level)?

Fortunately, many of these questions will have been addressed when you defined your BrandPicture.

Case Study: Midwest Hospital

The Midwest hospital mentioned in Step Two developed its positioning by answering each of the questions just mentioned. Its positioning follows our three-part outline:

Target Market: To users and potential users of Hospital X's services,

Business Definition: Hospital X is the premier hospital of choice that

Point of Difference: provides you with an attentive team of caring experts working together to provide you with the highest level of professional care.

Every word in this positioning has a specific meaning. Premier, attentive, team, caring, experts, highest level, professional care, and available all have action plans behind them, much like a Brand Vision does.

A positioning can be more aspirational than current to start with, as long as plans are in place to bring the positioning to life within twelve to eighteen months. Beyond that period, if you still have not "become" your positioning, the marketplace will start to lose faith in your ability to deliver on your promise.

Case Study: Hewitt Associates

One of our clients, Hewitt Associates, is one of the world's leading human resource management companies. Recently it redefined its positioning to this:

Target Market: To human resources clients around the world,

Business Definition: Hewitt Associates is the strategic HR services firm that

Point of Difference: improves business results through people by providing tailored innovations with measurable results.

By successfully redefining the business it was in, Hewitt was able to move beyond its position as a human resources helper to become part of a clients' strategic planning process. As a result, Hewitt has experienced incredible growth and has been able to increase its prices.

The Charles Schwab Story

Charles Schwab apparently understands the fine art of positioning. For years Schwab built its reputation as the lowest-cost brokerage firm that would help customers with all their stock market trans-actions. Most other firms charged higher commissions and, to new investors, seemed rather threatening. Not Schwab. In the early 1990s its positioning might have been described this way: "To stock market investors, Charles Schwab is the brokerage firm that allows you to buy and sell stock at the lowest cost."

As the 1990s progressed, however, the stock market exploded. Millions of new investors joined those who were already enjoying the bull ride. The newcomers became educated not just about the stock market but about the other investment options available. At the same time, the Internet also exploded, both as a learning tool and as a place to buy and sell investments.

Schwab saw an opportunity to reposition itself as these changes took place. It saw an opening and decided it could fill it first, as no one else appeared ready and able to do so. Thus in the late 1990s Schwab's positioning statement became this: "To self-sufficient stock market and mutual fund investors, Charles Schwab is the discount brokerage firm that provides everything you need to manage your own investments."

The differences between the two positions may seem slight, but the implications were great for how Schwab defined the business it was in, how it would compete, and how it would operate as a company. Note that the changes affected all three positioning components:

Target Market

Early 1990s	Late 1990s
To stock market investors	To self-sufficient stock market and mutual fund investors

Schwab recognized the shift in how investors were involving themselves in their financial planning and investment decisions. It also recognized that many new investors had entered the market.

Schwab also gave credit to the numerous investors who had taken it upon themselves to grow their own portfolio. Its old position said, "In the past you needed us and we were there to help you." Its new position says, "We are here if you need us." This is a subtle but powerful difference. In addition, Schwab recognized that mutual funds in the late 1990s are similar to bank accounts in the past—they are part of almost everyone's investment portfolio.

Definition of Business

Early 1990s	Late 1990s
Charles Schwab is the brokerage firm	Charles Schwab is the discount brokerage firm

Schwab decided early to connect "brokerage firm" and "lowest cost" together. For its target market, these terms became synonymous. But in the late 1990s, Schwab determined that it had to disconnect the terms to help redefine its business and increase margins.

However, because Schwab was known as a broker, it couldn't leave the term behind. So Schwab combined the concepts of "brokerage" and "low cost" into an amorphous phrase: discount brokerage. Note that this connects the two terms but doesn't promise "lowest cost."

Because Schwab recognized that discounts were going to be part of the price of entry for its industry, it decided to own the term "discount brokerage," even though the meaning of the phrase is nebulous (discounting could mean 1 percent less than Merrill Lynch's commissions or 10 percent less, for example). Schwab also knew that the market connected its brand with brokering, so it was still okay to be considered *the* brokerage firm.

Point of Difference

Early 1990s	Late 1990s
that allows you to buy and sell stock at the lowest cost.	that provides everything you need to manage your own investments.

Schwab's point of difference today is its ability to provide investors with everything they could possibly need, from advice on specific stocks to planning for retirement to helping investors manage all their financial needs. This is powerful because it allows for so much expansion and growth.

This point of difference recognizes that investors need to control their own destiny. It also compliments investors by saying "you're good, we just want to help make you better." This plays directly to an investors' ego and self-esteem—always important when buyers choose the brand that they want to be associated with. Also, it implies that whenever you need Schwab, Schwab will be there—that it is trustworthy. And it allowed Schwab to evolve new ways to deliver services—such as on the Internet.

Has this repositioning worked? Recently, *Money* magazine named Schwab the number one Internet discount brokerage firm, ahead of Merrill Lynch and other stalwarts. And Schwab's stock price continues to outstrip average market gains several times over.

Volvo's Positioning

Volvo touts itself in its brochures, other literature, and Web site as providing the best balance of safety, durability, and intelligent styling in family cars. As a result, Volvo's Brand Contract most likely features stipulations, such as that it sets the standard for understated, practical style; provides innovative safety features; and is designed to be highly functional and sturdy. For most consumers, all this shakes out to one simple message: Volvo equals safety. That is all that matters, because that is who Volvo is.

So when Volvo stepped away from safety and repositioned itself as a high-performance automobile, as mentioned earlier, it confused everyone—employees, stakeholders, and especially customers. Market share dropped, sales slumped, and some would say Volvo sold for far less than its value to Ford in 1999.

Volvo recently began a new ad campaign. One commercial shows a young couple in the front seat of their Volvo and a screaming baby in the back. "Maybe we should start with a dog first," says the woman to the man. No doubt this is an attempt to win younger customers, but I believe it also mocks Volvo's safety positioning and is therefore another assault on the brand, one by which long-term success may be traded for a potential short-term gain.

The Guiding Principles of Brand Positioning

So how does one create a positioning? How should one use a positioning? How do you know when to reposition your brand? And how does an organization keep a positioning alive? These are the most common questions about brand positioning. They are best answered by following five guiding principles (see the box).

Brand Positioning Guiding Principles

1. A brand's positioning should be updated every three to five years, or as often as needed to update the company's overall growth strategy.

2. Positioning should drive all of an organization's Brand Asset Management strategies, as well as revenue and profit streams.

3. Senior management has to lead the charge in implementing a brand's positioning.

4. Employees, not advertising agencies, bring a brand positioning to life.

5. A strong brand positioning is customer driven and fits with customer perceptions of the brand.

Let's examine each of these principles.

1. Update Your Brand Positioning as Necessary

The point of this is simple: take a fresh look at your brand's positioning on a regular basis to make sure it is still relevant to your target market, customer shifts, market trends and dynamics, and company goals and objectives.

An easy way to decide whether it is time to review or update your positioning is to look at your long-range strategic planning process. Most plans have a life cycle of three to five years and are updated, as needed, annually. This is the same mindset you should adopt when considering updating or changing your positioning.

I recommend looking at five brand positioning screens (see Figure 5.1) that should help you determine if your positioning should be updated. Your positioning has to address each screen, not just one or two. Let's look at each screen in more detail.

A. Value: Does Our Target Market Value the Brand Positioning?

- Does this positioning motivate customers to choose our brand over competitive brands?
- Does it speak to the key needs of our customers?
- Will it ultimately help win the loyalty of customers and, when delivered, keep them for life?
- Will it allow us to charge a price premium?
- Will it have value across segments, especially for our most profitable customers?
- Does it state a premise worth a purchase or at least a call to action?
- Does it allow our brand to cut across multiple segments with virtually the same positioning?

Figure 5.1. The Five Principles of Effective Positioning

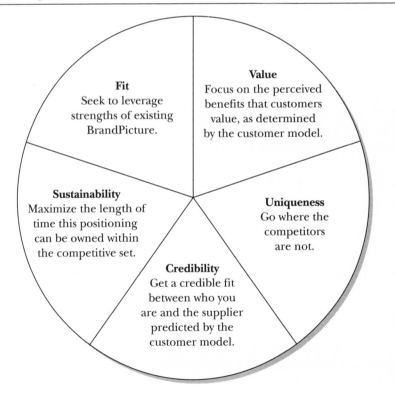

B. Uniqueness: Does the Brand's Positioning Exclude Competitive Offerings?

- Does the market perceive our positioning as something that only our brand and our company can deliver?
- Is our positioning clearly different from competitive positionings or does it closely follow another's?
- Are we trying to differentiate our brand just to be different or is it truly a unique and valued position?
- When mentioning this positioning to customers, without revealing your brand, do other brands come up too?
- Can our positioning be clearly communicated and readily understood?

C. Credibility: Is Our Brand Positioning Credible in the Marketplace?

- Will this positioning be credible to our customers or target market based on what they know about our brand?
- What must be delivered to make our positioning credible?
- Do customers view other brands as more credible in their positioning?
- From an internal perspective, is this positioning worth the investment required, or should we go with the "next best"?
- Can we realistically deliver on the positioning as promised?

D. Sustainability: Can We Own This Brand Position for a Long Time?

- Will this positioning remain valid over the next three to five years?
- How quickly might the competition copy it?
- Are we doing enough customer research to determine if needs and wants will remain similar to what they are today?
- What will it take to sustain this positioning internally and externally?

E. Fit: Does This Brand Positioning Fit Our Organization?

- Will it support our overall corporate objectives?
- Does it help us fill our long-range growth gap?
- Does it help drive momentum?

- Will it enhance our profitability?
- Will our employees rally around it?
- Can we measure our success by it in a consistent and meaningful way?
- Does it help focus our planning and day-to-day efforts?

All these questions represent an interview guide to use with your target market to determine which positioning statement you should use.

2. Brand Positioning Should Drive All BAM Strategies, Revenues, and Profits

Positioning is, in effect, your internal direction to execute strategies externally in the marketplace. Choosing what products and services you should offer, how best to reach your customers, what pricing strategy you should use, and how best to communicate your brand and its positioning should be directly linked to your brand positioning.

The Bookstore Brand Positioning War

The bookstore wars bring this principle to life. Assume only four book retailers exist: Borders, Crown Books, Barnes & Noble, and Amazon.com. Each has a unique positioning that targets a specific audience roughly as follows:

Company	Target	Business Definition	Point of Difference
Borders	Individuals looking for a community meeting place	Books, music, multimedia and on line	Fun place to go
Crown Books	Price-sensitive individuals, strip mall shoppers	Bookstores	Discount pricing
Barnes & Noble	Individuals looking for a quiet gathering place	Books, music, multimedia, and on line	Library-like setting
Amazon.com	Individuals who are Internet-active and shop on line	On-line books and music	Personalized on-line service

When we look at these positionings, a few obvious conclusions stand out. First, Borders and Barnes & Noble have similar positionings, but Borders is more socially oriented and "louder," whereas Barnes & Noble is library-like, individually oriented, and "quieter."

If you go to the corner of Diversey and Clark in Chicago on a Friday night, you can see both positionings in action. Both stores are packed, but Borders patrons are more likely to just be starting out their night; this is their meeting place. Barnes & Noble, however, may be *the* Friday night social activity for its patrons.

Crown Books has only two points of difference from the others: price and location. These may be important in real estate, but they sit at the bottom of the Brand Value Pyramid and are not differentiable in the bookstore category anymore, as others can and do offer the same discounts.

For several years, Amazon.com had a unique positioning as the only place to buy books and music on line. It is widely held up as a bellwether Internet stock and is one of the few that can actually see a profit on the horizon (unlike most Internet IPOs).

However, the recent past has not been kind to Amazon.com's positioning. Barnes & Noble has done an IPO of its Internet site and Borders is showing signs of becoming a strong Internet player too. All three recently dropped their prices on *New York Times* best sellers to 50 percent off list (I hope that policy was still in place if you bought this book on line!).

To stay competitive and viable, Amazon.com is in the process of changing its positioning and broadening it to include other on-line services, such as prescription medicine and auctions, similar to what eBay is offering. My guess is that Amazon.com will continue its current repositioning as the premier retail provider on the Internet and will continue to include offerings well beyond books and music. This will obviously have an impact on the message it communicates to its target audience, as it will have to expand to satisfy this new positioning.

Crown Books is the one in real trouble. It does not have much chance to succeed because its breadth of offerings is narrow, its discount strategy is undifferentiated, and its locations appeal only to strip mall shoppers. Even there, though, at the rate Borders and Barnes & Nobles are opening up, they will eclipse these locations.

Crown Books filed for Chapter 11 in 1998, after enduring three consecutive years of losses.

The interesting race should be between Barnes & Noble and Borders. Each owns a unique positioning, they both have captured consumers' desire for multimedia stores and alternative social gathering places, and both are successful in their own right. Coke and Pepsi have both survived. McDonald's and Burger King both have survived. Barnes & Noble and Borders will both survive. It will be interesting to see, though, which becomes the number one player.

Importantly, your chosen positioning should dictate how you operate as a business. It should give you guidance in directing all of your revenue and profit generating strategies, and it should help you remain relevant in the face of a continually changing and evolving marketplace.

3. Senior Management Must Lead the Charge

There are countless stories about senior management's belief in brand positioning and how its actions and behaviors help to show the organization and other stakeholders that its level of commitment is much more than lip service. Whether it is Bill Marriott's commitment to spending 80 percent of his time in his hotels or Richard Branson's many public relations efforts aimed at bringing the Virgin positioning to life, senior management can make or break a positioning's chances of taking hold and being a success.

At Harley-Davidson, for example, chairman Rich Teerlink and CEO Jeffrey Bleustein know their unfaltering commitment to the company's brand and to employees have helped make Harley-Davidson the success it is today.

These two executives recognize that the critical path to positioning success is through product quality, brand image, employees, and senior management's ability and desire to "walk the talk." Each is meaningless without the others.

Teerlink and Bleustein publicly attribute their success to the first three of those components, but insiders know that all four made Harley what it is today. This is the formula that has allowed the Harley brand to be popular with so many segments of the market, from AT&T CEO Michael Armstrong to Billy Joel to the Hell's Angels.

The Harley comeback story is well known, but not many know how senior management motivated employees to help bring Harley's brand positioning to life. First, Harley managers, like most employees in the company, are shareholders, which automatically increases their commitment, accountability, and ownership in the Harley brand. This in turn provides an immediate day-to-day passion for making the Harley brand as critical to them as it is to their customers.

Harley employees, although not all Harley bike owners, are all brand evangelists. They live the positioning and the symbolic status on a daily basis. They wear the clothes, give the tours, and attend the events. A Harley assembly plant worker is as popular at a Harley rally as is Jay Leno. It is like trying to find out the secret formula to Coca-Cola: customer and observers all want to know why it takes up to a year to get their Harley.

Senior management conducts focus groups by riding with customers. Harley dealers are treated with the same level of respect and importance as customers. And because many employees were at Harley when it almost went bankrupt, they have a greater appreciation for the need to keep the Harley passion, attitude, and energy always going. Management awards Harley employees bonuses linked to the warranty performance of their machines as well as to financial performance.

In short, Harley employees are the brand as much as the motorcycle is—this is the purest definition of a brand-based organization that I have seen.

4. Employees, Not Ad Agencies, Bring Positioning to Life

Once you arrive at the right brand positioning, it becomes absolutely critical to figure out how to bring that positioning to life. While a positioning must be externally driven, your internal team has to buy into it too, as they are the team that is ultimately responsible for bringing the positioning to life.

Harriet Gold, director of Brand Asset Management for Nicor, calls it "mobilizing the organization." Others would call it the single most important thing you can do to maximize your potential for success: train your employees on how the brand positioning has an impact on their day-to-day lives. I have seen organizations transform quickly once everyone in the company "gets it" and "lives it."

The goal here is to have your employees become brand ambassadors and bring the brand image, contract, and positioning to life.

What is important in maximizing internal brand positioning? Simply remember your AUDIENCE. In this acronym, each letter stands for an important element to consider as you train your employees to bring your positioning to life:

Awareness: Every member of your internal team should be able to state your brand positioning clearly.

Understanding: Your team should fully understand why the brand positioning was chosen and how day-to-day jobs are affected by it.

Direction: Provide your team with specific service standards or behaviors to adopt so they know how to deliver on the brand positioning.

Inspiration: Show your employees clips of the research you conducted, speaking to the virtues and importance of your new brand positioning—help them see the brand positioning as it is seen through the eyes of your customers.

Engagement: The positioning has to become relevant to every person in your organization, from your front desk receptionist to the CEO. You all have to walk the talk and all employees must understand how their and others' jobs will have to change.

Naturalness: If the right people are in place, a new positioning will soon become a natural part of their work life. (Often, a new positioning provides you with a report card on whether you have the right people in place to bring it to life.)

Criteria: Establish bonus criteria and MBO-like objectives, always remembering that what is not measured is not managed.

Education: Train your people to become brand ambassadors; you minimize risk and maximize positioning return by every dollar you invest in training your employees.

AUDIENCE is the quickest way to maximize your success potential for implementing your brand's positioning. Not acting on it almost guarantees that your positioning will not come to life.

5. Strong Brand Positioning Is Customer Driven

The need to be customer driven has been talked about a lot already in terms of screening criteria, but the actual process of "landing" on the right customer-driven positioning has not. To arrive at your desired positioning, analyze your data carefully. As mentioned, data inputs include customer needs and wants, your brand's strengths and weaknesses, core competencies, growth goals, competitive directions, and the like.

Again, if the BrandPicture has been done well, then most of this data has already been collected. With all that data in hand, you should be able to develop five to ten positioning statements that you feel are valid to test with the marketplace. One positioning statement may have to do with service, and others with high technology, dependability, brand heritage, or similar issues.

Here are sample positioning statements that were tested for the visual care company whose Brand Vision was discussed in Step One:

Visual Care Positioning Statement Alternatives

1. National network: With over 1,000 locations we offer the same quality care across the nation.
2. Highest-quality products: Our products are custom made and backed by a full, money-back return policy, so your satisfaction is guaranteed.
3. Most caring: We offer the greatest level of ongoing vision care with friendly, caring people who respect you as an individual. We listen to your needs.
4. Expert professionals: We have certified optometrists who will give you thorough explanations of test results and available solutions.
5. Comprehensive vision care: We offer a total vision care solution with unlimited follow-up visits for the lifetime of the products we sell.
6. Better sight: For more than thirty years we have helped people rediscover the sights they have been missing.
7. Best selection: We offer the widest selection and variety of style of any eye care provider. If we do not have the style you desire in our store, we will find it for you.

Each of these positioning statements should have already passed a few screens indicating they are valid to test with the marketplace. I highly recommend testing them in focus groups, where there can be a dialog between participants.

The positioning, brand image, and contract that my company recommended for this visual care company was based on the best elements of each of these positioning statements (see Figure 5.2). The positioning crafted without leveraging the rest of the Brand-Picture is often nothing more than a good tagline.

Your goal in conducting positioning research is not to come up with the winning positioning but to integrate the best elements of the various positionings tested. The process involves shaping and continuing to shape the positioning until you find the one that most strongly passes the five screens outlined earlier.

Positioning on a Shoestring

Money is helpful in implementing any program, but when it comes to implementing positioning it is generally far down on the list of priorities.

Many companies develop a brand's positioning on a shoestring budget. Some hire a couple of undergraduates who are trying to earn a credit by working a semester at a company and reporting back on what they have learned. These companies use their customer service or telemarketing department to conduct the research over the phone.

In other companies, management identifies eight or so key customers to act as their positioning customer research group, who will meet with them several times over a couple of months to help the company determine the right positioning. Internal positioning training can take place in the main lunchroom with a two-hour presentation by senior management and breakout sessions by functional areas afterward.

The point is that all this can be completed on a small budget if you think it through strategically and with a thrifty frame of mind.

Summary

If you don't take control of your positioning and create it yourself, others will do it for you de facto—and often not in your best

Figure 5.2. Arriving at Final Positioning: Visual Care Company Example

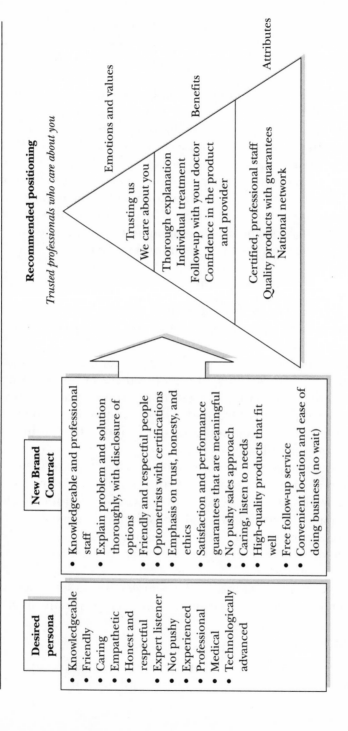

Desired persona

- Knowledgeable
- Friendly
- Caring
- Empathetic
- Honest and respectful
- Expert listener
- Not pushy
- Experienced
- Professional
- Medical
- Technologically advanced

New Brand Contract

- Knowledgeable and professional staff
- Explain problem and solution thoroughly, with disclosure of options
- Friendly and respectful people
- Optometrists with certifications
- Emphasis on trust, honesty, and ethics
- Satisfaction and performance guarantees that are meaningful
- No pushy sales approach
- Caring, listen to needs
- High-quality products that fit well
- Free follow-up service
- Convenient location and ease of doing business (no wait)

Recommended positioning

Trusted professionals who care about you

Emotions and values

Trusting us
We care about you

Benefits

Thorough explanation
Individual treatment
Follow-up with your doctor
Confidence in the product and provider

Attributes

Certified, professional staff
Quality products with guarantees
National network

interests. For years, the U.S. Postal Service allowed late night comedians to make fun of it because of the trials and tribulations many Americans have had with the Post Office at some point. Until the U.S. Postal Service embarked on its own brand campaign in 1997, its business was defined and positioned by everyone but itself.

Your positioning may be the single most important activity you conduct in developing and activating your Brand Asset Management strategy. With a well-crafted and well-thought-out positioning, the direction you need to go to develop your new products, extend your markets, communicate, price, and make use of channels should be fairly clear. In addition, your positioning should give total clarity, direction, and guidance to internal employees.

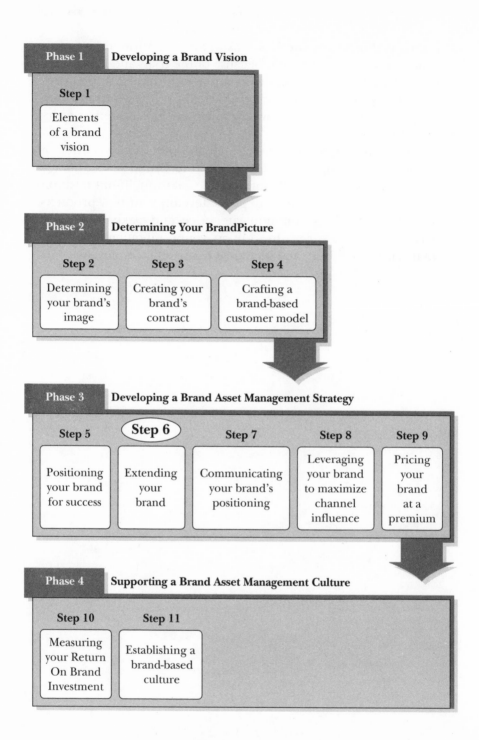

Extending Your Brand

As discussed in Step One, one of the best ways to fill your company's financial growth gap is to extend your brand by developing new products and services. There is no better way to fuel growth, close out the competition, and grow your BrandPicture than by extending the equity of your brand (see the illustration on the facing page).

Brand extensions, or brand-based innovations, leverage and integrate the strengths inherent within a brand to an identified, unmet market need. The reason brand extensions are so powerful is that the new product or service comes with instant credibility and a built-in endorsement, as the brand has already been accepted and proven in the marketplace by an existing product or service.

Brand Positioning as the Key to Brand Extension

What's new here is not the concept of brand extendibility, it's the mindset that connects the extension directly back to your brand positioning. Recall from the previous chapter that a positioning has three components: a target market, a definition of the business that the brand competes in, and a point of difference or benefit that is unique, credible, valued, sustainable, and fits with the brand and the company. Most brand extensions build off of one or more of these components.

Extending Your Target Market

Gillette's Sensor for women leveraged the definition of the business that Gillette is in and the Gillette brand benefit of the "clean shave" to dramatically extend its target market from only men to all adults who shave. Levi's Dockers leveraged its "comfort and durable" benefit to dramatically extend its target market and the definition of the business it was in (selling jeans).

Marriott's Courtyard by Marriott is another example of this. It leveraged the definition of the business Marriott was in (hotels) and the benefit (comfort and quality) to reach a target market that could not necessarily afford to stay at a regular Marriott or may have just thought of Marriott as a family vacation hotel instead of a businessperson's hotel. Sports Illustrated's *Sports Illustrated for Kids* and Cosmopolitan's *CosmoGIRL!* are also great examples of extending a brand's target market.

Extending the Definition of Your Business

Crayola's line of markers, paints, and clay is most likely targeted to the same customers as its crayon. The new line leverages Crayola's point of difference, "creative," but extends the definition of the business.

With IBM Consulting, IBM fundamentally changed the definition of the business it was in from "technology based" to "technology-based solutions."

Extending Your Point of Difference

With Go-Gurt Yogurt (basically yogurt in a tube), one of the top new products of 1998, General Mills' Yoplait leveraged its target market and definition of its business. The new product helped extend Yoplait's benefit within its positioning: the same great yogurt in a more convenient package.

Each time Intel comes out with a faster chip or Microsoft introduces a new version of Windows, they extend the benefits of their brands. Similarly, Blockbuster's new benefit of "guaranteed videos in stock" and FedEx's new drop-off time for packages of midnight in some locations are examples of building and extending on the defined point of difference.

Extending the Entire Positioning

Several recent new products and services have attempted to extend a brand's entire positioning. This usually occurs when a company is trying to enter a new market for the first time and has a brand whose strengths are recognized beyond the current target market and beyond the current definition of the positioning.

For instance, Caterpillar successfully introduced Caterpillar Footwear by extending its reputation and brand strength from the heavy equipment market. Although the construction-style boot that Caterpillar offers does not directly address an unmet market need, it does help to fill a niche for trendy, rugged footwear. This sort of extension may be considered risky, but if done well it allows a company to diversify its branded products and services and take a true portfolio approach to managing its brand.

The Gap has done this in a more subtle way with Baby Gap. It has extended its brand from the young adult market and now says, in effect, that The Gap now reaches out to parents with babies and toddlers because it is now in the business of providing clothing to customers from birth through adulthood. It is leveraging its reputation for stylish, high-quality clothes with a line that is baby safe and reasonably priced.

Baby Gap will probably thrive because it fulfills the marketplace desire for moderately priced, stylish baby clothing. In addition, The Gap's recent advertisements (such as *Gap Swing* and *Khakis Rock*) positively influence Baby Gap, as many customers shop at both stores.

Both Caterpillar and The Gap conducted extensive customer research to make sure that these extensions helped to build the brand, not diminish its strength.

When Should You Extend Your Brand?

Brand-based extensions can obviously have a direct impact on brand loyalty and brand value. A good rule of thumb comes from Bob Passikoff, president of Brand Keys: an increase in customer loyalty can increase the lifetime profits from a customer by as much as 100 percent. Thus, strategically leveraging your brand into smart brand extensions can ultimately help drive loyalty and the overall value of your brand.

Successfully extending your brand is tied to keeping current customers happy, bringing new customers into the brand family, and keeping the brand fresh. The goal of all brand-based extensions is always to increase the overall value and strength of the brand. In other words, innovate from a position of strength. Don't use your brand franchise to support weak ideas or products. Each brand extension should add strength to the overall brand identity, not take from it. Using your brand to support weak products and services will backfire and diminish the power of the overall brand.

Key Brand Extension Questions

Four questions are critical to ask prior to deciding whether to go forward with extending your brand:

1. Is the extension consistent with your Brand Vision?
2. Does the extension help uphold and strengthen your Brand-Picture?
3. Is the extension consistent with your overall positioning?
4. If the extension fails, will it be a major or minor setback for your brand?

Let's look at each of these questions individually.

Is the Extension Consistent with Your Brand Vision?

Determining the match of your brand extension with your brand vision depends on two things: how the extension reflects the needs in your financial growth gap and what role it plays in your overall development strategy.

The latest strategic move of Howard Schultz, the genius behind Starbucks' success, is relevant here. If you buy into the European experience—the special feeling that one experiences when buying a cup of coffee—then do you also believe that Starbucks in cyberspace can reflect that same experience? Is that a good, credible brand extension that is consistent with Starbucks' long-term vision?

His theory is that because of the incredible loyalty Starbucks garners from its customer base, anything with the Starbucks name on it will be a success. Apparently, Starbucks will encourage its customers to shop on the Web through Starbucks.com. Starbucks will partner with current Internet stars like eBay and Amazon.com, advertise through its own magazine, *Joe,* and will turn each of its stores into cyber-shops. It will be interesting to watch how this strategic intention turns out.

The goal for brand extendibility has to be aimed at adding value to the brand at the highest level, keeping current customers happy, and providing more choices and benefits to future customers.

Extensions Help Fill Your Financial Growth Gap

Step One discussed the Brand Vision and its linkages to corporate strategy. In planning for the future, you need a snapshot of where your brand is today and where you want it to go tomorrow. You should have a financial growth gap that dictates what percentage of the growth attributable to the brand should come from new products and services, new channels, price increases, mergers and acquisitions, and pure strengthening of the brand.

Brand extendibility expectations may range from small incremental growth to dramatic growth of the business and the brand.

Brand Extension Roles

In his book *Managing New Products*, Tom Kuczmarski talks about new products and the roles they can play in helping to fill a growth gap. I like to think about brand extensions as fulfilling certain roles also.

Brand extension requisite roles are extensions made to defend and bolster the brand as it is defined today. These extensions are usually termed line extensions, flankers, and revisions. Often they are aimed at matching a competitor's benefits, not necessarily differentiating the benefit from the competitor's. In addition, brand extension requisite roles are aimed at keeping your current customers satisfied by upgrading the benefits they are receiving. The words "more," "new," "improved," and "better than ever" are often used to describe a requisite extension.

A great example of filling a requisite extension role is the American Express Gold Card's recent new benefit offering of "Points Accelerator." This gives Gold Card members 1.5 American Express points for every dollar they charge. Revolutionary? No. A neat new benefit that will keep current Gold Card members satisfied and potentially add a few new card members? Absolutely. There is minimum risk, most likely minimum returns, but great potential for maintaining the strength of the brand.

Brand extension expansive roles are extensions that offer new expansions relative to the three components of the brand positioning. These extensions (many of which were discussed earlier) are aimed at dramatically growing the business. Expansive roles offer benefits that have not been received by the market before or offer an opportunity to get into a segment of the market that the brand may not have tapped before.

S. C. Johnson Wax's introduction of Glade Candles helped to dramatically grow the Glade brand air freshener business and helped SCJ redefine its business from odor masking to products that help enhance a home environment. This extension tapped an unmet need for relatively inexpensive candles at traditional food and drug stores. It capitalized on the strength of the Glade brand and the channels of distribution Glade owned. It also helped Glade increase penetration in the underleveraged male market segment.

In looking for ways to expand its brand beyond traditional markets, Eddie Bauer's management sought a fit between consumer need, its strong brand, and a new channel to leverage. Brad Larsen, brand manager for Eddie Bauer, says, "A successful example of channel expansion is the Eddie Bauer car seat. Where are they sold? Toys 'R' Us and Target—not places we normally correlate with our affluent consumer. However, after doing research, we realized that our consumer does go to those places for infant wear, children's wear, and other children's products. This was a good fit that allowed us to reach our consumers in a new outlet."

Case Study: Lego

To regain lost market share and the interest of children around the world, Lego, the $1.3 billion privately held maker of Lego blocks and other stalwart toys, had been seeking new ways to grow and extend its powerful brand.

I believe Lego could have joined the video game market, leveraging its name to sell high-tech software games played on a personal computer. However, the company chose to stick to what its brand is all about—those bright-colored plastic blocks.

Lego has approached the video and high-technology market in a different way that enables the company to acknowledge markets, leverage its strong brand, and not walk away from its building-block heritage. Lego "Mind-storms" are Lego blocks with embedded computer chips and light sensors.

These chips allow kids to program their computer with special software to add special effects to any Lego creation. This expansive brand-based extension has allowed Lego to remain a company dedicated to traditional children's products while extending into the computer age.

The Lego "Leg-acy" has continued in other ways. The company has consistently offered more complex specialty kits such as Lego space stations (a requisite role), has expanded its line to be age appropriate for all children from twelve months to twelve years old, and has recently opened its third LegoLand theme park outside of San Diego (an expansive extension).

The bottom line is that Lego is leveraging a strong brand into an even stronger and more profitable position in its markets through both expansive and requisite brand extension roles.

Does the Extension Uphold and Strengthen Your BrandPicture?

David Friedman, vice president of marketing at U.S. Cellular, says "the boundaries for good extensions are fundamentally those which the customer deems to be acceptable. That is a real challenge. The bottom line is that brand building, in part, resides in the mind of the customers, as do the opportunities for growth. Figure out the intersections of your brand's boundaries and those opportunities for growth and you will succeed."

Your BrandPicture should have taught you a lot about your brand. From the image it currently has to the contract it fulfills to the ways in which customers think about your brand compared to the competition, the BrandPicture helps you define where your brand is today and where it can go tomorrow. This second extendibility question helps you guarantee that your BrandPicture is not only upheld but strengthened over time.

Case Study: Ralph Lauren

Not many brands have transformed themselves into dynasties as Ralph Lauren has. And despite continuous pressures from the financial community not to, Lauren continues to invest in building the biggest and strongest powerhouse brand in retailing while continuing to build and strengthen its brand image.

How can Ralph Lauren possibly be in both Nordstrom's and Home Depot and retain its brand identity? Doesn't being carried in outlet stores degrade the brand? In reality, all these are helping to fuel record sales and further propel the brand.

Doesn't licensing take control of the brand out of Ralph Lauren's hands? Actually, the screens used for cobranded products, such as Sherwin Williams– Ralph Lauren paint, are probably tougher than internal Ralph Lauren screens, and the level of quality these licensees have to deliver is "best in class." What's next, furniture? Surprise! Lauren already offers furniture.

Lauren's portfolio of offerings allows it to experience incredible loyalty, an ability to charge premium prices, and an ability to regularly and successfully offer endorsed new products and services on a regular basis. The portfolio also allows Ralph Lauren to introduce its brand to those who may have not had exposure to it in the apparel world. If customers have a good brand experience in one product category, the brand has a higher probability for success in another category.

Obviously Lauren has to be careful and make sure the brand is consistently involved with the right fashion, channel, and image choices. If it loses sight of this or is driven by the short-term quarterly profit-and-loss spasms of the investment community, the long-term damage could be considerable. I am confident that Ralph Lauren will continue to make the right choices and continue to extend and enhance its brand image in very profitable ways.

Case Study: Disney's DisneyQuest

When you are at Disney's level on the Brand Value Pyramid (discussed in Step Two), the possibilities for brand extensions are endless. Disney has credibly gone into amusement parks, toys, movies, television, cable, publishing, cruise lines, and more because all of these experience-based products and services reinforce what the Disney brand stands for: wholesome family fun. Where they can't credibly extend, or where the association might harm the brand, it creates a new brand, such as Touchstone Pictures or Miramax.

DisneyQuest is an interesting new brand extension helping to fulfill an expansive role that I believe is fraught with high risk (to be discussed later in the chapter), though the potential return is correspondingly high.

DisneyQuest is Disney's attempt to bring the Disneyland and Disney World experience to Chicago by providing an indoor, interactive theme park. It features traditional "magical" rides and activities aimed at filling the need to go to Disneyland or Disney World when that is not possible. Also, because it is indoors it provides the Disney experience year-round, which is not possible outdoors in cold-weather states.

In addition, it provides Disney with an outlet to reach the important teenager market that it may otherwise lose when a child becomes an adolescent and decides that events that were fun a few years ago are now "uncool."

Disney has stated that if this works, it has plans to offer similar indoor parks in other northern cities, such as Philadelphia.

DisneyQuest provides a new benefit that could enhance the value of the umbrella brand and further reinforce its strong positioning.

Is the Extension Consistent with Your Overall Positioning?

Inconsistency with your Brand Vision, Contract, and image are forms of brand abuse. How do you know if there is inconsistency? Look at your price point, your target audience, your positioning, your distribution, and your overall image as a result of extending your brand into a new area. Is it consistent, like BMW offering high-end motorcycles? Or is it inconsistent, like Clorox offering laundry detergent?

The key questions to ask about consistency with your brand positioning are these:

- Does this extension add to or detract from what the parent brand stands for?
- Does it confuse current customers? If so, are you adding enough new customers to make up for it?
- If you are cannibalizing your current brand offerings through this innovation, are you at least increasing the price premium, like Gillette did with its Mach 3 razor relative to its Sensor razor?
- Can the marketplace clearly differentiate this innovation from offerings under your parent brand?

Consistent Extensions

Apple Computers stand for innovation, nonconformity, and the real beginning of the personal computer business. Apple rose all the way to the top of the Brand Value Pyramid in the 1980s and basically dominated the PC world. If you did not have an Apple, you were behind the times. The apple with a bite taken out of it is one of the world's best-known icons. After Bill Gates, there was no one better known in this industry than Steven Jobs.

Everyone knows that Apple lost its way for awhile. Jobs left, several others tried their hand at running the company (most notably, ex-Pepsi guru John Sculley), Apple's focus on Newton replaced the focus on Mac PCs, Dell exploded, IBM came back, and Apple almost never recovered.

But like someone sent from Central Casting, Steven Jobs came back, Apple became relevant again, many of the industry's top thinkers joined, and the brand made a strong comeback. In 1998 the iMac was introduced and was voted by many as the number one new product introduction of the year. It was colorful, it stood for connecting people (not being isolated in front of your PC), and it ran like a Mac has always run. The stock is back, the brand is as powerful as ever, and Apple continues to pump out new products. Purple computers are here to stay. In addition, HP, Compaq, IBM, and Dell have little credibility in matching this innovative offering—it just is not part of their respective BrandPictures.

Scott Snyder, marketing director at Johnson & Johnson, provides another great example of brand extension: "Creating the concept of Extra Strength Tylenol as a trusted pain reliever enabled us to go far beyond pain relief into related conditions with line extensions for virtually anything related to headache or fever. At first we were very cautious about extending the brand. As the world's largest brand name in over-the-counter medicine, there was a lot at stake. Slowly, we got into combinations that included cough and cold, sinus and allergy, sore throat, and the like.

"It made sense to people. Then we went to Non-Drowsy. We made increasingly bold and broad claims and we were surprised at how accepting people were. It became clear to us that we had a highly leverageable brand asset. Then we introduced Tylenol PM as a nighttime pain reliever. Although it was first marketed for pain relief, PM took on an entirely different role. The Tylenol name on the product gave consumers the confidence to take a sleeping pill. It became a huge business because millions of stressed-out Americans finally started taking something to help them fall asleep. In fact, we just launched a new medicine called Simply Sleep from the Makers of Tylenol. It is a nighttime sleep aid without the pain relief qualities. And it carries the associated brand equity: 'From the makers of Tylenol PM.'"

At Black & Decker, its powerful brand stands for the "handyman's tool manufacturer." Black & Decker helps Bob Villa wannabes actually succeed and accomplish projects they may have not been able to on their own. At the highest order, the Black &

Decker brand makes people more self-confident. The company has found a formula that, like John Deere, puts its brand at the highest level on the Brand Value Pyramid.

Its product extensions are consistent with that. For example, the Black & Decker Snake Light, introduced early in the holiday season, was an incredible success because the company addressed an unmet need in an innovative way and leveraged its powerful brand name to sell it. This product was aimed at helping consumers gain the flexibility needed when trying to see in areas not reachable with a conventional flashlight. The product was part of an overall string of innovations that helped reinvent Black & Decker.

When the Snake Light was introduced, the company was becoming known as a leader in cordless tools. From the original Dustbuster to power drills to the Snakelight, Black & Decker had hit on a success formula that met the demands of the market's need for convenience, cordless, and high-quality products.

Recently Black & Decker introduced the 24-volt version of its cordless drills, saws, power hammers, and the like. This will help Black & Decker become the first cordless toolmaker to make battery-operated tools that are as powerful as their corded counterparts, further driving its brand's value.

This series of innovations will help fuel sales of Black & Decker's other chargeable products too, such as lawn mowers, grass trimmers, hedge clippers, and its newest product, the cordless power sprayer—all having an extended usage relative to what they offered before.

The result is that Black & Decker is able to take advantage of and lead the growth of the power tool category. Cordless power tools are growing at an 8–10 percent annual rate, whereas the rest of the power tool category is growing at a 2–3 percent rate. Because of its strategy, Black & Decker has captured over 40 percent of the tool market in North America and 25 percent in Europe and is virtually untouchable on both continents. Black & Decker's most recent quarterly results saw revenues increase by 11 percent and operating profits by 24 percent.

Inconsistent Extensions

In mid-1999, Merrill Lynch announced plans to enter the on-line brokerage industry in order to capitalize on the huge market potential represented by customers buying and selling stock on line.

Merrill Lynch's president explained that the strategic move was due to market shifts and massive potential market share gains. He did not talk at all about the possible challenges caused by shifting strategy, such as alienating current customers who go to Merrill Lynch for the broker relationship, service, and expertise. Many people are more than willing to pay a $100 commission or more per trade for the kind of service and support a full-service broker can provide.

Merrill Lynch is running a serious risk that could permanently denigrate its brand image. Going to on-line trading might put it at parity with other traditional on-line and "bargain" brokers (such as AmeriTrade and E-Trade), leading current customers to think, probably for the first time, about how much they are spending on commissions. It may also lead customers to think that the company is abandoning its traditional customers and relationships to jump on the Internet bandwagon.

This concern was the motivation behind Lynch's recent TV commercials, which featured a rather worried-looking, middle-aged man being reassured by a Merrill Lynch broker that the company would still "be there." Yes, he is told, "it will all be there." "Even the bull?" the man asks. "Even the bull," the broker responds.

Although the icon and the message are needed, I believe Lynch is taking a chance. This shift could alienate its traditional, high-commission-paying clientele.

Another extension that will be interesting to watch is T. J. Maxx'n More, an offshoot of discounter T. J. Maxx. The company has determined it has the credibility to move into the home furnishings market. Offering everything from furniture to luxurious pillows to designer bedding to framed art to 100 percent wool rugs, T. J. Maxx is counting on the same market that goes to its stores today to get designer fashions at discounted prices.

But T. J. Maxx is not Ethan Allen. It has yet to establish credibility in the home furnishings arena and there is nothing in its latest ad copy that would suggest that, like its parent, this is also a discount store with famous brands. In fact, the tagline is Fashions for Your Family and Home. Great tagline, but I expect the same at Homemakers, Room and Board, and Carson's. Reaching the highest level of the triangle only allows you to credibly extend the value that you stand for. So far, T. J. Maxx has not followed that formula.

If the Extension Fails, Will It Be a Major or Minor Setback?

Will the extension further endear a customer to your brand, have a neutral effect, or have a negative effect that pulls a disloyalty trigger?

Consider DisneyQuest, discussed earlier. It is an attempt to expansively extend the Disney brand. But what happens if the brand extension fails, the benefit is not appreciated or valued, and DisneyQuest is a bomb? This important question has to be addressed through the customer model and through a process I will discuss shortly that focuses on the extension's short- and long-term benefits.

DisneyQuest is getting mixed reviews. One Chicago newspaper critic said, "It's the place where you pay $16 for three hours of standing in line, interrupted by a few modestly enjoyable distractions." This critic also states that Michael Eisner's initial gut reaction was to "kill the project" because it failed to truly exploit the Disney icons—even if it makes money. The critic goes on to say that Eisner should have stuck with his gut. Although in its early stages it has been popular and packed, DisneyQuest's contribution to the brand won't be felt for a few years.

What is the possible downside for Disney? EuroDisney is starting to recover after many years of poor performance, but it should have sent a message to Disney. The Disney brand is about an experience. If the experience is not a good one or is dramatically different from other Disney experiences, the brand could suffer a setback.

With EuroDisney, the American-style park was not customized to European needs. At DisneyQuest, Mickey Mouse and Donald Duck are not walking around greeting visitors, the atmosphere and ambiance is dark and uses some of Disney's "meaner" animated characters, and, incredibly, younger children cannot enjoy most of the rides and activities. How will this affect those same children's and their parents' desire to go to Disney World or Disneyland one day?

Brad VanAuken, former director of brand management and marketing at Hallmark, says, "You do have to be careful how far you extend the brand. You have to be very careful in clarifying what you stand for. At Hallmark, we were always riding that fine line of how far can we go with our positioning of caring shared, without losing its inherent meaning."

For example, Arm & Hammer Dental Care Baking Soda Gum went into national distribution in February 1998. This followed several baking soda-based launches over the last five years, including laundry detergent, dishwashing detergent, toothpaste, deodorant, and bleach. Church & Dwight's Arm and Hammer brand extension criteria appear to center on leveraging the good name and reputation of Arm & Hammer and baking soda's benefit of "clean and freshening" in every conceivable category where it might fit.

There are three problems with this: baking soda is a commodity, there are successful leaders in each category Arm & Hammer competes in, and the benefit is easily replicable. For example, Crest and Colgate immediately came out with toothpastes containing baking soda and, in effect, took Arm & Hammer out of the picture. Tide did not waste much time and neither did Dial or Sure in the deodorant category.

The fate of the gum is likely to be the same. Wrigley's or Trident will probably come out with a baking-soda ingredient soon just to knock Arm & Hammer out of the game. The bottom line is that Arm & Hammer has a sustainable advantage in baking soda as a baking ingredient, as a freshener in the refrigerator, and through a few other extensions. The rest are examples of what I call "brand abuse."

What could have been a strategy that made perfect sense for Arm & Hammer, allowed for credible extensions, and sustainable over time? Cobranding. If Arm & Hammer followed the Intel model of becoming a critical part (or ingredient) of other manufacturers' products, we could be talking about a massive success story. Imagine Crest with Arm & Hammer baking soda—that would be a powerful cobranded product.

Mercedes, however, may be committing the ultimate brand-extension sin. Its C230 sedan is listed at $30,450, is in the same showroom as higher-priced models, and may be taking up the bulk of Mercedes advertising energy today. In addition, new advertisements from Nissan Altima, comparing the two in terms of performance, luxury, options, and the like, may be a real embarrassment for Mercedes because Nissan is demonstrating that it is comparable on all fronts. The only difference is that the Altima is priced at $15,000. Another Nissan ad shows the Altima towing a new powerboat, implying that you can have both for the price of the C230.

How could Mercedes have traveled so far down the path from competing with Jaguars and BMWs to the Altima and the Honda Civic? It undoubtedly began with good intentions. Mercedes wanted to attract younger consumers or those with less disposable income to a class of car that in years past they would have never been able to own. The benefits are twofold: open yourself up to a new segment you did not have access to before and hope to gain a lifetime customer who will continue to trade up. Unfortunately, Mercedes has a lot of work to do to show that it can play in the $30,000 and $60,000 categories at the same time.

The biggest concern for Mercedes should be whether it is insulting the $60,000 car buyer who bought the luxury and prestige of owning a Mercedes and now shares the road with others who bought a Mercedes for half the price. Another problem is that some customers will not want to be associated with the lowest-priced Mercedes on the market. It may shout out to others, "I couldn't afford the expensive one."

How to Pick the Right Brand Extensions: A Four-Step Process

Every company needs to understand what its brand does and does not stand for before it tries to extend it in an uncharted direction that may not fit with the needs of the marketplace. A good process helps raise an organization's chances for success from luck (one out of ten successes) to high probability (seven out of ten successes).

A good process helps identify and avoid extension ideas that, although meeting a consumer need, are too far a stretch for the brand. For example, Owens Corning offering home installation for its insulation line is definitely a value-added offering, but is it credible?

This four-step process merges two powerful assets—knowledge of consumer needs (from the customer model) and the brand image and brand contract—to ensure that any new product concept that moves forward has already accounted for its fit with the brand and the impact it may have on it (see Table 6.1).

Table 6.1. The BAM Process:
A Head Start on the New Products Process

BAM Process	*Brand-Based New Products Process*
Five-year brand vision: Financial and strategic expectations ⟶	Step one: New products strategy
Customer model: Problems, needs and wants ⟶	Step two: Problem and need identification
Brand positioning: Future image and focus of brand ⟶	Step three: Idea generation and screening
	Step four: Concept development and business analysis

The box below shows how the Brand Vision and the individual components of the BrandPicture provide information that shapes and defines brand extension parameters for success.

A Brand Vision helps drive your brand extension goals and strategic roles.

The Persona and Contract help to determine brand strengths and weaknesses.

The Customer Model outlines needs, wants, and possible areas for growth.

The Customer Model outlines perceptions of your brand versus the competition.

The Customer Model helps define the extension boundaries for the brand.

The Brand Positioning helps to provide an overall screen for brand extensions.

Step One: Develop a Brand Extension Strategy

A brand extension strategy defines the role brand extensions will play in helping to fill to a company's financial growth gap, the strategic roles that brand extensions will fill, and the screening criteria that help determine which categories and new product concepts are most attractive to pursue under the brand.

Your brand extension strategy has to be in total alignment with the Brand Vision articulated in Phase One of the Brand Asset Management Process. The financial growth gap, discussed in Step One, enables us to see the size of the growth goal that needs to be achieved and what avenues are available to fill it. The strategy should allow you to maximize your brand extension potential by developing new products and services based on the strengths of your brand. Without a strategy, you are aimlessly seeking ways to stretch your brand. With a strategy, you should be able to develop a balanced portfolio of requisite and expansive brand extensions (see Figure 6.1).

Figure 6.1. Forms of Brand Extension

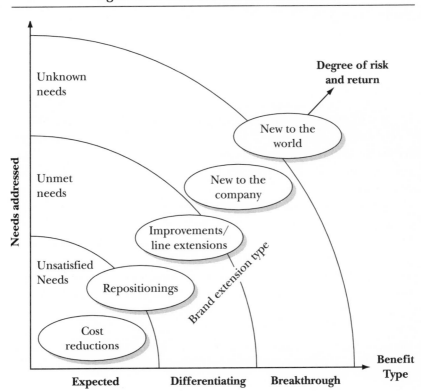

Your brand extension strategy should include desired three- to five-year revenue targets for brand extension efforts, brand extension strategic roles (as discussed earlier), and top management's expectations for and commitment to extending the brand.

The BrandPicture should help management recognize the inherent value of its brand in the market and where the brand can credibly go. By looking at the brand along several dimensions and relative to the competition, management will be able to focus all of its new product efforts on increasing the value of the brand. In addition, it will ultimately help the team focus its research efforts on credible brand-building efforts.

Step Two: Explore Problem and Opportunity Areas

The key here is to not focus on ideas, but rather on further defining potential growth opportunities. At this stage, gather and organize customer and market intelligence. This information then guides idea generation and concept development efforts. Try to come up with five to seven strategically focused, brand-based opportunity areas that will serve as a basis for generating ideas in Step Three.

For example, Burger King's Big Kids Meal reflects this needs identification process. Burger King realized that McDonald's Happy Meals target little kids perfectly and that the regular menu caters to adults and teenagers who want to think of themselves as adults. This leaves an in-between group that has never been specifically targeted: junior-high kids (eleven to fourteen years old).

Burger King took the simplest but most effective route of targeting an untapped market segment: it repackaged current offerings (such as a Whopper, sixteen-ounce drink, and large fries) and massively advertised directly to that segment. During development of this offering several questions were most likely asked: Does any other fast food company provide a meal that is focused on the junior high years? Does it appear that anyone will target this segment soon? Importantly, has McDonald's gotten there yet? The answers are no, no, and no. And yes, Burger King's Big Kids Meal has been a stellar success.

Step Three: Generate Brand-Based New Product Ideas

The objective of Step Three is to generate new solutions and creative approaches to the greatest need and growth opportunity areas identified in Step Two. The emphasis here should be on generating as many ideas as possible that will potentially solve problems and satisfy needs identified by consumers during the exploratory research conducted in Step Two.

Idea generation sessions should identify multiple solutions for problems and satisfy unmet consumer needs. These sessions are not traditional open brainstorming exercises. Rather, idea generation is a focused process aimed at creatively solving specific consumer-cited, not internally generated, problems.

These sessions can surface as many as several hundred targeted new-product ideas. More important than the quantity is that each idea be linked directly to a defined market need and a fit with the brand.

After all the ideas have been generated, it is time to move to idea screening. The first series of screens are consumer, strategic, and brand screens. These assess the degree to which ideas satisfy or address brand extension strategic roles and consumer needs and wants, and the degree of fit with the BrandPicture developed in Phase Two.

The top ideas coming out of Step Three will move forward to Step Four, concept development and business planning. These ideas will have passed all major screens and are deemed to fit well within the BrandPicture already developed.

For example, as discussed earlier, Cincinnati Bell Telephone (CBT) is a great example of how brand-based innovation comes to life. CBT is generally regarded as one of the premier telephone companies in the Midwest. The customer service, reputation, rates, quality, and variety of options it offers a residential or business customer are unparalleled for a company its size. A few years ago, CBT hired us to help fill its revenue and profit growth gap and to further extend its brand.

The strategy directed us to look into two specific market segments—single office and home office (SOHO) and medium-sized businesses. Focusing on the former, interviewees told us there were several problem areas that they could use assistance on, including the following:

- Helping my small company appear to be larger than it really is
- Lack of office support
- Limited budget
- Outdated or nonexistent equipment
- Expanding too fast to provide adequate sales support

Each of these need areas represents dozens of distinct product or service opportunity areas for any telecommunications company. For CBT, this eventually led to the successful introduction of the Internet Call Manager, which was described in Step Four.

Step Four: Develop Brand-Based Concepts and Conduct Business Analysis

The purpose here is to identify, based on the ideas generated in Step Three, a few high-potential, brand-value enhancing concepts ready for further development based on continued, positive feedback from the market and overall business attractiveness.

There are three parts to Step Four. The first part entails turning the twenty-five to thirty ideas into robust concepts. The second part involves prioritizing and testing the top five to seven concepts. The third part involves conducting business analysis on those concepts and narrowing them down to the top two or three that should move into prototype development. The types of questions business analysis should address are shown in Figure 6.2.

A well-crafted concept should describe the features and attributes, intended use, and primary benefits perceived by consumers. It addresses how the product might be positioned against competition and defines the primary purchaser. This is also a critical checkpoint for ensuring that the new product concept does indeed still fit with and enhance the value of the brand.

Summary

Successfully extending your brand should help you drive your brand's overall strength and value, as long as the four questions mentioned at the beginning of the chapter are addressed.

Figure 6.2. The Business Case: Pulling Together All Aspects of Product Development

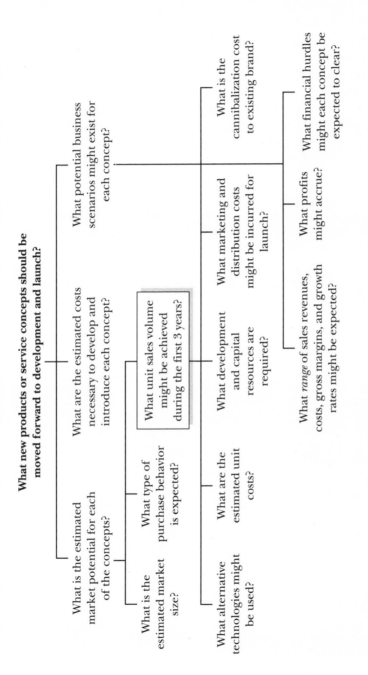

What new products or service concepts should be moved forward to development and launch?

What is the estimated market potential for each of the concepts?

What is the estimated market size?

What type of purchase behavior is expected?

What alternative technologies might be used?

What are the estimated costs necessary to develop and introduce each concept?

What unit sales volume might be achieved during the first 3 years?

What are the estimated unit costs?

What development and capital resources are required?

What potential business scenarios might exist for each concept?

What is the cannibalization cost to existing brand?

What marketing and distribution costs might be incurred for launch?

What profits might accrue?

What *range* of sales revenues, costs, gross margins, and growth rates might be expected?

What financial hurdles might each concept be expected to clear?

Many consider innovating and extending the brand to be the lifeline of an organization, especially in high-growth and rapidly evolving industries. It obviously requires a long-term mindset shift and commitment level to succeed. Recognition that brands can help fill your growth gap will only help to increase the internal and external value of the brand.

Companies that are successful in extending their brands ensure that they always have an active pipeline filled with a balanced portfolio of brand extensions, ranging from low risk–low return to high risk–high return. They treat innovation and extending the brand as a consistent and critical path to long-term brand survival and success. And they recognize that their brands can allow for a level of innovation success and consistent performance that may have not been available to them in the past and is most likely not available to their competitors.

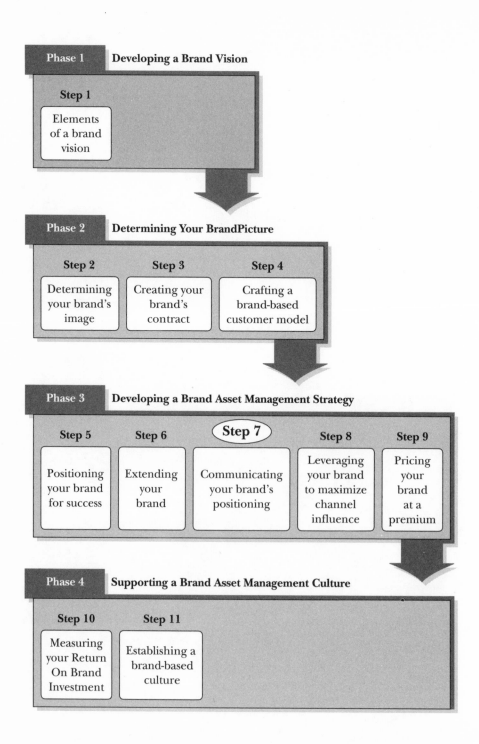

Phase 1 — Developing a Brand Vision

Step 1 — Elements of a brand vision

Phase 2 — Determining Your BrandPicture

Step 2 — Determining your brand's image

Step 3 — Creating your brand's contract

Step 4 — Crafting a brand-based customer model

Phase 3 — Developing a Brand Asset Management Strategy

Step 5 — Positioning your brand for success

Step 6 — Extending your brand

Step 7 — Communicating your brand's positioning

Step 8 — Leveraging your brand to maximize channel influence

Step 9 — Pricing your brand at a premium

Phase 4 — Supporting a Brand Asset Management Culture

Step 10 — Measuring your Return On Brand Investment

Step 11 — Establishing a brand-based culture

Communicating Your Brand's Positioning

Brand-based communications (see the illustration on the facing page) are aimed at developing and implementing the communications strategies that will help bring your brand's positioning to life. Ultimately, the right mix of strategies will maximize your potential for brand success.

Successful brand-based communications assumes that you have the other foundations in place, as shown in the box.

Corporate Strategy $\longrightarrow$ Brand Vision $\longrightarrow$

BrandPicture $\longrightarrow$ Brand Positioning $\longrightarrow$

Brand-Based Communications Strategy

The last stage shown here—a brand-based communications strategy—is the basis for successfully communicating your brand's positioning to your target market.

Managing the Brand Is Not Just Managing Communications

The most difficult mindset shift for managers to make—regardless of industry, size of company, or experience—is that branding is about more than just communications. Communications is one of many tools needed to execute a successful Brand Asset Management strategy. Unfortunately, many companies still believe that the advertising agency, not internal managers, should take care of branding.

As you will see in this chapter, communications in Brand Asset Management go way beyond advertising. In fact, a good brand-based communications strategy covers the following areas:

- Advertising
- Public relations
- Event marketing and corporate sponsorships
- Trade and sales promotions
- Consumer promotions (point of purchase, coupons, refunds, contests)
- Direct marketing (catalogues, Internet, mailings, fax, e-mail)
- Internal employee communications

Each of these will be discussed in more detail later in the chapter.

Another crucial shift in the mindset is to start viewing dollars spent on brand-based communications as investments, not costs. P&G is a great example; it recently announced that it was raising the stakes to make sure that its agency's advertising campaign hits the mark. P&G is requiring its agencies to reduce their fees and enter into a risk-sharing arrangement based directly on the effectiveness of their recommended campaign in increasing sales.

Becoming an AUTHOR

Most companies focus on communications' execution but pay too little attention to its goals and objectives. The AUTHOR model, which describes the six stages of impact communications should have on your target customer, provides an effective approach to linking brand-based communications to your Brand Vision, Brand-Picture and brand positioning. It enables you to be like any author—in control of all your communications efforts. The six stages are:

Awareness: First, you must create awareness for your brand.

Understanding: Once you have achieved awareness, your communications efforts should lead your target audience to clearly understand what your brand stands for—that is, its positioning.

Trial: Once your customer understands who you are and what your unique points of difference are, concentrate on generating trial and inducing customers to try your brand.

Happiness: After a trial of your brand, the customer had a good experience and has a very favorable impression of your brand.

Only one: This is the most important stage of all—getting the customer to think only about your brand in your category. This is the position of power, which allows for premium pricing and credible and expansive extensions. This loyalty position is now yours to lose.

Referral or recommendation: The ultimate sign of brand satisfaction is when customers are willing to put their own reputation on the line by referring your brand to a peer.

The AUTHOR model is especially useful for keeping the big picture in mind at all times.

Five Principles for Successful Brand-Based Communications

There are five guiding principles that will help you implement a long-term brand-based communications strategy:

1. Use all communication strategies to help achieve your corporate strategy and brand vision.
2. Let your BrandPicture and brand positioning largely determine the right communications strategy to execute.
3. Use an integrated marketing communications strategy to get maximum return from all dollar investments.

4. Execute your communications strategy well across the organization.

5. Create internal involvement, education, and metrics to determine the success of communications.

These principles along with the AUTHOR model should help any company that wants to maximize its brand communications efforts to have both the right mindset and the right expectations.

Many of these principles are embraced by a few recent winners of the American Marketing Association's EFFIE awards. The EFFIEs are one of advertising's highest honors and generally go hand in hand with a company or brand achieving a major strategic goal, along with well-executed advertising. Here are four brief EFFIE examples, with the challenge, strategy, and results stated for each.

Case Study: Ray-Ban: "Definitely Ray-Ban"

The challenge: Ray-Ban had experienced sales declines as the brand became outdated and was viewed as too limiting, too masculine, and not very competitive.

The strategy: the Ray-Ban ad campaign was aimed at challenging consumers' existing perceptions of Ray-Ban by creating a new Brand Persona (modern, intelligent, and confident) and creating a contract and positioning tied to personifying itself as the sunglasses expert. Its goals included appealing to current customers, noncustomers, nonusers, women, and younger consumers.

The results: Ray-Ban's sales have stabilized and appear to be rising again.

Case Study: BMW: "The Ultimate Driving Machine"

The challenge: 1997 threatened to be the first year BMW would concede its number one position in the high-performance luxury car market. BMW had no new product launches, whereas tough competitors like Mercedes, Lexus, and Infiniti had many.

The strategy: BMW decided, because its BrandPicture was so positive, that what it really needed to focus on was further leveraging its strong positioning with an intensive communications campaign.

The results: the "Ultimate Driving Machine" campaign solidified BMW's strategic position as the best car in the market. Commercials reminded and convinced competitive drivers and shoppers why they should choose BMW. BMW maintained its number one position in the market without any new product introductions.

Case Study: State Farm Insurance: "State Farm Understands Life"

The challenge: reverse a declining trend and address parents' needs to protect and nurture their children.

The strategy: State Farm's intent was to change its brand associations and contract, leverage an updated customer model, and launch a new positioning. The tagline has two meanings: State Farm understands parents' challenges, dilemmas, and especially their unique needs; and State Farm has the expertise in life insurance you need.

The results: the campaign helped increase life insurance sales by 36 percent.

Case Study: TheStreet.com: "Addiction"

The challenge: people were not aware that TheStreet.com is an independent financial news and market performance Internet source.

The strategy: this campaign was solely intended to help bring TheStreet.com's BrandPicture and positioning into the forefront. The measure of success would be how much broad awareness had been created. Its goal was to induce trial with those who are "addicted" to playing Wall Street.

The results: the campaign pulled in 125,000 subscribers, 10 percent of whom paid $100 for a one-year trial subscription.

Hewlett-Packard conceptualizes and implements brand-based communications relying heavily on the five guiding principles. HP's "Invent" campaign, for example, was a corporate-wide, bold communications shift that was developed to move the company away from an overreliance on specific products and into the broader technology market. HP's ads and communications were changed from generic product ads to ads showing how HP products help customers make connections with those around them.

The critical communications shift for HP has been from a functional or product-based focus to a focus on products' problem-solving capabilities and the consequences for people. In thumbnail form, this example of HP's transformation synopsizes all five principles (and will be discussed throughout this chapter).

Let's look now at each guiding principle in detail.

1. Use All Communication Strategies to Achieve Your Corporate Strategy and Brand Vision

At this point, you have set your corporate vision, identified your corporate goals, and identified the potential impact your brand can have on this vision. Senior management has reached consensus on the company's direction, and everyone understands the near-term and long-term brand goals. The Brand Vision should have helped to set the right financial and strategic goals for the brand. And you have set realistic expectations for the timing of when your brand-based communications will start to have an impact on sales.

With our clients we try to set realistic timing expectations:

Recommended Brand Communications' Timeline for Impact

First 18 months	Build awareness, recall, and understanding
Month 19–month 36	Start to see results of communication efforts
Month 37–month 48	Loyalty is built and word-of-mouth spreads

Of course, the amount of time needed to produce results can vary with the strength of the brand, the type and size of the company, its available resources, the nature of the market, and many other factors. Priceline.com reached 70 percent unaided awareness within a year as a direct result of its massive advertising budget.

The point here is to set reasonable and realistic expectations and constantly remind yourself that your Brand Vision is dictating strategy for three to five years, not one or two.

2. Your BrandPicture and Brand Positioning Help Determine the Right Communications Strategy

The BrandPicture plays a significant role in shaping brand-based communications. The brand image defines the associations and the persona that the marketplace uses to identify a brand. Together the Brand Vision and BrandPicture show how large a gap exists between where management wants the brand to be and where it really is. This bit of "reality therapy" provides a first glimpse of realism into what is needed to actualize your brand-based communications efforts. Your brand positioning helps you aspire to a future position that will help you bridge this gap.

At Hewlett-Packard, for example, managers looked at the gap between corporate strategy and HP's brand vision. Amy Kelm, worldwide consumer brand manager, states, "The Hewlett-Packard brand had traditionally been a very strong brand. A decentralized organization and communications strategy, however, had allowed the brand to become fragmented in the minds of our customers. We had to face the reality that the brand was underutilized and not reaching its potential."

Hewlett-Packard was trying to fill the gap between how it was perceived and what its brand vision said it should be tomorrow.

"Because we wanted HP to be more relevant and differentiated in the market," continued Kelm, "we needed to understand what associations our customers had with the brand. They told us they believed HP to be very scientific, technical, and professional. They told us we had superior quality and reliability, and that they most often associated us with printers, obviously one of our largest and most visible product categories. Also, they told us they believed we had become somewhat quiet, slow, and passive. Our goal had to be to make the brand more relevant to our target market and also overcome the perceived limitations in innovation and approachability. "We saw this as a unique opportunity to go back to our roots. HP is a company with tremendous history. Started by two young men in a garage in 1939, HP was the original start-up. It was a company driven by engineers with an obsession for building quality products. In being a start-up, the company had defined itself through inventive thinking, seen not only through the products they developed but through the management philosophy they practiced as well. It was a company that worked collaboratively and moved quickly. We were extremely proud of our background and recognized the need to make the brand's heritage relevant once again.

"The word 'invent' captured the spirit of this repositioning and became the company's new brand statement. By blending the associations customers currently had with the brand, with the attributes that had originally defined the brand, we were able to communicate HP as a newly energized, fast-moving, and focused company.

"In addition, we knew that with a brand statement like 'invent' we would have to reinforce this promise through all our communication.

This included both visual and verbal forms of communication. We had to create an identity system that was new, innovative, and representative of the new HP."

MasterCard International was in a position similar to that of HP and needed to reposition its brand to reach its longer-term goals and objectives. The result of this repositioning is best seen through MasterCard's successful "priceless" campaign.

For years MasterCard was considered to be a standard, functional credit card with no emotional tie to it (compared to American Express's "don't leave home without it" campaign, for example). The "priceless" campaign is about the emotional ties people have with one another, the kind of ties that don't have a price tag. These ads imply that MasterCard can make life simpler so people have time to focus on the things that money can't buy, such as time for conversation with a child.

General Nutrition Centers' recent communications focus on its expertise in the nutritional arena, clearly reflecting its understanding of wellness and its quality products. Its ads show how its products improve well-being and overall health.

Ads for GNC's Women's Ultra Mega describe it as the most comprehensive formula designed specifically to meet women's needs. It describes each of the thirty-six vitamins included in a timed-release tablet and what each can do for the body. It also states that this product has no sugar, artificial colors, flavors, or preservatives. In addition, it has no wheat, dairy or soy additives, all thought to have potential negative side effects on some women.

What might the GNC brand contract promise through the Ultra Mega line? My description would include the following:

- Caters to the special needs of women
- Helps a woman feel as healthy and as good about herself as possible
- Includes all the vitamins a woman needs on a daily basis with an explanation of what each does
- Is safe; has no preservatives or artificial ingredients
- Is backed by knowledgeable employees in GNC stores to help explain the virtues of the vitamin
- Is available at any GNC store

3. Use an Integrated Marketing Communications Strategy

There has been a lot written recently about the virtues of integrated marketing communications (IMCs). Here's a summary:

Integrated Marketing Communications: Principles

- Ensure that all communications deliver a consistent message linking back to the brand and communications strategies.
- Appoint an IMC director and obtain support from the CEO.
- Train everyone involved in communications to think IMC.
- Create multimedia campaigns instead of one based on a single instrument.
- Always look for opportunities to blend various communications tools in order to deliver more sales per dollar than using one instrument alone.
- Track all promotional expenditures by product, promotional tools, stage of product life cycle, and observed effect as a benchmark for improving future use of these tools.
- Create a philosophy of the capabilities and cost effectiveness of each communication tool.

The primary objective of integrated marketing communications is to force you to think about every way you communicate your positioning with the outside world. It forces you to consider every communications vehicle you have, what your budget in total and per vehicle is, what your timing is, and similar matters—and to link all of it back to your original brand-based communications goals and objectives.

Seven basic communications vehicles, each with pros and cons, are available to you. You cannot simply pick and choose among them; each should be leveraged to help bring your Brand Asset Management strategy to life. These vehicles, as mentioned earlier, include:

- *Advertising:* selling messages intended to build awareness, create an image, and eventually lead to a sale
- *Public relations:* nonpaid, third-party endorsement of one's product or service

- *Event marketing and corporate sponsorships:* paid endorsements of one's products or services through leveraging an event
- *Trade and sales promotions:* an inducement, usually something other than the product itself, with the intention of accelerating the purchase decision. These may include demonstrations, trade allowances, and the like
- *Consumer promotions:* an inducement for a consumer to buy a product or service (such as coupons, rebates, contests)
- *Direct marketing:* leveraging catalogues, the Internet, mailings, faxes, and e-mails and relationship building to help make sales
- *Internal employee communications:* making sure that everyone inside your organization understands what the brand stands for and what role they play

Advertising

Advertising is the most visible and dynamic form of communicating with an audience. Barry Krause, president of Publicis & Hal Riney, explains: "In advertising, our goal is to turn facts into feelings. It's the key to success for an advertising agency. We need to do the best job possible of uncovering relevant brand facts and then turning those facts into positive feelings.

"Ultimately, people make decisions for emotional reasons. Churchill said never underestimate the power of emotion in decision making. No matter what the decision is, the more important it is, the more emotion is involved. But we always need to rationalize our emotion so we can explain it to others. The ultimate goal of branding is to endear people to your brand. Those brands that find ways to endear people to them will win."

Krause tells the story of how Serta Mattress turned facts into feelings. "Serta had the most boring focus groups. People had very little to say about mattresses and did not know the difference between brands. They only buy one mattress every ten years. We called it the s-trap: they're all the same—Sealy, Simmons, Serta, etc.!

"We heard from consumers, 'The first thing I do is cover up the brand name with a mattress pad and then a sheet, and never look at the brand name again.' We asked customers what they look for in mattresses. Their answer was they wanted a comfortable mattress. We were getting nowhere in our research."

"Finally, one woman said, 'When I'm awake, I'm not thinking about a mattress; when I'm in bed, I'm asleep. There is only one fleeting moment, when I slip under the covers, that I think about my bed and, at that moment, I know if I will have a good night's sleep.' There was the emotion we were searching for. That was the key insight. There was the opportunity. The 'Serta Moment.' We built a campaign around that moment and the Serta Perfect Sleeper went on to become the market leader."

Don't confuse creative tactics with branding. There is a range of creative tactics that advertising agencies use to drive their communications recommendations and brand success. Often these tactics get mistaken for what the brand stands for. Instead they should be viewed as a way to creatively bring a brand to life. Some of my favorite creative brand-leveraging tactics in advertising include these:

Shape: the Absolut vodka bottle and the Classic Coke bottle

Jingle: Alka Seltzer's old jingle (plop, plop, fizz, fizz . . .)

Spokespersons: all the celebrities appearing in the Got Milk? campaign; Mr. Whipple for Charmin; Mr. Peanut, who has his own traveling hot rod; Michael Jordan for Gatorade; and Wendy from the Snapple ads

Symbol: Starbucks' mermaid-like figure

Color: the red that Compaq owns and the blue and gold that Continental owns

Taglines: It's the Real Thing (Coca-Cola); Where's the Beef? (Wendy's)

Songs: Jump, Jive and Wail by the Brian Setzer Orchestra for Gap Khakis; Coca-Cola's *I'd Like to Teach the World to Sing;* Bob Seger's *Like a Rock* for Chevy

A good creative brief will help you work with your ad agency. Effective advertising is directly correlated with the working relationship you have with your agency. Great agencies bring brands to life. Their focus has to be on the current needs of their client, as well as the long-term health of the brand. The best client-agency relationships I have seen include a crisply written brief that *must* be led by the client.

A creative brief is the direction a client gives to the agency. It should outline several specifics:

- Positioning
- Competitors' positioning
- Goals and objectives
- Target audience
- Message
- Creative screens
- Practical considerations
- Budget

In addition, the creative brief should emphasize a number of tangible issues about the advertising:

What is important to customers and what drives them to a purchase decision?

What does the competition look like?

What should the ads accomplish?

Who do they target?

What benefit should be emphasized?

What kinds of ads are acceptable and align with the brand?

What form is it in?

What will this cost?

Clients should write the creative brief for several reasons. It forces them to thoroughly think through what they are trying to achieve, gives an idea what type of agency should be sought, and provides an indication of whether the budget is appropriate considering what they are trying to achieve. Also, the brief serves as a good screen to judge if the advertising is effective once it has been created, and it forces the client to determine beforehand how much additional research may need to be done if the positioning is not solidified.

Too often the agency takes control of the brief and the client stays behind the scenes. This is generally a recipe for disaster because it can lead the agency to overemphasize creative executions—

looking for the most innovative or creative or daring way to bring the advertising to life—at the expense of the bigger picture. This in large part is due to how agencies have been traditionally defined and an agency's need to show its value.

Often the quality of an ad strongly suggests that the company did the essential work of creating a brief. For example, the Saturn commercial featuring Julie getting her first car is probably one of the best commercials ever made. The entire spot defines, elaborates on, and ultimately builds Saturn's powerful brand. The research that went into developing the brand message is obvious; in addition, Saturn's contract is clearly articulated, the Saturn persona is shown, Saturn's customer model is clear, and its positioning is clear. Saturn management obviously knew what it wanted to accomplish prior to bringing the ad agency on board.

Licensing is another form of advertising. In recent years more companies have used licensing to build their brands. Traditional licensors like Disney, movie studios, and sports teams come to mind, but licensing is becoming more and more popular for nontraditional companies (such as Yahoo!) to boost someone else's noncompeting brand along with one's own.

For example, General Motors recently launched a separate business to license GM's brand names to other companies that, as GM puts it, "have a marketplace advantage that can accelerate you past the competition." The theory is that by making Buick, Pontiac, Oldsmobile, Cadillac, and Intrigue licensors to other products that are strong brands in their own right will enable these licensors to benefit by implied endorsement.

Obviously GM must be careful not to overextend its brands or license them to organizations that may hurt them. In addition, licensees must be careful that the GM brand actually adds value to their offering and that, from a customer's perspective, it fits.

Public Relations, Event Marketing, and Sponsorships

Public relations is the least often used but potentially most powerful communications tool at your disposal. Good PR offers companies an opportunity to get second- and third-party endorsements in an effective, efficient, and economical way.

For Cincinnati Bell Telephone's Internet Call Manager, the single most effective advertising it had was a review of the service on the local evening news. The review generated more leads than all other marketing efforts combined. Similarly, stories on documentary programs like *Nightline with Ted Koppel* have been known to generate thousands of leads.

A good PR strategy determines which public relations vehicles present the best opportunities to bring *positive and good* attention to your brand. At AT&T, for example, CEO Michael Armstrong recently did the keynote address at a major television technology exposition to further define AT&T's intentions about getting into the cable television industry. At Intel, CEO Andy Grove says that the company's defining moment came in the course of its public relations effort to handle the microchip crisis back in 1994.

There are many opportunities to use public relations, including newspaper and magazine interviews, favorable stories about the company and its people, and building a good reputation for corporate social responsibility.

Ed Faruolo, vice president of CIGNA Corporation, in a recent speech talked about the power of CIGNA's sponsorship of a PBS series based on William Bennet's *The Book of Virtues*. He shared with the audience a letter that he received:

> Although you've advertised extensively, I've paid no attention to CIGNA until I saw your prominent sponsorship on the "Book of Virtues" cartoon series on PBS. I made a note to myself to thank you for sponsoring quality programming of such a moral caliber, but I unfortunately set things aside for lack of address. Then I ran into an ad about Reggie White in *Time* magazine, talking to the charitable organization you both work for on behalf of CIGNA. I'm impressed!
>
> I know very little about you, but I am now seeking as much information about your organization as I can find. It is the carefully directed generosity of companies such as yours which quietly defines a standard for morality and decency in our country. I wish you the best, and look forward to purchasing a CIGNA product, because now I know my dollars will produce even after I've spent them.

This letter is the result of leveraging public relations in a very public way to help spread your message without necessarily tooting your own horn. By the way, Ed, you just received more public relations by being in this book.

Sponsorships and event marketing are other ways of creating goodwill. Here are some notable examples:

- IBM hosting the U.S. Open
- 3Com and Qualcomm sponsoring the San Francisco Giants and 49ers and the San Diego Padres and Chargers ballparks, respectively
- Hallmark's television productions
- Visa's sponsorship of the Olympics
- Saturn's annual tent party for all Saturn owners
- Harley-Davidson's annual motorcycle rallies

What is most important about event marketing and sponsorships is that you don't need a seven-figure budget to get maximum impact. Indeed, the reverse is often true.

For instance, is your market the local literati? Sponsoring a local RIF (Reading Is Fun) program will win you enormous goodwill as well as sales. Similarly, high-visibility sponsorship of a local or regional PBS radio or TV program or station can cost a tenth as much as making an impression through other media. The magic questions, of course, are: Is it where your customer is? Is it important to your customer?

Not all public relations are positive. Tragedies such as the Exxon *Valdez*, Tylenol pill tainting, tainted Perrier, Audi crashes, and the tainting of Sara Lee's Ball Park Franks and Coke products in Europe demonstrate that a company's response to tragedy can either build its brand or destroy it. The keys to handling negative public relations, according to Bob Roemer, former director of emergency response and training at Amoco, include the following:

- Be up front and honest.
- Be quick to respond.
- Be empathetic.
- Detail the steps the company will take to avoid the problem in the future.
- Detail what action the company will take to help remedy the current situation.
- Give specific action steps for customers to take, if necessary.

- Deliver any message of this magnitude from the highest level within the organization—if possible the president or CEO.

Roemer also stresses things you must do before a crisis occurs to make sure you have the best chance of handling it well:

"Usually, if you see a company that doesn't do a good job of handling a crisis, you can trace it back to one of three things. First, they don't have a plan to handle the crisis. Second, they have not rehearsed that plan.

"When the actual crisis occurs, if you haven't rehearsed it, people will start arguing. You sit in a boardroom and the lawyers don't want you to send out a press release, there is panic, and you are wasting valuable time by not communicating.

"Third, the company takes a defensive posture tied to the incident instead of showing empathy. What you are really trying to defend above all else is your reputation. That is the absolute key to being successful in handling negative public relations. If the lawyers have their say, and you end up defending your legal position, you are going to lose your public relations and public opinion battles. Most times, losing those battles are more costly than losing the legal ones."

The recent Coke crisis is a case in point. Coke has faced very few crises in its history, so the three horrible events that occurred over six weeks in Europe in the summer of 1999 were a shock. Potentially contaminating bacteria strains were found in Coke products in three parts of Europe within days of one another. It resulted in the recall of all Coca-Cola products packaged in .33–liter glass bottles and the recall of 180,000 half-liter bottles of Bonauqa Plus mineral water (a Coke product).

Coke did not handle the situation well. It was accused of responding too slowly and being defensive. In addition, Coke was accused of not fully disclosing everything it knew about early occurrences of illness from the tainted Coke.

In line with Roemer's analysis, this was a company not prepared for a crisis. Coke took a road of defensiveness and denial that is not what consumers and retailers expected from the number one brand in the world.

Crisis experts say that you must have a crisis plan in place to combat negative public relations and disasters. I suggest even going through several unannounced internal trial runs to help get the company prepared for a crisis that will hopefully never come.

Many would say that Exxon and Perrier will never recover the asset value of their brands because of the way they handled their respective crises. But others such as Tylenol and Amoco continue to flourish and grow in the face of their tragedies. Consumers accept mistakes and tragedies if they are handled well. If not, the tragedy will continue, trust and the desire to affiliate with that brand will diminish, and the company may never recover.

Our Brand Asset Management For the 21st Century study, mentioned in Chapter One, shows that less than 50 percent of companies have any kind of crisis plan in place. If you believe that your brand is one of the most important and powerful assets you own, then the least you can and should do is to prepare for the worst.

Sales and Trade Promotions

The ex-chairman of J.C. Penney once said that you can have the best advertising and communications plan in the world and the strongest brand, but if you cannot get that customer to go "the last eighteen inches" in the store to make the purchase, then you have ultimately failed.

Sales representatives bring your message directly to your target market. It is critical for them to understand what you are trying to accomplish with the brand. You need to figure out how to align your goals for the brand with the goals of your sales reps to accomplish a win-win situation—increasing sales and building the value of your brand.

As Jack Welch, legendary president of General Electric, once said: "Get everyone to agree to the same reality." If you buy this then you have to get your salespeople involved in building and developing your BrandPicture. Have them take part in the development of the BrandPicture and play an active role in reaching the answer. They are the ones closest to your customers on a daily basis. How could Ford not have a couple of star sales representatives at top dealers, such as Larry Goodman at Highland Park Lincoln Mercury outside of Chicago, involved in building a brand strategy that the sales reps will help execute?

Leveraging your sales reps' customer knowledge will allow you to build a more robust customer model, especially as it relates to determining customer purchase criteria and the overall purchase process customers go through in choosing one brand over another. Let your sales representatives help you understand why your positioning will work or not work.

Trade partners are another matter. You have less control over them, they do not owe you much, and most likely you are not their only supplier. They want to make money and will usually go where the money is. They exert, as discussed in the next chapter, an incredible amount of power in the market and thus directly affect your ability to achieve your goals.

Your goal has to include becoming intimate with your trade partners. Get them involved in the promotion you are trying to launch. Get them involved in the design and the details and let them be rewarded in a way such that both of you win. Brokers and retailers like anything that will increase foot traffic. A new product draws traffic. A new promotion draws traffic. Use the word "new" often and you will move closer to getting the trade to help you achieve your overall Brand Asset Management goals and objectives.

Consumer Promotions: Not Generally Effective for Building a Brand

Consumer promotions is probably the vehicle that companies abuse most, especially with respect to coupons and discounts. These may help draw traffic, but if used too often they condition customers to wait for the coupon or the next big sale.

When McDonald's left "food, folks and fun" several years ago, it deserted a campaign that was directly linked to what the brand stood for. Over the next decade, McDonald's fumbled around trying to find itself again after targeting adults, trying to compete on price, and the like. The more price promotions Burger King or Wendy's offered, the more likely that McDonald's would follow suit. Soon enough, everything was priced at 99 cents, profits plummeted, and McDonald's stock and brand image shrank.

The reasons are obvious. Recall from Step Three that McDonald's for years rested on top of the Brand Value Pyramid. It was associated with powerful values—family and kids and fun and trust. But the company seemed to forget what it had taken so many years to accomplish and started competing on the lowest common denominator of the Brand Value Pyramid: cost.

We are in an age when the consumer wants to negotiate the price of virtually everything. Priceline.com (the Internet travel agent) is further driving that mindset home as it tells customers to pick their destination, determine how much they are willing to spend, and submit that offer. If the offer is accepted, the consumer is better off. This is ultimately a business founded on a consumer promotion. Note, for example, that Priceline.com's name could be recalled by twenty-five million adults just six months after the company was launched.

This is why you have to be very specific about the goals and objectives you are trying to achieve with a consumer promotion. Effective consumer promotions drive traffic, enhance awareness, increase trial, and build the brand. That means gaining and keeping new customers and enhancing the brand's overall image, rather than focusing on price.

Direct Marketing: Costly but Effective

Direct marketing is by far the most explosive marketing communications vehicle today. Sales through the Internet and through catalogue shopping recently topped $500 billion. Companies like Fingerhut are solely in the business of marketing and selling through catalogues and the Internet.

Less time to shop, more options, more women in the workplace, and more computers in the home makes this a critical communications tool. It seems like yesterday that buying through the Land's End or L. L. Bean catalogue was all the rage. It was unique, different, cool, and very satisfying. Today these cataloguers are no longer unique (but still popular) because you can buy the same sort of products through Amazon.com, eToys, or countless other Web retailers.

When a company looks at building its brand through direct marketing, the goals are similar to those in consumer promotions. Direct marketing has to help a company achieve its intended goal (such as 5 percent penetration and 1 percent sales) and increase the brand's overall value and image. Direct marketing also has to help build a relationship between the customer and the direct marketing vehicle itself (such as the catalogue or the Internet).

When a relationship is built, then direct marketing has had a positive effect on the brand. When a relationship is not built or the direct mail approach is perceived to be invasive, then you have taken away from the value of the brand.

In addition, companies should look at direct marketing as an opportunity to get to know more about their customers than is possible with any other marketing tactic. Direct marketing is the foundation of database marketing. Think of the information you can obtain through this form of marketing: name, address, income level (potentially) or sales numbers, shopping preferences, likes and dislikes, other people's names and numbers (if the customer is sending gifts), and the like.

Pottery Barn, Victoria's Secret, and Banana Republic, for example, have all established a unique and personalized relationship with their customer base. They have built a strong and loyal following of customers who buy a particular level of quality, style, and variety. These sellers don't disappoint, and so their customers do not distinguish between buying at the retail store or via catalogue.

All three of these retailers have further extended that relationship into the home by allowing their loyal store- and catalogue-shopping customers to shop on the Internet. The impact on store foot traffic has been negligible, but the impact on sales has been tremendous. Impressively, one very rarely sees any of these brands using discount-driven promotions to support a sale.

Starbucks recently launched an interesting direct marketing vehicle. *Joe* is an in-store magazine that carries articles, stories, unique photographs, and sexy advertisements throughout. The tagline under the title *Joe* reads, "Life Is Interesting. Discuss."

Joe helps Starbucks accomplish much. It suggests that coffee is the perfect complement to intelligent, interesting conversation, discussion, and rumination. The magazine reinforces the image of product use as well as the use itself. Also, advertising from outside companies promoting products that are consistent with the Starbucks image reinforces both images. For that matter, the number of Starbucks ads reminds readers about the power of the brand and the unique position it has. As an economic proposition, the outside ads make the magazine self-supporting.

Amazon.com has built a phenomenal retail brand relationship over the Internet. Although it will continue to be attacked by numerous competitors, today Amazon.com has an incredibly loyal customer base for many reasons:

- It was first to market with this service.
- It is widely regarded as "the little engine that could," relative to Borders and Barnes & Noble—but don't tell that to founder Jeff Bezos.
- The service is excellent.
- The pricing discounts and special offers are attractive; the on-line book reviews are valuable.
- Its direct marketing efforts continue to remind customers about who it is.
- It has begun to add other value-added services, such as auctioning and toys.
- It continues to create unusual products and services based on knowledge of customers' preferences.
- It has created a unique gift-giving opportunity with Amazon.com gift certificates.

Finally, Amazon.com collects so much valuable information on its subscribers that renting the list is a viable business in its own right.

4. Execute Your Communications Strategy Across the Organization

Once your three-year BAM strategy has been set as discussed in Step One, you should develop a corresponding three-year game plan. Remember, the Brand Vision defines goals and objectives in a three- to five-year time frame, as does the AUTHOR model.

Case Study: Pella Windows

Pella Windows, the number two U.S. window manufacturer, restaged its brand a few years ago. Pella had not capitalized on its unique product differences and had become somewhat complacent in differentiating itself from competitors like Andersen Windows and Marvin Windows.

Randy Iles, senior vice president of marketing and sales, and Jerry Dow, senior marketing manager, knew they had to act to stem the tide of competitive inroads into their markets. They also knew that to achieve this longer-term vision of the company, well-executed, well-integrated communications would be critical.

Once they clarified their Brand Vision and had a clear understanding of what their brand stood for in the marketplace, it became clear what Pella had to do. It had to answer the following questions and develop an integrated Brand Asset Management strategy when it learned the answers:

- How do we best reach current customers? How do we best reach future customers? How do we best reach past customers?
- How do we best balance the customer and the channel when the channel has such an influence in the purchase decision?
- How do we increase the five minutes someone thinks about windows when building a house, relative to the thousands of minutes they spend thinking about other aspects of the house?
- How do we leverage the powerful yellow-and-black Pella logo and its equity better?
- How do we make sure everyone in the organization knows what Pella is trying to accomplish?
- How much will this cost? How should we measure results? How do we know if we are getting our marketing and branding dollars' worth?

Jerry Dow states, "Our singular positioning has to be targeted differently to each segment we are trying to reach. One ad would not be effective or appropriate if it is used across all the segments we serve. Each message has to be tailored and executed differently, according to the specific target market we are trying to reach. But the overall message and end result of the communication has to be the same."

Tailored messages relative to the positioning, once again, have to come from the marketplace, meaning you must know specifically what is important to each target market you are pursuing and what communications vehicles will help to best communicate to each.

The positioning Pella had chosen (as it was unique, valued, credible, fitting, and sustainable) was tied to its high-quality product and image. Once the positioning was agreed upon, the next question was how to leverage the right communications vehicles to bring the positioning to life.

Pella started with the mindset that every contact it had with customers should be integrated, no matter when or where it was taking place. It also realized the need for a simple, straightforward message that was easy to understand.

Following are some of the ways Pella executed its new positioning:

- Came up with a relevant tagline—"Viewed to be the best"—that took hold internally and externally as Pella's mantra
- Developed catchy print ads that are unlike traditional window ads—the window

is the hero of the advertising, and each ad focuses on a different Pella feature
- Developed outstanding television commercials; Y&R New York came up with several, including one called "Elopement" that won several major awards (including a gold EFFIE and an Emmy nomination)
- Deployed a consistent look and feel to independently owned and operated Pella store locations
- Replaced the graphics on all service trucks so they look the same and feature the Pella logo prominently—Pella views these as traveling billboards because the trucks traverse the country
- Trained customer service reps to answer questions, educate consumers, and always focus on selling the virtues of Pella products
- Increased its image and presence at major trade shows
- Focused on innovation, bringing out new products consistently and revitalizing old products so they remain relevant
- Increased pull-through with do-it-yourself consumers through a greater presence at retailers that cater to such consumers
- Focused on public relations and gained a memorable spot on *Good Morning America*

Pella set up a three-year strategy including specific annual goals: year one, build awareness and invoke trial; year two, further build awareness, strengthen image, build preference, increase trial, increase market share by one to two points; year three, further strengthen image, preference, and loyalty, increase repeat purchases and word-of-mouth.

The biggest challenge for Pella was making sure their focus and efforts were appropriately balanced between the channel and the consumer. Pella could not risk alienating either one, as it would result in the entire brand-based communications strategy failing or being suboptimized.

Consequently, Pella equally focused its efforts on both pushing the product (through the channel) and pulling the customer (through communications efforts). The end result has been a dramatic increase in sales, a solidified position in the marketplace, and overall share gains relative to the competition.

Case Study: VW Beetle

The VW Beetle has hit on all cylinders for brand-based communications in the last several years. Sergio Zyman, ex-senior vice president of Coca-Cola, believes that the VW revolution over the last five years is a great example of giving customers a reason to want your product.

In a recent *Business Week* interview, Zyman stated: "The marketing and advertising of the Beetle presents a reason to buy. If you are the kind of driver [VW seeks], the select few, you have this optimistic personality and you do not take life too seriously. Your personality matches the personality of this car. That's a reason to buy. This is your car. It's not about price at all, it's about what this product means to you, how it fits into your life."

There are numerous reasons why the Beetle relaunch was such a success. First, VW hit on a major trend of nostalgia. It had one of the best-known names in the automotive world and, although dormant for many years like Harley-Davidson and Schwinn, had the power to come back.

There were teaser ads. There were billboards every few blocks (or so it seemed). There were great commercials. There was the dealers' showroom and all the salesmen "pumped up" for the reintroduction. There were the great colors and, of course, there was a great product at a great price. The Beetle again had relevancy and again was a big success.

Why? VW had a clear vision of what it wanted the brand to stand for in the marketplace, understood its past BrandPicture and desired BrandPicture, and had every functional area involved in implementing and executing the strategy.

Case Study: Yahoo!

Yahoo!'s external communications strategy for the most part has been nontraditional, but management has focused on approaches that are consistent with the Yahoo! brand, all ultimately aimed at building brand loyalty. Some of its communications tactics and philosophies include the following:

- Number one source of awareness: word of mouth
- Work the Web by advertising whenever possible
- Get television stations to put their news on Yahoo!
- Get employees to Yahoo! their cars, boats, and body parts
- Have a strong presence at art, music, and food festivals and events
- Regularly tie in with companies with much larger budgets (such as NBC and Ben & Jerry's)
- Aggressively license the name for products and services
- Cobrand where appropriate (such as with Visa and MCI)
- Make advertising stress that Yahoo! is a consumer brand, not a technology brand

5. Create Internal Involvement, Education, and Metrics

I will say more about these in Step Eleven. Simply stated, unless every employee is intimate with what you are trying to achieve with the brand and its communications, you put at risk the overall success of the brand.

I recommend a minimum of three months to communicate and educate your internal team on what you are trying to achieve externally with the brand and what employees' role should be. One wrong communication about your brand from just one of your employees can lead to many others' misunderstandings.

Amy Kelm at HP sums up well the role employees need to play in bringing brand-based communications to life: "When we began to roll out the brand, there was a question of where to start. You have a new positioning, now how do you execute it? We got lots of internal employees involved to help us drive out executional strategies. By sitting down with internal cross-functional teams to outline and brainstorm all of the places that the brand interacts with consumers, we built ownership and accountability for delivering on the brand promise. They helped us discover that we had to look at things like service and support in a whole new way."

In developing your brand-based communications plan, it is critical to think about every stage of communications that a customer may have with your brand. Similar to the AUTHOR model, good communications plans lay specific communications strategies and tactics for all of a customer's encounter with your brand—before buying, during the sale, and after the purchase. Tables 7.1 and 7.2 are examples of the depth I believe is required.

Communication measures have to go beyond awareness and recall, the two most widely used communications metrics in use today. Rubbermaid has 100 percent awareness and recall but its stock underperformed for several years and was sold to Newell in 1998 at a discount from where it was several years before.

The key to success here is to pick the five or six metrics that will have the greatest impact on your brand's performance, ones that are easy to measure, repeatable, and aimed at making smart business decisions. Metrics for the sake of metrics is useless. Metrics to help you make better and more informed business decisions is priceless. The ROBI Eight metrics are discussed in Step Ten.

Table 7.1. Communication Plan for Service Firm A

Key Media Targets	Reach and Frequency	Creative Direction
Primary • Men and women 45+ • Women with families *Geography* • Northern states	• The goal in our brand communication plan is to maximize reach, with frequency being a lesser, though also critical goal. • Maximize reach by using multimedia strategy. • Reasons for high frequency: new brand and new campaign, low awareness, clutter of competing information.	• All ads must be integrated into a single campaign to promote brand image. • New brands require emotional appeal—longer spots, high quality. • Quality must break through the competitive clutter. • Plan to have three creative themes: general ads, service area–specific ads, and seasonal ads when interest is high.

Summary

Branding is not just about communications but about developing the right brand-based communications strategy to help bring your brand positioning to life and ultimately reach your overall Brand Asset Management goals and objectives. The primary goal of all brand-based communications efforts is to drive the asset value of your brand. With this goal always in mind and your communications goals and objectives well articulated, the approach you take should be fairly straightforward.

Determine your communications goals (such as to help drive new product sales), determine your target audience, and understand the most effective way of reaching that target and how best to drive measures such as awareness, understanding, trial, preference, and loyalty. Brand-based communications should always be aimed at helping your brand build a relationship with its customers and at closing the sale.

Table 7.2. Communication Plan for Service Firm B

	Advertising	Public Relations	Direct Marketing

Vehicles	• Television
	  – Broadcast
	  – Local cable
	• Local radio
	• Print
	• Outdoor
		• Media relations
		  – Press releases
		  – Community relations
		• Expertise marketing
		  – Community involvement
		  – Community education
		  – Experts on the road
			• Direct mail
			• Consumer newsletter
			• Website
			• Mall information center (kiosk)

Rationale	• Maximize reach. • Enable an emotional sell (visual and verbal communications). • Achieve parity with competition.	• Inexpensive way to demonstrate expertise through care for the community. • Fulfill mission. • Build awareness of our experts through expertise marketing.	• Support dissemination of more in-depth information, such as information about specific expertise areas. • Facilitate access to information through website. • Control timing, messages, and distribution through consumer newsletters.

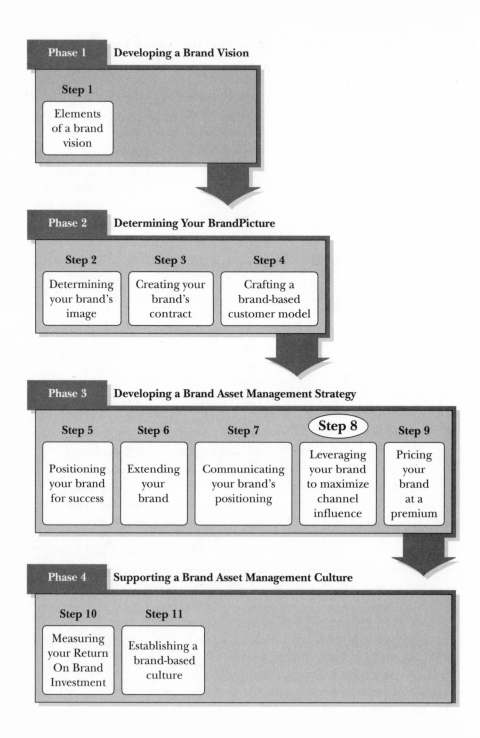

Leveraging Your Brand to Maximize Channel Influence

Who controls the channel? This is the most critical marketing and business question managers face today. The answer depends on who you ask among the intermediaries that touch a product before it gets to the final customer.

Three primary shifts in the channel landscape make this question even more difficult to answer: the spread of superstores such as Wal-Mart and Home Depot, the increasing presence of direct mail, and the onslaught of e-commerce. These have worked together to keep manufacturers and service providers on their toes, forcing them to be nimble and to consider new ways of maximizing control over the channel.

Effectively leveraging your brand as a channel driver can be the surest and smartest way to control your destiny (see the illustration on the facing page). The stronger and more valued your brand is, the more loyal its adherents and the more likely that you will be able to exert control on the process of getting products to customers.

But between you and your customers are one or more intermediaries who exert some degree of control over the channel (see Figure 8.1). The strength of your brand can help you determine whether you should work with, through, or around other channel members.

This chapter has two goals. The first is to describe the changing landscape of channels and why it has become increasingly challenging to manage them. The second is to explain how brand strength can be used in dealing with channel members and to maximize leverage within your channel.

Figure 8.1. Channel Intermediaries

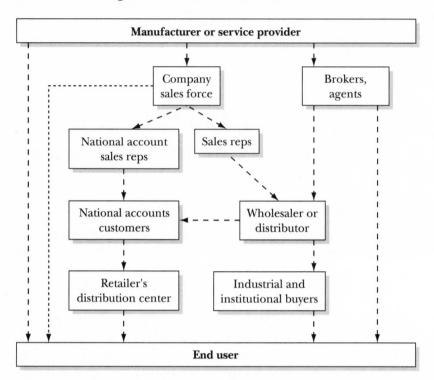

The Changing Landscape of Channels

When I was at Proctor & Gamble, the channel model was straight-forward. P&G (the manufacturer) used its sales force for larger accounts and distributors for smaller accounts. When P&G came out with a new product like Liquid Tide, the sales force would carry the news to the channel and the channel would get fired up because a promotion or a trade incentive was generally tied to it.

In addition, the sales force, distributors, and retailers would be excited about creating new foot traffic as a result of the massive communication and promotional expenditures P&G would put into a new product introduction.

Since that time, almost everything has changed.

Superstores and Category Killers

Wal-Mart had the biggest impact on P&G's traditional channel approach to conducting business. Basically, in the early 1990s Wal-Mart decided to tell P&G how to run its brands. Increased slotting allowances, no guarantees of shelf space, increased private label products, and the shift of who owned the customer were just a few of the major issues P&G had to confront, as did other consumer packaged goods manufacturers.

Along these lines, one of the "big boxes" recently shocked its top vendors (Black & Decker, Stanley Tools, Snap-On, and others) by issuing a memo stating that Home Depot wished them well in each of their recently announced Internet plays and that it looked forward to competing with them directly in the future. The implication was that the suppliers were no longer going to be part of this big boxes franchise. Last I heard these vendors had not gone forward with their Internet strategies.

The Internet

Toys 'R' Us is in a position similar to that of Wal-Mart and Home Depot in its category. For the most part, if you want to sell toys you have to go through Toys 'R' Us. But the Internet may change that. eToys, for one, is trying to take over Toys 'R' Us's enviable position. Interestingly, Toys 'R' Us recently tried its hand at e-commerce, but most customers were disappointed. Toys 'R' Us later announced that, to gain back the good graces of on-line customers, it would provide free shipping and handling for all gifts bought on line.

As you would expect, channel rules have changed most dramatically and visibly recently because of the Internet, where you can now pick a car and choose the options, the dealer you want to pick it up from, the financing you desire, and the delivery date. You can plan vacations without a travel agent and negotiate the price without talking to a human being. You can buy books without stepping into a bookstore; you can order all your groceries, down to the color of the banana, without ever leaving your home.

Across industries, customers can access the manufacturer or service provider directly. They can bypass the middleman for the first time ever and possibly get much better service and turnaround times than they had received from the middleman. There are frustrations with the Internet, but relatively new providers such as eBay, E-Trade, and UBID have helped launch an industry that relies on convenience, broad product and service selection, and high levels of customer service. No industry today is immune to the power of the Internet.

The Internet world is even beginning to see internal e-commerce competition. It used to be that Amazon.com competed against traditional brick-and-mortar stores such as Crown Books, Borders, and Barnes & Noble. But the latter two now have added their own .coms, and eToys and BUY.COM are both selling children's books.

Similarly, although eBay supposedly owns the on-line auctioning category, recently UBID and Amazon.com have entered the field and have slowly started to eat away at eBay's once dominant share.

The Internet also provides an opportunity for direct selling that has challenged even the holiest of channel strategies. Tupperware recently announced that it would start selling its products on line to complement its home-party direct sales approach. Its stock jumped 24 percent the day the new strategy was announced.

A recent *Fortune* cover story showed ultraconservative turnaround king Arthur Martinez, CEO of Sears, and sears.com creative chief Michael Vaughan posing together to indicate "the e-volution of big business."

Direct Mail

In addition to the Internet, the increased importance of direct marketing—in all of its forms, from mail to catalogues to telemarketing—as a sales channel is remarkable. Direct mail is becoming an increasingly important way of selling in both consumer and business markets. Catalogue sales are at an all-time high.

Traditional bricks-and-mortar establishments such as Pottery Barn and Crate and Barrel now derive and depend on catalogue sales for a great deal of their annual revenues. Direct mail technology has also created a smart database that can target specific catalogues and mailings to a specific customer's interests.

The increased importance of superstores, the Internet, and direct marketing are just a few of the more obvious reasons that the term "disintermediation" is being used more and more frequently in business circles. The channel game is becoming more and more complex.

Brand Power Is Channel Power

DuPont's Stainmaster carpeting proved this point back in the mid-1980s. For decades carpet retailers controlled the carpet industry. These retailers told manufacturers what margin they would make and how much carpet they could pass through to the retailer. Retailers also told manufacturers that they would carry several different carpet lines and focus on selling the one that provided them with the highest margin. A typical 1980s channel power structure is shown in Figure 8.2.

Figure 8.2. Channel Power Structure

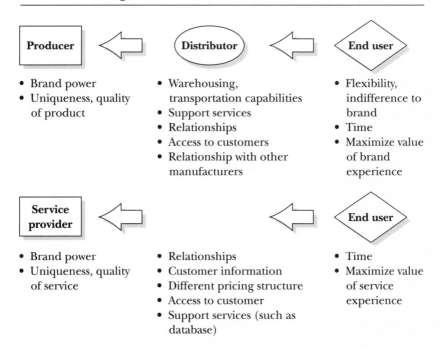

When Stainmaster treatment was invented, it provided carpet manufacturers with a benefit that would become a staple. The benefit of easy stain removal forced retailers to carry the product. DuPont's Stainmaster became the brand of choice and manufacturers turned the tables on their old channel partner.

The Stainmaster brand sparked strong enough consumer demand that consumers would ask for it by name. If the retailer did not have Stainmaster in stock, the consumer would go elsewhere. Thus the power in the channel shifted to the manufacturer for the first time—and by customer insistence (see Figure 8.3).

Building your BrandPicture will most likely show you to what extent you can control your channel and how to do it. In the analysis of your brand's image, you gained perspectives on your brand's unique competitive strengths and advantages. Within the Brand Contract, you identified expectations set by the marketplace that you need to abide by.

The customer model helped recreate the customer's purchase experience and the criteria they use in making a purchase decision. The model also helped to identify and differentiate the

**Figure 8.3. DuPont Stainmaster's Use of Branding
to Capture Channel Power**

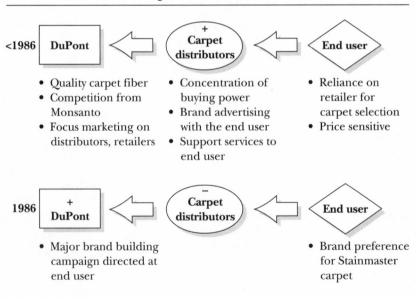

decision makers from the decision influencers. The customer model also helps you understand where the power resides within your various channels and how much control or influence you currently have and could possibly have in the future.

Subsequently, your brand positioning should have given you enough information to determine what role your brand could and should play within the channel to maximize your long-term position and effectiveness.

Three Questions to Determine Your Brand's Channel Power

Regardless of recent shifts in the channel, the same three fundamental questions that have driven channel strategies for years still hold. Address them and you will know whether you can take more control within your channel and the role your brand can play in the process:

1. Where is the power in the selling process?
2. How can your brand help you maximize channel power?
3. How can your brand help you maintain channel power?

Let's explore each of these questions.

1. Where Is the Power in the Selling Process?

Traditionally, managing the channel involved managing the countless intermediaries, both direct and indirect, that may be involved in getting your product or service into customers' hands. These intermediaries typically include wholesalers, brokers, distributors, retailers, and resellers.

The more direct your selling effort, the more control you exert over the final outcome. The more indirect your selling effort, the less control you exert and, generally, the less percentage of dollars you receive as a result of the sale.

The key first step in your brand-based channel efforts is identifying all the channel members and their impact on and relationship with your brand. The chain may be long and complex. For instance, in the consumer packaged goods world, the supply chain may look like this:

Manufacturer ⟶ Company sales force ⟶
National account sales reps ⟶ National account
customers ⟶ Retailer's distribution center ⟶
Individual retailer ⟶ End user

For a meat processor, the channel may include the following:

Grain farmer ⟶ Feed supplier ⟶
Livestock farmer ⟶ Packer ⟶ Distributor ⟶
Food service organization ⟶ Grocery store
or restaurant ⟶ End user

And for an insurance company the channel structure might be this:

Underwriter ⟶ National sales force ⟶
Local sales force ⟶ Broker ⟶ End user

Acknowledging these complex channel structures forces you to be concerned with much more than just getting your product or service made. You have to build relationships throughout the channel, you have to understand the hot buttons of each player, the leverage each has, the impact they have on whether a sale is made, and how, if at all, your brand can influence the role each plays in getting your brand into the hands of the end user.

There is an inherent struggle for power within a channel, generally between the producer and everyone else. The producer's cards include owning the product itself, the technology and R&D to manufacture it, and the brand.

If it is a multibrand conglomerate, the producer may hold another card—additional name brands that the channel members' customers want or even demand. The producer's leverage is the degree to which end users demand a particular brand from an intermediary.

Kellogg's, General Mills, PepsiCo and S.C. Johnson Wax all have this kind of brand power. They have the ability to cut deals in their favor throughout the chain because of their ability to provide so many products, across so many categories, with so many well-known brands. They have the clout to tell retailers "take Mountain Dew or you won't get Pepsi" or "take Vanish or you won't get Pledge."

These megabranded companies hold so much power because of the strength and diversity of their portfolio of brands. It does not hurt that most of the brands in these portfolios are powerful and evoke high degrees of loyalty. So for a channel member (such as a retailer) it's not a matter of losing one megabrand but of losing many.

The Gap, for example, built a brand and changed the channel rules simultaneously. When The Gap started out, it was dependent on Levi's as its primary pull into the store. Levi's dictated the rules and The Gap listened to survive. But more than a decade ago The Gap stopped carrying Levi's altogether and carried only its own private-label branded jeans. An interesting question to ask now is, which one is the "All-American" brand icon?

Similarly, Starmark, the pre-owned Mercedes car dealerships owned by Mercedes-Benz, has taken away some of the power from other used car dealerships because now it is *the* destination for those who want to buy the best preowned Mercedes. The only way Starmark survives in the highly competitive used car market is by having one of the strongest brands in the world in its showrooms.

But what if you don't have such brand power? The challenge for most companies is that their brands do not exert the same type of combinative power as the megabrands, so their power to control is not as strong.

One approach is to get key channel members involved in building the BrandPicture and the brand positioning. This may seem ludicrous to you at first, but to channel members it is a clear indication of the respect you have for their opinion and the desire you have to get them involved in helping your brand succeed.

What is in it for them? You should come up with an incentive that will matter to them, but more importantly they will probably view this as a sign that you want to build a relationship with them. Also, it's an ego stroke for them just to be asked for their opinion on such an important matter.

For you, getting channel members involved will add a lot of value to your customer model and your overall roll-out plan. So you potentially can get two benefits for the price of one.

2. How Can Your Brand Help You Maximize Channel Power?

As power keeps shifting in the channel game, companies that are nimble enough to change strategy as the rules change will survive and thrive. The question to continually ask and answer is: How do I most effectively get my products and services to my target audience and what role will the brand play in helping me do that?

One way is to completely reinvent the channel. There have been computers and coffeehouses for years, for example, but Dell and Starbucks repackaged their offerings, focused on how customers wanted to receive their offerings, and consistently invested in building their brands with dollars and by making sure their customers had good experiences (which led to loyalty and strong word-of-mouth).

Dell is a channel story that became a brand story. It built its business on traditional direct marketing, whose basic tenets include finding out what people want to buy and selling it to them in a way that is most convenient to them—where they control the purchase process. If you succeed in doing this like Dell has, you start to build trust. Once you build trust, you can start to build loyalty. Once you build loyalty, you have triggered a high probability of repeat sales and strong word-of-mouth. In doing all of this, as Dell has, you can build a relationship with a customer, which is the ultimate sign of control.

Michael Dell started a business—computers by mail and telephone—in college to help students and others get computers less expensively than in a store. He figured that by bypassing the channel and creating a direct relationship between customer and manufacturer he could pass on the savings to students.

Dell still follows the same strategy today with its multibillion-dollar business. But now Dell controls the manufacturing of the computer. It recently bypassed Compaq as the number one PC seller in the world. The biggest change for Dell now is the addition of another direct vehicle—selling computers on line, giving customers one more channel to its products and services.

At Starbucks, what started as a brick-and-mortar retail business evolved into something more by drawing customers into its channel. By focusing on the highest level of coffee quality and on the "coffee experience," Howard Schultz created a destination channel. This same formula has been used in building Starbucks' coffeehouses across America and across the world in a systematic way. As at Dell, the brand became the power base that allowed Starbucks to leverage new channels and bring its brand to as many consumers as possible. From United Airlines to offices around the world, Starbucks is available to all who want it.

Sony continues to provide the highest quality, most innovative electronic entertainment equipment. As a result, the Sony brand draws ever more customers and retailers. Sony made itself valuable to customers by setting the standard for both innovation and quality, and to retailers by becoming a destination brand. Customers looking for the best in electronics seek out a Sony retailer. If a retailer does not carry Sony, a customer will most likely seek out another retailer that does.

The popularity of the Sony Store in downtown Chicago is indicative of how strong the brand is. The Sony Store is a prototype store for displaying innovations as well as for showcasing popular Sony products that have been around for awhile. It also serves as a consistent and gentle reminder of the power that Sony can exert over the retail channel. The store is always crowded and customers are always asking, "Where can I buy this?"

Dell, Starbucks, and Sony all rely on the single concept they own and, as a result, their channel power continues to grow. How can you do the same? To control your channel, you need to understand channel members' needs. The key to any relationship is to know what is important to your partner. Most channel members have simple and similar needs relative to the customers they serve and to the supplier or manufacturer they work with. Here are some examples.

Channel Member Needs Relative to Customers
- Highest-quality product or service
- A brand that is a drawing card—one that generates foot traffic
- Superior customer service (whether supplied by the channel member or the manufacturer)

- Fair pricing that allows the customer to save money while covering the channel member's required margin
- Sharing of costs for special promotions
- When needed, education on how best to use the product or service

Channel Member Needs Relative to Suppliers

- Highest-quality product or service
- Superior service to back up the offering
- Brand that is a drawing card
- Brand that allows for premium pricing to help the channel member meet the margin needs of channel constituencies
- Funding to support promotions tied to the brand
- Education on the brand and its goals and objectives
- Information on customers and the changing marketplace
- Decision power—helping you to drive strategy

These lists are not exhaustive, but they are fairly inclusive; more important, the similarities between the two lists are striking.

Let's combine them into five categories of needs that channel members have. By focusing on these five needs, maximizing the control you have over your channel, through your brand, seems a lot less daunting.

Key Channel Member "Hot Buttons"

1. *High quality product or service*—there is no stronger draw than having the best product or service available. Consumers will generally pay more for high quality and will go to another store if the one they are shopping at does not have the brand in stock.
2. *Education and training*—to help sell the product and strong service support after the sale (for both the channel member and the end customer).
3. *A brand that is a drawing card*—the stronger the brand, the more likely the channel member will want to be connected to it. Channel members, as much as possible, strive to satisfy customers' needs and wants.
4. *A reasonable pricing strategy*—one that allows all channel members to get their cut. Stronger brands command higher prices,

which means more dollars for all intermediaries involved in the sale.

5. *Funding to help promote the brand*—this is always important as it speaks to a channel member-supplier partnership and relationship. The more it appears that both sides are contributing to the final sale, the more likely there will be a stronger commitment to sell your brand.

Often a brand is not strong enough on its own to exert control on the channel. This is where cobranding relationships are sometimes born. Kellogg's Right Start cereal was instantly accepted because of the Kellogg cachet tied to it. Similarly, AOL's acquisition of Netscape allowed Netscape to own a much more powerful channel control position.

Cobranding between K-Mart and Martha Stewart may have saved the former. K-Mart almost disappeared a few years ago in the haze of its last blue-light special. Did the repackaging and redesign of the stores save K-Mart? No. Martha Stewart in large part did. Her brand is one of today's hottest drawing cards and she has helped to drive foot traffic into K-Mart. K-Mart, in turn, was able to use Martha (the brand) to draw in many well-known brands. Now K-Mart is likely to be one of the big four retailers to survive over the next ten years (along with Sears, Wal-Mart, and Target).

3. How Can Your Brand Help You Maintain Channel Power?

One of the most important aspects of channel management is purchasing process. By controlling customer perceptions before they make the purchase, while they are making it, and after they make it, you increase your chances of building brand loyalty. As mentioned earlier, the stronger the loyalty, the stronger the relationship your brand has with its customers and the more likely you will maximize your control of the channel.

In effect what you are leveraging is a traditional push strategy, in that you are controlling the entire brand experience and thus having customers drive channel requirements, instead of the other way around. Most companies do not pay attention to all three aspects of the sale and thus miss a great opportunity to exert control over the channel process.

The Presale: Setting the Stage for the Brand Purchase

Without communicating effectively and introducing, informing, and educating customers about why your brand should be the brand of choice, you are leaving too much of the purchase decision out of your control.

Saturn, for example, did a great job of preconditioning the market for months prior to the introduction of its new car series in 1999, which took its average car price from $12,000 to well over $20,000. Saturn created interest, trained dealers, made sure current Saturn owners were informed about the new car line, and made sure enough inquiries were made prior to the introduction that it would be a success.

Saturn banked on the fact that the "Saturn experience" had created such goodwill that customers in the market for a new car at a higher price would want to try out its new line.

Probably the master of effective presale activities is Disney. Disney does everything right to build its brand and to pull people into Disney stores. One way it does so is through its movie studio.

Every Disney movie release is preceded by massive advertising, previews in the theater, songs from the soundtrack, and merchandising partnerships with fast-food restaurants and toy stores. Before *Tarzan* opened, millions of dollars had already been spent by consumers on *Tarzan*-related items. Millions of children saw the teasers for *Tarzan* when they saw *A Bug's Life* at the theater or on video. In addition, the Disney Store provides the perfect outlet for Disney merchandise—before, during and after the event.

In addition, Disney treats each customer that walks into the stores or attractions as "guests." Employees are called "cast members" and each door an employee walks through says "stage" on it. This reminds all employees that their role is to delight, help, and entertain.

The Brand Promise Is Delivered at the Sale

Once consumers decide to buy in your category, you must persuade them to choose your brand. The point of sale is critical because that's where the sale is consummated or lost.

Crossing "the final eighteen inches" depends on the sales representative, the point-of-purchase material that is leveraged, the details of why your product or service is better than the rest, the incentives you provide, and the strength of your brand. Whether you are selling long-distance service over the phone or seeking a washing machine decision at Sears, if you do not control that "final eighteen inches" you have lost out—most likely to another strong brand.

Company stores such as Nike Town and Warner Brothers have the advantage of drawing customers only to their brand simply because that's all they carry. Similarly, stores within stores, such as Polo and DKNY within Bloomingdales and Saks, gives those powerful brands an edge in closing a brand-driven sale.

The brand promise is delivered at the sale. The brand contract has been agreed upon and the expectations are set. So if FedEx does not deliver on its overnight delivery promise, or Amazon.com takes a week to deliver books instead of the three days it promised, or there is one rude employee at Nordstrom's, any presale advantage that the brand had goes away. Channel member effectiveness in closing the sale is what separates great brands from others.

Postsale Management: Where a Relationship Is Born

A product or service provider's ability to maintain a relationship with a customer after the sale is becoming increasingly important as retention of and additional sales to current customers is a critical element for those companies who have built strong brands.

Lexus is famous for building relationships after the sale. It provides free loaners when an owner's car is in the shop—which, by the way, will always be an upgraded, brand-new Lexus. Lexus also provides an automated system that connects its dealers across the country so that service done in Chicago can be called up by a dealership in Sacramento. Saturday morning pancakes, follow-up phone calls, reminders of service needs, birthday cards, and the like all help Lexus build a successful relationship with its customers and maximize the potential for total satisfaction, repeat business, and referral business.

Building Your Brand on the Internet

Leveraging the Internet as a channel strategy is becoming more of a norm than an exception. The Web, as discussed earlier, provides a channel of distribution that is yours for the taking. However, your brand has to earn its place on the Web and, importantly, the Web has to be able to support your overall BrandPicture, including your image and contract as well as your positioning. The Internet has to be able to help you build your brand, not detract from it.

From many discussions I have had with successful Web retailers, it appears that there are a few key factors a Web-based retailer has to consider. As you explore the Web's role in your brand strategy, keep these ideas in mind:

- Clearly articulate your goals. Too many Web strategies do not take into account other channel members, which results in a direct threat to existing channels.
- Get channel members involved in your Web design. The worst thing you can do is create a site that will serve as a new channel for your customers without getting the current members of the channel involved.
- Make sure all Internet activities you execute are totally consistent with your non-Web strategies and tactics—colors, names, prices, and the like.
- Make sure using the Web is easy for your customers. Their ability to navigate easily and find the information they want is critical to their having a good experience with your brand.
- Leverage customer insights and competitor websites to most effectively build your website. Build in what customers tell you is most important to them.
- Set the right expectations. Think of your website as an opportunity to gather customer information first and to make a sale second. Companies have never had such an incredible opportunity to gather such relevant and current data before.
- Use the site to build customer relationships. Yahoo! prides itself on being able to serve sixty million users uniquely. Yahoo! also recognizes its unique relationship-building power with its on-line users (the first electronic birthday card a customer receives is usually from Yahoo!).
- Build in a checks-and-balances system that allows you to get feedback from your customers so you can improve your website.

Citigroup recently announced its intention to leverage the Web and stretch its brand name. Its Internet service, called e-Citi, links to Citigroup's retail bank, brokerage, and credit card businesses globally. The challenges for Citigroup are similar to those that many face when deciding to adopt an Internet sales strategy:

- Can Citigroup effectively compete with first-movers, such as E-Trade and Ameritrade?
- Will the Citigroup brand image be maintained?
- Will e-Citi's service be consistent with off-line service levels? Can Citigroup sell e-Citi internally despite it being a direct threat to current channels?
- Can e-Citi make money on the Web? (It has lost over $200 million on it so far.)
- Will e-Citi be able to differentiate itself from the herd of financial players that already are or are about to play in this space (such as Chase Manhattan and Merrill Lynch)?

Those brands not selling on line today are already several years behind those that are. The brands that are on line recognize that the competition and the expectations of customers are changing daily. To stay relevant, the on-line brand has to stay up to date.

Summary

Brand-based channel strategies offer companies a unique opportunity to exert as much control within their channel as possible. Knowing your customer through your BrandPicture and recognizing where the power lies within your channel will help you develop a strong brand-based channel strategy and allow you to control your channel instead of it controlling you.

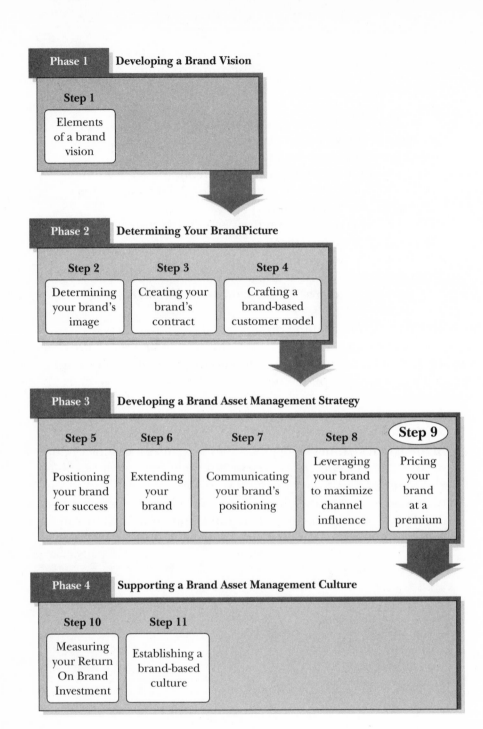

Pricing Your Brand at a Premium

Every step we have taken so far has been guided by the conviction that your brand truly is an asset. Determining the right price for your brand could be the single most important determinant of whether you are getting true asset value from your brand. Brand-Based Pricing is a strategy that ensures you will think of your brand as a lever to help you raise your brand's price point or improve your brand's margins to achieve the goals that the strength of your brand allows.

This is the last chapter in this book describing Brand Asset Management strategies (see the illustration on the facing page). It is positioned last because to fully realize the pricing and margin benefits your brand provides, you have to know the positioning you will adopt for your brand, as well as the innovation, communications, and channels strategies that you plan to execute as part of your overall Brand Asset Management Strategy.

In this chapter I talk about the ways a company can capture and leverage the premium price the brand is receiving relative to the competition. This is the ultimate test of whether you are managing your brand as an asset. Then we will discuss a pricing model that allows you to work your way up to maximizing the price of your branded product or service.

Premium Pricing Reaps the Value and Benefits of Your Brand

If you have leveraged your brand as an asset, you have put yourself in a position to charge a premium price, enjoy higher margins, and reap the other incredible benefits that this asset value provides. Let's look at these benefits.

1. *You can price your brand at a premium price relative to the competition.* The stronger the brand, the greater the potential to charge a premium compared to the price of the closest competitor. Strong brands deserve high prices—they have earned it.

In the first chapter of this book I noted that our most recent customer-based Brand Asset Management study shows that, on average, customers are willing to pay up to a 19 percent price premium for the brand they are most loyal to within a category, regardless of category.

Evian water is a good example because it is the market leader and basically invented the category, and it continues to demand and get fifty cents to a dollar in price premium over its closest competitors—Poland Springs, Aquafina, and Crystal Geyser, even though it is consistently challenged by new entrants such as Coca-Cola's Dasani.

2. *You can launch new products more cheaply than the competition.* Peter Zandan suggests that the stronger the brand, the quicker customers are to buy and try new products. Recall our discussion in Step Six of how a strong brand gives instant credibility and a strong endorsement to any new product launched under its umbrella.

The introduction of iMac in 1998 is a perfect example of this theory. Apple was able to garner quick acceptance and market share as well as hit its margin and payback goals in a relatively short time.

The competition between P&G's Swiffer and Pledge's Grab-It shows the advantage a strong brand has over a new brand, regardless of the dollars invested. P&G spent lots of time and money to create the technology for Swiffer, which is best described as an electrostatic dust mop for hard-to-reach places (such as ceiling fans). P&G put millions of dollars behind the development and launch of this new brand.

In a relatively short time, though, Pledge was able to replicate the technology of Swiffer and leverage its in-house knowledge and its strong brand name to quickly take any advantage away from Swiffer. Grab-It is currently number one in market share, can't be kept on the shelf, and is dropping a nice profit to the bottom line. Swiffer is struggling.

3. *You can recoup development and launch costs sooner.* The stronger your brand is, the more likely consumers are to try a new product endorsed by that brand. The sooner they try it, the sooner you will recoup your development costs and achieve your return on investment (ROI) goal.

When a new product is endorsed by a strong brand, Zandan also found that customers are more willing to put their own reputation on the line, referring new products to others three to six months sooner than they would for other, weaker brands. This lowers the cost of acquiring new customers and, again, allows you to recoup your investment faster.

4. *You can lower your acquisition costs for new customers, which directly affects your bottom line.* Companies like ADT and Brinks have the unique advantage of offering a service (burglar and fire alarm protection) that plays off the emotion of fear. Once customers know they need to buy a burglar and fire alarm system, they usually think only of these two brands. This industry and these brands realize several benefits that many other brands can only hope for.

Ron Davis, chairman of Security Associates—a company that monitors alarm systems for customers of over 3,000 independent alarm systems dealers—claims that local dealers get many of the same benefits and can charge premium prices for expanded services.

5. *Loyal customers continue to pay premium prices for your brand, increasing the profitability per customer.* As discussed earlier, the longer you retain a current customer, the more profitable that customer becomes and the more willingly that customer pays a premium price for your brand. Managers of strong brands recognize that retention tools such as frequent flyer points are inexpensive ways to keep customers loyal, while still charging a premium price.

Who are the pros at leveraging their loyal customer bases to charge premium prices and garner a greater share of profit from loyal customers? I would nominate Sony, Disney, Nordstrom's, Starbucks, FedEx, Xerox, Heineken, Lexus, and The Four Seasons Hotel chain. All of these brands have had the fortune of becoming strong brands with high levels of loyalty, positive customer perceptions, a strong contract and image, and the ability to consistently charge and get a premium price.

6. *Premium pricing allows you to exert greater control over your channel.* A strong brand that is priced at a premium allows channel members to be able to make their cut more readily without eating into your cut. On the other hand, because of the strength of its brand several years ago, Black & Decker was able to muscle several percentage points from the channel and back into Black & Decker's pockets. Channel members basically had two choices: continue to carry Black & Decker products at reduced margins or not carry them at all.

7. *You can more readily seek out cobranding and licensing opportunities that will drop dollars right to the bottom line.* Cobranding and licensing the brand is becoming widespread. Obviously, the challenge is making sure that you do not stretch the brand too far just to reap more dollars. The General Motors example was mentioned earlier. Hallmark's business is in large part driven by license arrangements with brand icons (from Disney to Dilbert).

Starbucks on United Airlines and McDonald's in larger Wal-Mart stores are two other great examples of this.

8. *You can leverage your brand across many target segments to own a category without diluting the value of the brand.* For example, Marriott leverages the benefit of its brand perfectly with its brand portfolio:

Marriott Hotel Brand	Brand Price Point	Target Margin
Marriott Vacation Club—Vacation Villas	Highest	High-end family vacationers
Marriott Marquis	High	High-end prestigious business travelers
Marriott	High-medium	Average business traveler
Residence Inn	Medium-high	Extended business traveler (made to feel more like home)
Courtyard by Marriott	Medium	Business travelers and sales reps looking for good value and local (suburban) convenience
Fairfield Inn	Low	Inexpensive, extended family travel

These hotels are priced and prioritized according to the additional benefits and value a business traveler or vacationer gets. What goes into Marriott's value formula? Attributes and benefits such as quality, service, image, convenience, and amenities.

These eight benefits of leveraging your brand as an asset demonstrate that if managed and executed well, your brand will help you drop dollars to the bottom line. This will occur in one of two ways: by allowing you to charge a premium price or by helping you improve your margins by lowering associated brand costs such as those for customer acquisition.

To reap these benefits, it is important to understand how to reach a premium price point for your brand that the marketplace will accept.

Premium Pricing Is Brand-Based Pricing

Here's a quote that sums up the power of a brand name and the benefits one can enjoy from it:

"An orange . . . is an orange . . . is an orange. Unless, of course, that orange happens to be Sunkist, a name that 80 percent of consumers know and trust." —Russell Hanlin, CEO, Sunkist Growers

Brand-based pricing allows you to leverage the findings from your BrandPicture, integrated with your brand's positioning, to determine the price you will place on the product or service your brand is supporting.

The purest way to think about the advantages a branded product has over a nonbranded product is by looking at a category that has both—a branded product and a few "generic" products. A brand-based price is the premium price the market is willing to pay for the branded product relative to the nonbranded product.

A Coffeehouse Example

Let's think about two neighboring coffeehouses that offer exactly the same South American coffee, medium-roast and brewed, in exactly the same size cup. One coffeehouse is called Jim's and the other is the nationally recognized and popular Sunbucks.

Sunbucks is a well-known, highly respected nationally branded coffee and coffeehouse. In the annual report of the publicly held

Sunbucks, management states its goal that "every Sunbucks experience should be the same—inviting, inspiring, and reliable." Sunbucks does indeed allow its consumers to enjoy the same great Sunbucks taste practically anywhere in the world. It also sells several ancillary products and has recently opened up restaurants.

Jim is well known in the neighborhood and has a sign on his front door that says "best coffee in Chicago."

Let's assume that a total of 500 customers drink coffee every day in this neighborhood—and that number rarely varies much except when Sunbucks is running a big promotion that draws coffee drinkers from other neighborhoods.

Jim charges $1.25 per twelve-ounce cup of coffee to his daily 200 customers. Sunbucks charges $1.75 per twelve-ounce cup to its 300 customers. Thus, Sunbucks enjoys a $.50 premium per cup of coffee over Jim's.

On average, Jim sells $250 worth of coffee per day ($1.25 × 200), and Sunbucks sells $525 worth of coffee per day ($1.75 × 300). Sunbucks thus enjoys a $150 premium every day ($.50 × 300).

In addition, because of its strong brand and national presence, Sunbucks is able to take advantage of certain economies that allow it to earn a 50 percent gross profit per cup of coffee sold. However, a portion of that margin has to go right back into marketing and brand building. So Sunbucks earns a 40 percent net profit margin. Partly because Jim does not have the same buying power as Sunbucks, he is only able to enjoy a 25 percent gross profit per cup of coffee.

This results in Sunbucks enjoying a 27 percent net profit margin premium (40 percent – 25 percent = 15 percent, and 15/40 = 27 percent) over Jim's. Let's also assume that Sunbuck's does enjoy high loyalty because of its strong brand and that Jim has been slowly but surely losing customers.

Sunbucks has been able to achieve a lot as a result of its national brand, reputation, economies, and high degree of loyalty, relative to Jim's coffeehouse: high brand price and profit premiums, greater ability to sell additional products and services, and an ability to afford promotions and potentially buy some of Jim's customers. My guess is that Sunbucks could also take a price increase without really affecting the number of customers it serves.

In sum, Sunbucks is able to enjoy the advantage of charging a premium price for its branded products and all the additional benefits that go along with that strong position.

Scott's Lawn and Garden

Here's another example. If a manufacturer came out with a lawn care fertilizer that helped to retard grass growth so that homeowners would need to mow their lawn once a month instead of weekly, how would the manufacturer value price this product? The company would first figure out how much it costs to mow a typical lawn for a month. For simplicity's sake, let's assume a homeowner spends $15 a week or $60 a month for lawn mowing, every month. Then $44.99 becomes the ceiling price for this fertilizer, because with it a homeowner only has to have the lawn mowed once a month ($60 − $15.01 = $44.99, or a one-cent savings over what is currently being spent).

So the company has a fertilizer that provides incredible value. It knows that the pricing range could be anywhere between $3 (the typical price for a bag of fertilizer) and $45 (the ceiling price identified). Most likely $45 is too high, as a well-derived customer model probably would not support it.

But what if the manufacturer happens to be Scott's? How would that name affect the price? Well, it has just added the following to its already highly valued product:

- Scott's high brand awareness, recognition, and credibility
- Scott's reputation for the highest level of quality within the lawn care market
- The recognition that Scott's has the financial backing to have tested this product multiple times for performance and safety
- Scott's 1–800 number, which will be answered by someone who knows what he or she is talking about
- Scott's wide distribution, so the product is accessible and customers can buy it at a name-brand store, like Home Depot (which will stand behind the products it sells)
- Scott's status as a publicly held company, so this product will be watched by a lot of experts

- Scott's brilliant CEO, Chuck Berger, who is always focused on the customer
- Scott's many ancillary products that customers can use to support their lawn care efforts

Thus, the strong brand name maximizes the price premium. My guess is that Scott's could easily charge and get $15 to $20 for this product.

Pella Brand Supports Price Positioning

Jerry Dow, senior marketing manager at Pella Corporation, says, "Our brand enables us to position our product. While we manufacture a product that is in a very competitive industry, we believe price is a big indicator of whether or not, from a marketplace perspective, we have achieved our positioning.

"Pella has been around for seventy-five years, has established a reputation for a high level of quality and value, and thus can price accordingly. For this to work, though, like everything else in branding, you have to achieve your stated positioning and have the entire organization rally around it and make it come to life."

Brand Loyalty Drives Your Ability to Charge a Premium Price

Look back to the Brand Value Pyramid in Step Two. As you might assume, brands at the very top of the pyramid are given permission to charge and get higher prices. These brands are generally more valued and garner a higher level of loyalty.

Because loyalty and premium pricing are intimately linked, it is important to know what drives brand loyalty. For instance, if you are a brand manager at Nabisco and the brand that a consumer is most loyal to is Fig Newtons, then it behooves you to know what drives this level of loyalty, how you can nurture it, and how you can potentially attract new customers, based on the loyalty of others.

Table 9.1 shows how customers articulate the factors that keep them loyal to brands. Each consumer was allowed to choose three factors as a very important driver of loyalty.

Table 9.1. Brand Loyalty Factors

Loyalty Factors	Consumers (percent) Stating This Factor Is Important to Driving Loyalty
Tier One	
1. Provides high-quality performance	70
2. Performs dependably and consistently	61
Tier Two	
3. Is one I have used for a long time	33
4. Provides me with high value for the price	30
5. Fits my personality	26
6. Effectively solves my problems	26
Tier Three	
7. Delivers truly unique benefits	15
8. Is supported by good customer service	11
9. Is environmentally friendly	5

Interestingly, price ranks fairly low: fourth. This list reveals what a company should focus on to drive brand value and, ultimately, to price the brand at a premium. The list demonstrates that the focus should be not on price or cost but on benefits provided and value received, which translates into brand loyalty. High levels of brand loyalty ultimately allow for premium pricing to occur.

Loyal Consumers Will Pay a Premium

We recently conducted a study of consumer brand loyalty in which we asked consumers to give examples of brands they are most loyal to in a particular category, and the price premium they would be willing to pay for that brand vis-à-vis a competitive brand. A few examples of this relationship between loyalty and price premium are shown in the following list:

Brand Most Loyal To	Premium Consumer Will Pay Relative to Closest Competitor (percent)
Coke	50
Tide	100
Lancome	100
Volvo	40
Heinz	100
Heineken	30
Northwest Airlines	20
Local cleaners	30
American Express	50
Hertz	30
Pampers	50
Hyatt	20
Local Jiffy Lube	25
Honda	20

What does this list suggest?

- Premium pricing opportunities are not bound by categories.
- Products and services are equally open to a premium pricing strategy.
- Loyalty is a strong driver of overall satisfaction and ability to charge a premium.
- A brand has to continue to earn brand loyalty to continue to justify premium pricing.

The House of Pricing

So how do you know what price you can place on your branded product or service? Of course there is no automatic answer, but here is a simple approach I like to use to get started in thinking about the right price to ascribe to a branded product or service. I call it the House of Pricing.

Think of working your way up through the floors of a house as you are working your way up through different price points. You start with the "basement" price, the lowest price you can charge for your branded product or service. Ultimately, you'll climb to the "rooftop" (or highest) price you can charge.

Basement Pricing—The Lowest Price You Should Charge for Your Brand

Basement pricing is very similar to cost-plus pricing in that it is the very lowest price you could or should charge and still make a few dollars. This level of pricing is typically used for commodity products and services or for products or services that are being used as a cash cow to fund other products or services. The two inputs into basement pricing are product or service costs and the minimum amount of profit (translated into dollars) you need to make above cost to satisfy internal hurdles.

First Floor Pricing

First floor pricing brings competitor pricing into the pricing mix. This can work either for you or against you, depending on how the competition is pricing its product or service. This is often a good strategy to adopt when you are entering a market for the first time and competitors have already established some of the pricing ground rules. This input is competitor pricing.

Second Floor Pricing

The second floor is where you can start to realize some premium pricing benefits. It is here that you start to look at a traditional model of value pricing, particularly the degree to which you can offer this product or service exclusively for some period.

Sony's original Walkman and 3Com's original Palm Pilot were both priced at a premium because they were the first to market with a highly valued technology (although you could say that Apple's Newton came before the Palm Pilot). Within second floor pricing, you have great pricing power when you own an exclusive benefit. The two inputs into second floor pricing include value of the benefit you are delivering and exclusivity of the offering.

Top Floor Pricing

Top floor pricing takes us up to the next level, at which you have not only an exclusive offering of the benefit you are providing but also deep marketing and channel dollars behind the benefit. Lucent, for example, is a strong brand with exclusive ownership of certain benefits and incredible marketing and distribution power behind it. The two inputs into top floor pricing include distribution power (owning the channel) and marketing power (the more you can tell the marketplace about your brand, the more likely you are to maximize share potential and desire for your product or service).

Rooftop Pricing

Rooftop pricing takes into account the power of your brand. To take full advantage of rooftop pricing, your overall BrandPicture has to be strong and your brand's positioning has to be powerful, as it was in the preceding example for Scott's fertilizer. The only input for top floor pricing is the added value that your brand brings to the product or service you are offering.

An Example: Windex Outdoor

To demonstrate the House of Pricing, consider Windex Outdoor. The prices used here aren't necessarily the actual prices and values as Windex sees them. The fact that the typical price of a bottle of Windex is priced at $2.99 and that Windex Outdoor is priced between $7.99 and $9.99 helps to set the parameters for this model.

As background, Windex Outdoor leverages the strong brand image and contract associated with the Windex brand and the unmet need homeowners have for finding an easier way to clean the outside of their windows. The actual product is a specially formulated version of Windex in a trigger bottle that attaches to a garden hose and allows for the right concentration of water and Windex to wash twenty-four windows to a "streak-free shine."

Let's assume that it would cost $100 to professionally clean a consumer's outdoor windows annually. Let's also assume the consumer would use Windex Outdoor once a year. From this information, we already know that the price range of Windex Outdoor could potentially be between $2.99 (the price of regular Windex) and $99.99 (the price of professional window cleaning, less a penny).

Basement Pricing = $2.99

The cost of regular Windex is $2.99.

First Floor Pricing = $5.00

There are no competitors for this product except window cleaning services and using a bottle of Windex or Glass Plus on a ladder, with a bucket and a roll of paper towels. Washing your windows this way costs at least $5 for supplies.

Second Floor Pricing = $7.20

The value of this product, above and beyond out-of-pocket costs, has to be tied to the time it would take homeowners to wash the windows themselves, the safety risk involved, and other benefits. This has to be worth at least a 20 percent premium, so we are at $6.

In addition, these benefits will most likely be owned for at least three years, as the patent is most likely protected and no current competitor (such as Glass Plus) could credibly offer a similar product. This should be worth an additional 20 percent premium. We are now at $7.20 for Windex Outdoor.

Top Floor Pricing = $8.40

There will be great distribution and promotion effects as this product touts its own benefits and leverages the strength and heritage of the Windex brand. In addition, consumers can buy Windex Outdoor at food, drug, and mass-market stores instead of just specialty lawn and garden stores. This again has to be worth another 15–20 percent premium.

Rooftop Pricing = $10–11

In measuring the equity of the Windex brand, it is found that loyal consumers would be willing to pay a 20–30 percent premium over the competition's price because of what the Windex brand brings to this product. (I don't know that this is exactly true, so I have taken an average of the price premiums consumers stated they would pay for the brands they are most loyal to earlier.)

However, you have to assume that not everyone is a loyal Windex user; some may be familiar with the brand without having experienced it. In addition, the customer model would probably dictate that there is a mental barrier to charging more than $10 for a product like this. Taking this into account, we should probably subtract a few percentage points. So the final brand-based price for Windex Outdoor is $9.99.

Again, this example is meant only to illustrate how one should think about traveling up through the House of Pricing to arrive at a brand-based price.

Summary

Brand-based pricing challenges traditional approaches to pricing. It allows you to fully enjoy and leverage the power of your brand. The marketplace in general agrees that a strategy like this is not only acceptable but expected.

In addition, the strength of your brand will correlate with the pricing strategy you adopt. This strategy and philosophy should allow you, through the margins you are able to garner, to recognize and enjoy the true asset value of your brand.

Supporting a Brand Asset Management Culture

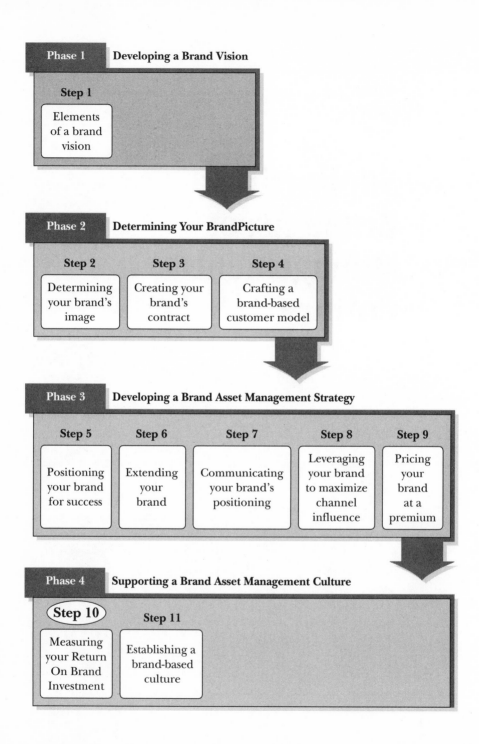

Phase 1 — Developing a Brand Vision

Step 1 — Elements of a brand vision

Phase 2 — Determining Your BrandPicture

Step 2 — Determining your brand's image

Step 3 — Creating your brand's contract

Step 4 — Crafting a brand-based customer model

Phase 3 — Developing a Brand Asset Management Strategy

Step 5 — Positioning your brand for success

Step 6 — Extending your brand

Step 7 — Communicating your brand's positioning

Step 8 — Leveraging your brand to maximize channel influence

Step 9 — Pricing your brand at a premium

Phase 4 — Supporting a Brand Asset Management Culture

Step 10 — Measuring your Return On Brand Investment

Step 11 — Establishing a brand-based culture

Measuring Your Return On Brand Investment (ROBI)

The adage, "What is not measured is not managed," is at the heart of this chapter. Measuring brand performance as the Return On Brand Investment is one of the most complex, yet critically important, aspects of managing your brand successfully (see the illustration on the facing page).

In the past, the only two metrics that seemed to matter were awareness and recall, both created primarily to measure an advertising agency's success. Scoring high on unaided awareness was the ultimate sign that the agency was doing a good job and that more consumers could recognize your brand name. The only problem with this mindset was that recognition and awareness and recall could not be correlated to success for the company—only to success for the agency.

I can still remember calling the head of public relations at a Fortune 100 company several years ago to talk about how successful they are in measuring their brand as an asset. She told me that the company had finally reached the highest level of success, 100 percent awareness and recall scores. What she did not mention was that the stock was down for the fifth straight year and sales were going down simultaneously.

Our recent study, *Brand Asset Management for the 21st Century,* confirmed that there is massive dissatisfaction with how companies are measuring their brand's progress. In fact, only 40 percent of companies currently measure brand value. Of those 40 percent, only half are satisfied with the methods they use. Therefore, more than 80 percent of companies are unhappy with their brand measures.

Over the years, we have created or worked with nineteen different metrics. Every company has different needs, so we kept on creating different metrics. Over time, though, eight metrics in particular consistently helped our clients and we now refer to those as the ROBI Eight—the eight measures of Return On Brand Investment we recommend using. Before we look at the ROBI Eight, let's talk more generally about the benefits of metrics and about the nineteen metrics we have used in the past.

Choosing the Right Metrics for Your Organization

In general, good metrics allow an organization to strategically grow its brand by doing the following:

- Providing an ongoing understanding of how your brand is performing internally and externally
- Starting to provide you with information about returns on investments and beginning to allow for a return on overall marketing and branding strategies
- Helping to sustain organizational focus and consistent communications
- Helping you to allocate resources more effectively in the future
- Providing information that can be used in employees' bonus criteria

David Friedman, vice president of marketing at U.S. Cellular, describes the role of metrics in a similar way: "We ask three questions: How satisfied are you? Would you recommend our product and service to others? Would you repurchase our product or service if you had to start over? We measure all of this and then benchmark ourselves against other companies. We are a services business and have to look and act like the best out there."

Similarly, Anne Greer at 3M puts it this way: "Metrics help us understand what drives loyalty in a particular market, so we can focus on expanding or improving those activities that will strengthen the brand. A loyal customer is a customer who gives the brand a 'top box' rating—or the top score of 'five' on each of three questions." Following are the questions 3M asks:

- Overall, how satisfied are you with (brand)'s products and services?
- The next time you purchase (product category) products, how likely are you to repurchase (brand)'s products and services?
- How likely are you to recommend (brand)'s products and services to friends and associates?

Qualities of a Good Metric

How do you know if a metric is good or not? The simplest answer to that question is whether you can make a business decision based on the information that metric provides. If you cannot, then the metric has provided no more than "nice-to-know" information.

Four additional guidelines help determine whether you have chosen the right metric.

First, a metric has to be *simple to use.* If the data that have to be collected and analyzed are not fairly straightforward, you will find yourself spending more time on the process of measuring the brand than actually using the information the metric provides. No one has ever shown a correlation between metric complexity and metric value.

Second, a metric has to be *consistently accessible.* If you only have the time, dollar, or people resources to activate a particular metric every three years, it probably is not worth investing in. As a rule of thumb, you should consider only metrics that can be measured every six months.

Third, the metric has to be *repeatable* in terms of how you gather the data. If you deviate from the formula or method you used last time you measured *xyz*, you might as well start over. Brand metrics are only useful for comparing apples to apples. For instance, if you are measuring how well the marketplace understands your positioning and you are interested in how you are progressing with that metric, you have to go back and talk to the exact same group of customers again, or to a group of customers of the same profile as before. Otherwise you cannot make an accurate comparison.

Fourth, as mentioned earlier, if a metric does not *help you to take action,* then you probably have found a metric that is what I call a "nice-to-have," not "a need-to-have." For instance, if you discover that your brand is not helping you to keep current customers (and their subsequent loyalty), you have some nice information, but it would be fairly hard to determine what action to take. However, if you find out that you are losing customers because you consistently break your Brand Contract by providing a level of customer service that is too low, then you know you need to make some changes to customer service.

The bottom line is that if you cannot make a business decision as a result of the metric, you should probably move on to another metric.

Nineteen Metrics Worth Considering

A number of metrics should be considered to see which can be of most use to a company. They include the following:

1. *Brand name knowledge, awareness, recognition, recall:* measures strength of the brand as reflected by customer's ability to identify the brand under varying conditions
2. *Positioning understanding:* identifies the level of market understanding of the positioning and selling message, by target market or segment
3. *Contract fulfillment:* measures the degree to which your brand is upholding its Brand Contract
4. *Persona recognition:* measures the degree to which your brand is consistent with its persona
5. *Association laddering:* similar to the persona recognition metric; helps determine if your brand's value is ascending, descending, or staying in place on the Brand Value Pyramid
6. *Acquired customers:* counts customers claiming they have come to your company based on the strength of the brand
7. *Lost customers:* counts customers claiming they have left your brand either to go to a competitive brand or because they no longer participate in the industry you serve
8. *Market share:* looks at the percentage of potential customers (those participating in your category) that are using your brand
9. *Current customer penetration:* estimates the amount of additional products or services you can sell to current customers based on the strength of your brand

10. *Customer loyalty:* measures the degree to which customers continue to purchase your brand and how long that loyalty has lasted

11. *Purchase frequency:* measures the degree to which your brand can help drive the frequency of purchases within your category (for example, Can I get a customer to buy one more candy bar a month than they are today?)

12. *Community impact:* counts the number of positive public relations "hits" your brand gets over a given time

13. *Brand regard:* describes how consumers feel about your brand and talk about it to others

14. *Referral index:* determines the percentage of new business resulting from a customer, influencer, or other stakeholder recommending your brand to a potential new user

15. *Customer satisfaction:* provides a "score" for customers' degree of satisfaction with your brand's product or service performance

16. *Financial value:* reports the financial value of your brand in the marketplace (if it was to be sold to another company)

17. *Price premium:* finds the percentage of price premium your brand is able to command over private-label brands, as well as key competitor brands

18. *Return on advertising:* shows the financial return on advertising expenditures

19. *Lifetime value of a customer:* a metric deserving special discussion, which follows

The lifetime value of a customer is a measure gaining popularity within the branding community. The concept is straightforward but powerful: to quantify the relative worth of a loyal customer. Let's use Coke as an example. The following numbers are hypothetical:

Let's imagine Sara drinks a Coke a day and started drinking Coke when she was fifteen years old. Let's also assume a Coke costs fifty cents. Every year she spends $182 on Coca-Cola. This is a seventy-year habit, so she has spent $12,775 over that time.

In addition, as a parent she has spawned another two Coke drinkers whose lifetime value may be similar, so she is at $37,000. Moreover, Coke has consistently raised its price so that $37,000 is actually $40,000.

The lifetime value of a customer illustrates the importance of keeping customers loyal to your brand and the power they may have in influencing others to become loyal to your brand too. The more accurate the data for this metric, the simpler it becomes to predict future earnings and sales potential.

How Many Is Enough?

Despite the fact that 3M has hundreds of brands and thousands of products, the core of its measurement system is the simple "top box" measure, which is as relevant in its health care markets as in its industrial and consumer markets. U.S. Cellular uses just three metrics. Coca-Cola measures its brands on a global basis, every month, across twenty-four different measures.

I think a reasonable goal for measuring ROBI would not reach Coke's level of depth and sophistication. Try to keep your efforts simple. Focus on leveraging the mix of ROBI measures you believe will be most powerful for guiding your company's progress in Brand Asset Management.

I recommend picking four metrics to start with—two qualitative and two quantitative. Get those metrics right, make them useful to your company, and after a few successful years of measuring those four, add another four to ultimately reach something like the ROBI Eight that I discuss next. Once you get beyond eight metrics, you'll reach a point of diminishing returns.

The ROBI Eight

As mentioned earlier in the chapter, I find eight metrics in particular to be most useful in measuring Brand Asset Management progress. The ROBI Eight (see Table 10.1) are a mix of quantitative and qualitative metrics aimed at helping an organization reach Brand Asset Management success. The ROBI Eight help a company accomplish four things in particular:

- *Stay focused on maintaining and improving upon your BrandPicture.* This is especially important if there is a large gap between your current and desired brand image and brand contract.

Table 10.1. Assessing Brand-Based Value: The ROBI Eight

Qualitative Assessments—Semiannually

Brand Awareness	Brand Positioning Understanding	Brand Image Recognition	Brand Contract Fulfillment
Measures current awareness, understanding, and recall levels tied to your brand name	Measures current awareness of positioning and selling messages to check effectiveness of segment-specific communcations	Measures how the Brand Persona and associations are perceived and where corrections or changes are necessary	Measures the level of customer satisfaction with the performance of the elements of your Brand Contract

Quantitative Assessments—Annually

Brand-Driven Customer Acquisitions	Brand-Driven Customer Retention and Loyalty	Brand-Driven Penetration or Frequency	Financial Brand Value
Measures actual new customers you are attracting or acquiring as a result of your BAM efforts	Measures the number of customers you would have lost if not for your BAM efforts	Measures the number of customers buying more products or services from you as a result of your BAM efforts	Measures the price premium your brand is able to command vis-à-vis the competition multiplied by units sold (for similar variable)

- *Determine the impact your branding efforts have on maintaining and building loyalty with current customers.* Loyal customers are more apt to give you and your brand a higher share of their wallet, recommend you to others, and give you a second chance if the brand does not live up to expectations.
- *Understand how your branding efforts have affected your ability to attract new customers.* Ideally, new customers should turn into loyal customers.
- *Determine whether your positioning is well understood by the marketplace.* Your Brand Asset Management Strategy is driven by your

brand's positioning. If the marketplace does not recognize or understand your positioning, you have most likely under-achieved in your branding efforts. This directly affects the preceding four goals.

Obviously, these goals all have a central aim: determining whether you are using your brand investment dollars wisely and getting the returns you are seeking.

Brand Asset Management's ROBI Eight demands a fundamental understanding and ongoing measurement of the value of the brand as an asset from two perspectives: qualitative perceptions, which are based on market perceptions and purchase behaviors related to your brand, and quantitative perceptions, which are based on the financial and market impact your brand has on future earnings.

Qualitative Metrics

Of the ROBI Eight, the following four metrics are qualitative.

1. *Brand awareness:* This metric provides detailed data regarding the level of awareness, recall, and understanding of your brand. It closely mirrors the traditional recall and awareness measures that advertising agencies use. A mix of aided and unaided responses to this metric will help you best gauge progress along this brand awareness metric.

Two particular areas you want to include in this metric are brand awareness, the percentage of respondents who are aware of the brand name; and brand recall, the percentage of respondents who recall your brand first when asked about the category it competes in.

Although this measure is typically used by advertising agencies to determine the effectiveness of their advertising campaigns, I recommend getting more involved in this measurement to understand more implications of the responses you receive.

2. *Brand positioning understanding:* This metric identifies the level of market understanding of your brand's positioning, so you can see whether your positioning is effective and working.

This measurement should be conducted across a representative sample of your brand's customers and noncustomers to get a good indication of the level of understanding and comprehension they have of your brand's positioning. For example, Nordstrom's wants to know whether its chosen positioning of the highest level of retail service is taking hold. The same is true for FedEx and guaranteed delivery, and for Volvo and safety.

This may be the most important metric of all, as it is a true indication of whether your positioning and related BAM strategies are working. United Airlines decided to pull the plug on its "Rising" campaign, discussed earlier, because the market found this positioning to be counter to what was actually happening with the airline.

Once United adopts a new positioning, it will need to see if this one is taking hold. As we have seen throughout this book, you have to back up your positioning with actions to support the implications of your brand image, contract, and customer model. Thus, it is important to differentiate the positioning metric from the awareness metric. This metric assumes there is already awareness of the brand, but now you want to understand what specifics your consumer is aware of.

3. *Brand image recognition:* This metric helps you understand how well the persona you are projecting is taking hold and to what extent the associated benefits are being realized. If your brand image is something you are aspiring to (meaning you are not there yet), then you have to adjust your expectations of the metrics accordingly.

Brand image recognition is measured across a representative sample of your customers to determine their understanding of your brand's persona versus what you had intended the brand to personify. As discussed in Step Two, here are some typical traits that you may want to see if the marketplace perceives in your brand: dependable, younger, stable, energetic, friendly and warm, knowledgeable, and empathetic.

In addition, within the metric of brand image recognition, you need to better understand the level of benefits a customer ascribes to your brand. Going back to a few of the Brand Value Pyramid examples in Step Two, if your company is John Deere, Saturn, or Ralph Lauren, it is clear what answers you are seeking.

If the persona or associations are much different than what you have defined in your BrandPicture, a few image adjustments probably need to be made.

4. *Brand Contract fulfillment:* This metric helps you determine whether your brand is fulfilling its contract in the marketplace. In other words, is your brand performing on the expectations and promises it has made to its customers?

This metric should give you a straightforward report on how you are performing on every Brand Contract stipulation and promise you and the marketplace see as critical to achieving your Brand Vision. As discussed in Step Three, a good Brand Contract should include both the promises that you are guaranteeing today, as well as those you want to include in your Brand Contract tomorrow.

I like the metric for Brand Contract fulfillment because a strong brand implies a strong level of trust. Sticking to what you promise drives trust, which drives loyalty. A company should treat its Brand Contract as sacred and legally binding.

Quantitative Metrics

The other four of the ROBI Eight tools are quantitative metrics.

5. *Brand-driven customer acquisitions:* This metric counts actual new customers you are attracting or acquiring as a result of your Brand Asset Management efforts.

New customers are measured as the total number of customers buying your product or service today minus the total number from some moment in the past. Win-back customers are measured as the total number of former customers who have come back to your brand or who were not in the database during your last measurement.

This measure resembles typical sales measures, but it is aimed specifically at identifying the number of customers who have bought your brand as a direct result of your Brand Asset Management efforts. The challenge with this metric is your ability to understand why a customer bought your branded product or service, and your ability to specifically link the purchase to your BAM efforts. Giving respondents a number of reasons to choose from will help you gain more specifics about the buying decision.

6. *Brand-driven customer retention and loyalty:* This measures the number of customers you would have lost if you had not activated your Brand Asset Management strategy. This measurement is

aimed purely at understanding the degree of loyalty customers have to your brand.

This is another difficult factor to measure, because it entails asking your customers if they have considered leaving your brand since the last measurement period. A good approach for this metric is to ask customers what other brands they considered purchasing since their last purchase and then why they chose your brand.

Specifically, you want to see which other brands and new brands have entered your current customer's decision set, specifically why the customer did not choose any of the other brands that have surfaced, and why they decided to stick with your brand instead.

7. *Brand-driven penetration or frequency:* This measures the number of existing customers who are buying more products or services from you as a result of your Brand Asset Management efforts. It is determined by looking at current customers who have purchased new products or services that you have offered as an extension of your brand.

In addition, you need to be able to capture new revenues associated with these branded extensions in order to fully understand the level of success and the implications of your extended brand.

This measure will help you answer two critical questions: (1) How extendable is my brand? and (2) How far are my customers willing to go with my brand? Starbucks was able to get into ice cream and protein drinks. Arm & Hammer wasn't able to get into chewing gum successfully. This measure can also help you get closer to being able to place a lifetime dollar value on your customers.

8. *Financial brand value:* This measures the price premium your brand is able to command over competing brands within your category. I suggest you try to determine the premium you are able to receive relative to a private label or commodity version of your branded product or service and two or three of your closest competitors.

Not surprisingly, three-quarters of all respondents to our best practices study claimed they did not place a financial value on their brand. For the 25 percent who did measure value, the most commonly used measurements are net sales and profit, and the lifetime value of the customer.

This metric, used in the Sunbucks example in Step Nine, tells the dollar or percentage value consumers ascribe to your brand vis-à-vis competing brands. A logical next step is to multiply the premium (or percentage) by the number of units you have sold to get an absolute dollar value relative to your competition.

One additional step you can take with this metric is to apply a few assumptions, like category growth, price increases you anticipate, and the number of new customers buying your brand, and project for the next three to five years what premium or value you will receive by more effectively leveraging your brand. This should help you discover whether you are achieving some of the goals of brand-based pricing—to drive revenues, reduce costs, and improve your profits.

This dollar amount ultimately represents the revenues or profits attributable to your brand. This number has many uses, including how it has appreciated since your last measurement period, how it is appreciating compared to your competition's brand value (if you can get comparable competitor data), and most important, whether the asset value of your brand is appreciating over the long term.

Summary

Determining the right brand metrics for you to leverage to gauge how effective your branding efforts have been is critical to your long-term branding success. The focus of measuring your ROBI, and of eventually getting to the ROBI Eight, is to be able to make meaningful decisions as a result of the information you have collected.

If used consistently, ROBI metrics ultimately help you determine whether your Brand Asset Management efforts have been effective.

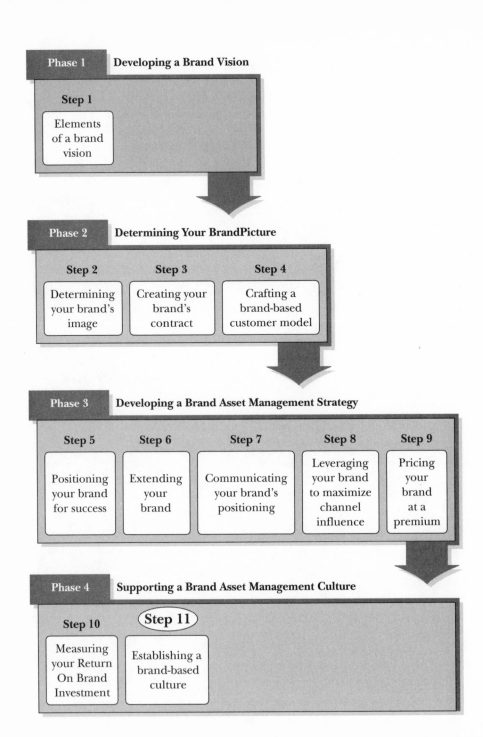

Phase 1   Developing a Brand Vision

Step 1

Elements
of a brand
vision

Phase 2   Determining Your BrandPicture

Step 2

Determining
your brand's
image

Step 3

Creating your
brand's
contract

Step 4

Crafting a
brand-based
customer model

Phase 3   Developing a Brand Asset Management Strategy

Step 5

Positioning
your brand
for success

Step 6

Extending
your
brand

Step 7

Communicating
your brand's
positioning

Step 8

Leveraging
your brand
to maximize
channel
influence

Step 9

Pricing
your
brand
at a
premium

Phase 4   Supporting a Brand Asset Management Culture

Step 10

Measuring
your Return
On Brand
Investment

Step 11

Establishing a
brand-based
culture

Establishing a Brand-Based Culture

One of the best ways a consulting firm can show its value is to have its recommendations implemented. If the final report sits on the shelf, the consulting firm has failed. Similarly, you can develop the best strategy in your industry, one that will help you achieve your Brand Vision and that recognizes and leverages your BrandPicture (see the illustration on the facing page). But without internal, cross-company commitment, your BAM strategy will most likely sit on the shelf and you will retreat to old habits.

This chapter centers on three subjects: (1) creating a brand-based organization, (2) inhibitors and success factors, and (3) the three factors needed to create a brand-based culture: senior management leadership, employee involvement and motivation, and internal communications and education.

The Benefits of a Brand-Based Organization

Take a fresh look at how you are set up internally, how close your culture is to where it needs to be, and what level of human and dollar resources will be put into activating your BAM strategy. These three factors will directly affect your chances of achieving the benefits of BAM. As outlined early in the book, these benefits, once again, include the following:

- Clarity in decisions and their execution
- Greater profits and returns

- Market share gains
- Endorsement for new product introductions
- Ability to charge premium prices
- A lever for attracting the best employees
- A rallying point for current employees
- Customer loyalty, which in turn drives repeat business
- Clear, valued, and sustainable differentiation from the competition
- A more forgiving marketplace when mistakes are made
- Greater shareholder and stakeholder returns
- Company-wide confidence

Each benefit helps companies maximize the power of their brands and reap the results of a brand-based organization. A few additional benefits of the BAM strategy, from an internal perspective, have to do with the effect of a brand-based culture on employee relations:

- It allows each employee to see how they fit into the grander scheme of the organization.
- It helps make career tracks and financial rewards straightforward and clear.
- It confirms that the customer, the employee, and the brand are the things to focus on.
- It provides a statement to the entire organization of senior management's commitment to branding.

If you talk to employees at Microsoft, Hallmark, Coca-Cola, or John Deere, you'll hear a pride that cannot be found in most companies. Pride breeds ownership. Ownership breeds action. Action breeds results. Results breed pride, and the Brand Asset Management circle continues to go around.

Vicky Shire, vice president of marketing at Nicor, believes that her organization gets it. "You need to get the whole organization to live it and it has to be a continuous effort and continuously fed. You need to continue to talk about it and educate others on a regular basis. Internally the momentum has been phenomenal for employees too. It is a feeling you have, a part of the culture. People want to be associated with the brand here. The pride is infectious."

Brad VanAuken, former director of brand management and marketing at Hallmark, says, "The brand is what it is today because of our founder, J. C. Hall, and his marketing vision. Our ability to keep consistent in our message over time has also played an important role. Another key driver of having a strong brand is having a corporate culture that reinforces the brand promise.

"If you ask employees, you may not be able to get them all to articulate exactly what the brand stands for, but they can capture the essence of it in their response. Many, many years ago, someone in the creative department developed a statement that talked about what we do. The basic theme of it was that Hallmark helps people express their feelings and touch others' lives. The last line of it says something to the effect that 'few companies in America can claim such a privilege.' It brings tears to people's eyes almost every time it's read. Everyone in the creative community (as well as many in other areas) has had this on their desk forever."

I am talking about creating a brand-based culture where the word *asset* is not just a buzzword but a word that everyone adopts as their own. Think about that for a moment. If every employee believes that the brand is an asset and should be treated as such, they also believe that part of their role is protecting and building that asset.

The Long-Term Future of Brand-Based Organizations

Brand-based organizations are a logical advance in the evolution of business organizations in the United States. To see this, let's first look at the steps that went before.

The Previous Evolution of Organizations

Since the mid-twentieth century, we have had several different types of organizational constructs in the United States, each having a specific focus and each laying the groundwork for the next organizational shift.

Focus on Economies of Scale

After World War II, organizations focused on economies of scale and maximizing production capabilities, partly to meet the demands of the economic boom after the war. A factory-based, production-oriented structure served organizations well by producing economies that helped achieve the goal of profit maximization.

Focus on Manufacturing Quality

The next era focused on quality in manufacturing. Deming had taught the Japanese all about quality circles and total quality management in the 1950s, and the United States finally started to catch up in the late 1960s and 1970s. Large-scale industrial empires were built following Deming's advice. Certification classes on quality were initiated and the United States started to catch up with the quality management of the rest of the world.

Focus on Creating Demand

The next era was defined as a demand-side and sales era. In the late 1970s to early mid-1980s, the focus was on sales and creating demand. Many companies dictated what they believed the customer wanted and, ultimately, where the customer should go to buy the product or service they wanted. In this company-centric era, organizations focused on what was best for the organization but not necessarily for the customer.

Focus on Mergers and Acquisitions

The next era was the merger and acquisition period of the late 1980s. Companies focused on buying market share (generally at very high multiples) and on reinventing themselves after the acquisition. New entities were built, organizations integrated at a rapid pace, and a new generation of conglomerates were formed, like RJR Nabisco.

Focus on Reengineering

Many of the companies that had completed a merger or acquisition were left with duplication and excesses. They were in need of consolidation and better integration, which led to the creation of reengineering in the late 1980s and early 1990s. Reengineering aimed to rework companies that were fat, unprofitable, and operating suboptimally. This helped result in companies that were meaner and leaner, yet still not true fighting machines.

Focus on the Customer and Company Growth

It makes sense that the next major organizational trend got back to focusing on the customer. Customer-centric organizations were formed around what customers wanted and how they wanted to receive the product or service. This helped drive our current shift to a focus on growth and stock price appreciation. The primary modes of this growth are again mergers and acquisitions (except this time they are done with consolidation in mind from the outset), innovation, and managing the brand more smartly. Additionally, the minor revolution called e-commerce has helped fuel this growth and may ultimately lead to another shift.

Why a Brand-Based Organization Is the Next Logical Step

This leads us to the brand-based organization, which takes the customer-driven organization a step further. It demands seeing customers in terms of how they think about brands.

When a customer thinks about making a purchase in a category (whether it is long-distance service or toothpaste), usually a few brands come to mind as part of that customer's purchase set. In the future, companies who focus on getting a customer to think about their brand first, once the decision has been made to make a purchase in that category, will be successful. Recognizing that a brand, rather than the product or service, drives sales should motivate companies to organize around the brand.

For instance, the washing machine industry, which includes Maytag, Whirlpool, General Electric, and a few others, does not drive sales. If they did, customers would be drawn to buy a washing machine just because these companies tell them to, regardless of whether they needed a new washing machine.

Instead, the right approach is to get the customer to think of your brand first, once they have decided to make a purchase in the category you compete in. Many industries are already set up this way, with automotive being the one that probably leverages this model best.

Barriers to Implementing a Brand-Based Organization

Why haven't more companies recognized the importance of organizing around the brand? Several factors, in particular, hinder an organization's ability to adopt this type of mindset. Let's look at these inhibitors in more detail.

Few companies have set up brand-based career tracks, so managers continue to think in terms of short-term brand decisions that get short-term results to show their value to the rest of the organization. Pressure to report on performance every quarter reinforces the tendency to make short-term decisions that may result in near-term successes; unfortunately, these may come at the expense of long-term brand value. Also, few companies have the word "brand" in their employees' bonus criteria, formulas for base salary increases, or promotion criteria.

Many companies think that promoting their managers from one brand onto another is positive for both the employee and the company. They see exposing managers to more brands as increasing the value of the managers to the company. Unfortunately, the day a manager moves to another brand is the day that person's brand-specific knowledge is lost.

At the top of many organizations is someone with finance or operational experience but little marketing or branding experience, so the value of the brand is underappreciated.

Global organizations often have different managers in different regions around the world running the brands. This can easily lead to inconsistent global brand management. Few organizations have high-level, cross-functional task forces or committees responsible for the brand.

Many organizations look at awareness and recall as the only measures for branding success. If this is the case, it seems logical to house all branding efforts in the marketing and communications departments, or even to view branding as the advertising agency's responsibility.

Traditional brand management thinking can push responsibility for the brand down to the most junior members of the marketing team, as the organization chart in Figure 11.1 shows. Such a branding organization is best described as a hierarchy:

The senior vice president of marketing sees the whole picture, is responsible for the one- and three-year brand plans, has to make the tough budget trade-offs, and reports directly to the president or CEO along with five to ten other senior vice presidents.

⬇

Figure 11.1. Typical Brand Management Structure

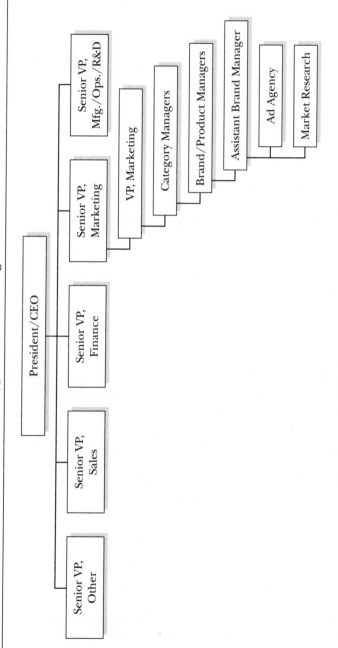

The vice-president of marketing has a high-level perspective on what the company is trying to accomplish with its brands.

↓

The category manager is responsible for making sure the annual plan is being executed and all brands in the category are coordinated. If there are not other brands, this title might be divisional manager. This manager has decision-making authority and is the person accountable for reaching goals and objectives.

↓

The brand manager is in charge of day-to-day operations and coordination of the brand. Brand managers work closely with the sales and distribution departments to make sure promotions are being implemented and deliveries are on time.

↓

The assistant brand manager is in charge of getting all the data collected and the statistics in place to help make decisions at a higher level.

This organizational construct pushes brand responsibilities down the organization so that the person who should have the most accountability for the brand has the least.

The New BAM Construct Puts Responsibility at the Top

A new style of organization, from basic structure to cross-functional teams, can help the company change to a brand-based organization.

New Organizational Norms

A brand-based organization demands that the brand report directly to the top of an organization (see Figure 11.2). It strives to find efficiencies across branding efforts. It puts career tracks in place that result in an employee striving to become, for instance, vice president of Tide or vice president of Courtyard By Marriott.

Figure 11.2. Strategic BAM Organization

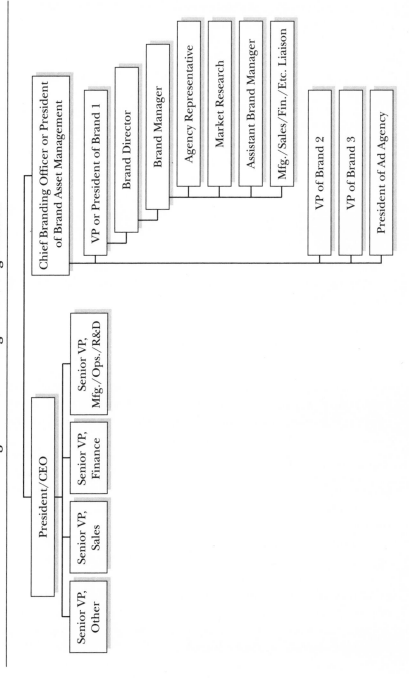

This type of organizational structure will create controversy. How can an organization have someone in charge of the brand so high up? Is this person as high up as a COO? Another way to look at this is that the COO, president, or CEO runs the cost side of the business while the chief branding officer (CBO) runs the revenue side of the business.

A brand-based organization resolves the question of whether the brand should be siloed within marketing or be a cross-functional activity. It also dictates that senior executives have bonus and stock options determined, in part, by the performance of the brand.

This structure allows your organization to send a clear message to stakeholders and shareholders. The message is that you are serious about branding and it is not just the theme for the first few years of the millennium. In fact, this business approach will allow your organization to always make sure that the customer and the brand come first.

As Brad VanAuken, the former Hallmark executive, says, "This is not just about marketing, but about creating a culture that reinforces your brand promise. All of a company's processes, functions, and resources have to reinforce that promise. To work, it has to start at the top."

In order for this belief to take hold within an organization, senior managers have to become both brand ambassadors and brand czars. At the highest levels, management has to believe first of all in the power of the brand and second that brand has to be managed across the organization.

Without having brand accountability at the top of an organization, decisions will likely be suboptimized. In addition, if you believe that the brand is one of the primary mechanisms to fill the growth gap, it makes sense that the brand organization reports to the top.

Look at what happened at 3M. Anne Greer describes it this way: "Our CEO has sponsored Brand Asset Management for almost two years. A corporate-level committee has the responsibility for increasing the asset value of our brands and ensuring the health of our brand portfolio. The committee, chaired by the VP of corporate marketing, is a cross-functional group consisting of executives representing business units, the senior vice president of R&D, and senior staff experts in trademark law and brand strategy.

"One of the reasons our brands—such as Scotch and Post-it—have been so successful over the years has been because of the consistent executive support. When I worked with the Scotch brand in the 1970s, the veterans of the business made sure the newcomers understood the brand. These leaders invested in the brand, monitored the health of the brand, and made sure their organizations were equipped to deliver the brand promise.

"So the new Brand Asset Management is really based on 3M's heritage, infused with new techniques and designed to make brand management even more effective in the future."

New Organizational Entities

Companies may consider erecting a few new BAM entities to further promote the mindset that the brand is critical to long-term success and that the brand has to be supported at the top. Here are some good new possibilities:

- *Chief branding officer (CBO):* As mentioned earlier, this person has the ultimate responsibility for the performance of the brand and its accompanying strategy. In a perfect world, there would be a CBO for every major brand in the organization. Where a CBO exists, that person would head up the BAM steering committee. The CBO would also have to make sure that brand decisions are made consistently, around the world.
- *BAM steering committee:* This includes senior-level executives, cutting across functional areas. The committee's main objective is to help establish linkages between all functional strategies and the BAM strategy. The CEO has to be the head of this committee unless there is a CBO.
- *BAM director's committee:* This group of middle- to senior-level managers would be responsible for making sure the BAM strategy is executed. This group too would be cross-functional, and to succeed, it would need a connecting person (possibly the CBO) from the BAM steering committee helping to direct this committee. This group is focused on action, whereas the steering committee is more focused on strategy.
- *BAM teams* (see Figure 11.3): These would be the day-to-day personnel within the organization that make sure the business

is running in a brand-based way. Again, these teams are cross-functional, and they have a connecting person from the director's committee. Each circle in Figure 11.3 outside the core team represents a team that oversees one or more brands.

- *BAM outside advisory council:* This group would be BAM practitioners and strategists from outside industries, who can share lessons learned and successes with the branding teams. It would be wise to have this council share their experiences with both the steering committee and the director's committee.

Motivating Employees in a Brand-Based Organization

Organizations that have succeeded in building a brand-based culture have a few common traits. They have strong motivation and

Figure 11.3. Example of BAM Team Structure

reward systems to keep managers motivated to make the best BAM decisions possible. They have longer-term career tracks that motivate employees to want to stick with the brand in the long term. Also, they have demonstrated the commitment of senior management to BAM.

Motivators and Rewards

Employees respond to the things that motivate them the most—usually career promotions, stock options, and the like (see Figure 11.4). Unfortunately, most companies do not have brand-oriented career tracks in place. In our best practices survey, 72 percent of respondents said their organization does not have such a career track.

By setting up brand career tracks that focus on the consistency and longevity of the manager's relationship with the brand, a company can maximize the long-term quality of its Brand Asset

Figure 11.4. Motivating Employees: Survey Results

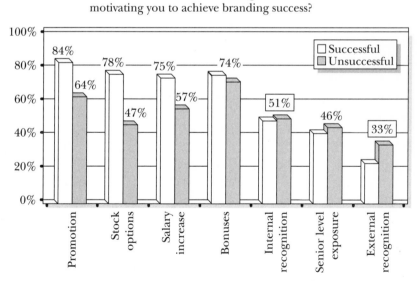

How effective* are the following rewards in motivating you to achieve branding success?

* Effective = % of respondents
  rating a 4 or 5 out of 5

Management efforts. Smaller companies that have only one or two brands in their stable may provide a good brand-based organizational model for larger companies.

For instance, Dad's Dog Food needs to focus on promoting only its Dad's brand name and its Kibble Select brand name. This tends to promote a model for managing the brand effectively and for the long term.

Apart from career tracks, the best motivation system may be the right combination of individual and firmwide bonus structures tied to the success of the brand. Each employee's annual goals should be tied to that individual's contribution to brand-related efforts, and the organization as a whole should have brand-based rewards that everyone gets to participate in. This way, both the individual and the entire organization are responsible for the brand's success.

Jay Luttrell, director of product research and development at Citigroup, says, "It is critical to link rewards to the metrics you want and vice versa. You need to make both very clear, with little room for interpretation."

Recruitment for BAM Success

Once you have decided to adopt a BAM strategy and rally your organization around that strategy, it should become apparent what type of professionals you would want to have going forward within your organization. The key to successful recruiting for a brand-based organization is to hire new employees and managers who already embrace ideas and qualities consistent with managing the brand like an asset.

The focus should not just be on hiring the best marketing people you can find, because this is not just about marketing. You need to hire the best brand-oriented individuals across all functional areas. Rather than focusing only on the functional experience of candidates, consider their personal attributes.

The people you want will tend to be entrepreneurial and goal-oriented, good motivators and good team players. Customer orientation is a must, and brand experience and understanding are desirable. New hires should be willing to let a portion of their salary be variable, not guaranteed, if it offers a potentially higher total compensation than they would get in similar jobs.

Jean Leon Bouchenoire, brand equity director at Compaq Corporation, says, "We have a 'can do' group of people with a 'can do' attitude, and therefore nothing is impossible. We also have some of the best minds in the business to do it. By having a top brand, and being a top tier company, we can recruit the best."

The Critical Role of Internal Communications and Education

Without effective internal communications and education about what your brand strategy is, how each and every employee within the organization can carry out that strategy, and what the benefits of Brand Asset Management are, your chances for success are minimal at best. The reason for this is simple—without employee buy-in and real behavioral changes, you will have minimized your ability to control your BAM strategy. Unfortunately, most companies do not believe their employee communications and education are very effective.

Successfully implementing a Brand Asset Management strategy cannot be viewed, as one senior executive put it, "like our corporate values [project]. We did the project, reported the results, put up banners around the lunchroom, put the values on the back of our business cards, and then it was back to business as usual. To succeed, we have to be talking about changing behaviors, not just changing communications. We have to be talking about the top priority of the organization, not just one of ten initiatives the company is focused on."

The ultimate goal of internal brand-based education and communications is to start to put the pieces in place for creating a Brand Asset Management culture, one in which the vision is well understood, the BrandPicture is upheld, the positioning is embraced, and the brand-based strategies are implemented. Ultimately, you want your employees not only to want to help you build the strategy, but to drive it, protect it, and own it.

Three Examples of Effective Internal Communications

Hallmark, 3M, and Nicor offer three tales of success in using internal communications to promote a brand-based culture.

Hallmark

Hallmark is managed in a very brand-based way. It has a select group of internal managers who are totally focused on brand training and education. The purpose of the training is to make sure that Hallmark's brand promises are clear and specific, and to provide brand dos and don'ts that every employee can easily follow.

Hallmark has regular internal brand training; an in-depth, brand-based intranet site; internal publications; and a speaker series where outside brand practitioners come and speak about branding efforts within their organization (such as Disney and Starbucks). The company even places daily brand promise reminders on the start-up screens of employees' computers.

What is also impressive about Hallmark's brand-based culture is that it consistently focuses on conducting internal assessments of employees' perceptions of the brand with the intent of focusing on gaps between internal perceptions and marketplace perceptions. By conducting this type of assessment, Hallmark is better able to determine the specific brand-related areas of training and education that are needed to increase success.

3M

Anne Greer at 3M likes to call 3M's brand training and education "The Seven Steps to Mobilizing Employees and Maximizing Your Branding Efforts." These seven steps are

1. Secure management leadership, commitment, and sponsorship.
2. Create cross-functional teams; without them you cannot be assured that the brand promise will be fulfilled.
3. Facilitate ongoing learning and education across the company.
4. Involve a cross-functional team in strategy development. Getting employees to help develop the strategy improves the likelihood the strategy will succeed.
5. Be specific about functional area members' roles and expectations relative to achieving brand success.
6. Ensure that all internal systems are aligned. If you make changes, make sure your internal infrastructure and systems support those changes.

7. Measure consistently. Set up a few metrics and consistently measure them. Make improvements based on them.

Greer says, "Successful delivery of a brand promise depends on virtually every employee—from the executive who runs the business, to the scientist who refreshes a brand through product innovation, to sales representatives and other 'front-line' people.

"In order to ensure this level of involvement, 3M relies on a variety of educational approaches. For instance, we have a series of one-hour interactive training modules that teach a business team the key concepts in segmentation, brand promise, customer relationship management, and measurement. The idea is to learn the concepts, then apply them immediately to business."

Nicor

Similarly, Harriet Gold at Nicor talks about her five-pronged attack to enhance brand-based communications and get employees to be part of the strategy success:

1. Hold focus groups with frontline employees.
2. Create cross-functional teams to address customer issues.
3. Hold company-wide events for employees.
4. Redesign all internal communications.
5. Sponsor a company-wide education program.

Vicky Shire, vice president of marketing at Nicor, says, "My department has to be the first and best source of information for our employees. The key is figuring out how to get this information to employees quickly and in a manner they can understand and apply. For instance, one strategy may be to provide information to a supervisor and have them be responsible for sharing that information with their people. We also have a corporate publication and a weekly publication that includes recognition for brand-building employees.

"In addition, we always publish our TV schedule for commercials as well as customer letters that have singled out an employee for providing that unconditional customer service we talk about. We have asked our employees, before they hang up the phone or leave a job site, to ask customers if there is anything else they can do for them. One older woman asked a meter-reader if he could take the garbage out to the street—and he did it, with a smile. We believe it is the little things that make a difference to our customers, as much as it is the bigger things, and we always try to keep our employees thinking as if they are in the mind of our customer."

The Cross-Functional Approach

Hallmark, 3M, and Nicor all use cross-functional team representation as a key driver of BAM success, and one effect is a faster spread of communications throughout the company. Successful Brand Asset Management in each company involves all functional areas starting with phase one. Each company relies on the help of a dedicated cross-functional team to craft the Brand Vision, develop the BrandPicture, and determine the right brand positioning and strategies for success.

These cross-functional teams ultimately help do the work, set the strategy, and champion the BAM implementation and training efforts internally. In addition, the teams serve as strong communication links back to their functional areas. A good cross section of functional members plays several roles on a Brand Asset Management team, including

- Providing tremendous insight into the project from a company perspective, as well as from the functional area they represent
- Getting input from key players in their functional area as needed
- Keeping their functional area up to date on the progress of the project
- Leading the communications and education efforts that need to take place to successfully get full company buy-in, participation, and ownership

Four Tools to Effectively Communicate Internally

Four tools, in particular, have been used effectively to help employees understand the goals and objectives of a BAM strategy and the roles they can play.

1. *Have employees relive the project and the research you have conducted.* The goal here is for employees to fully understand how you arrived at the Brand Vision, Brand Persona, Brand Contract, and so on. You may want to take them back to the original objectives of the project, the desired outcomes, the process that was used, findings from the process, and most important, the final conclusions and recommendations.

In developing a Brand Asset Management strategy with the largest hearing aid manufacturer in the world, Beltone, we decided the best way to reach employees was to tell the project story and have employees relive parts of the project, as much as possible. Viewing customer research was at the top of the list.

Our team proceeded to go through more than thirty hours of focus groups, trying to find representative comments from current Beltone users, current competitor users, and nonusers who were expected to buy a hearing aid within the next two years. Ultimately, we wanted to have employees feel like they were with us at the focus groups. Our team felt we could present reports until we were blue in the face, but that showing a video compilation of representative comments from users and nonusers of Beltone products would have the biggest impact on Beltone employees.

2. *Make sure employees understand the end results you are seeking.* Too often management neglects to communicate the desired end results to employees, many of whom are responsible for implementing the agreed-upon goals and objectives.

Without the end goal in sight, it becomes very difficult for employees to see how they fit into the bigger picture and why they should care. The key here is to bring the goals and objectives down to a level that is important to employees: how it may affect their functional area and what they have to do next.

3. *Make sure employees understand what specific actions to take.* Employees need to hear specifics as to what is now expected of them. They need to hear how their day-to-day activities will change, why they will change, and how they will be evaluated as a result. Because what is not measured is not managed, employees do need to hear specific actions and standards that they will now have to abide by.

For instance, if you are a service company, the brand contract may translate into several tangible actions employees need to embrace and activate. For example, a brand contract may dictate any of the following:

- Customer service should pick up the phone on the first ring.
- Customer service should be given authority to solve problems online.
- Billing should develop different payment options that are tailored to customer needs and wants.
- Sales representatives should be renamed relationship managers and some of their bonus criteria should change along with that.
- New product development should not be a marketing function only but a cross-company function.

4. *Give employees the game plan for the rollout of your BAM strategy.* Not only do employees need to know what changes will be made and why, but they also need to know how long they will have to prepare and train for the changes. They need to know when their performance will start to be measured and the specific targets they should be trying to reach. Without making this tangible and real for your employees, do not expect real results.

Ways to Communicate

There are several approaches to communicating your new Brand Asset Management strategy to employees. Without question, there is no better way to communicate than in person and from the top of the organization.

For example, senior management at Nicor held a brand kickoff, a weekend evening tent party for all employees and their spouses and significant others. The CEO stood in front of a couple of thousand people touting the rationale for branding the company and what was behind the new positioning—"unconditional personal service to each and every customer." The fact that the full BAM strategy was unveiled, the new commercials were run, the new logo was shown, and family was included made it a special event that provided momentum for the conversion to a Brand Asset Management organization.

Some of the best demonstrations by senior management of their commitment to branding are these:

- A culture that supports branding
- The CEO's vocal support of the branding
- The company's focus on product development, research, and marketing
- Including brand managers in key meetings
- Continued increases in brand investment
- Including brand performance as part of performance evaluations

Set Up an Internal Communications Plan

Once the big "show" is executed, the challenge becomes having the organization get ready for the external launch. The best way to think about such a complex project is to use a format that outlines for each internal target audience what the goals and objectives are, what the timing is, who is responsible for what, and how much it may cost to have this executed and how success will be measured.

For one internal constituency it may look like this:

Target audience	Customer service representatives
Communications vehicles	Senior management roundtable, follow-up meetings, and company newsletter
Objectives	Educate, inform, and discuss operational changes
Frequency	Weekly meetings until fully implemented; monthly meetings thereafter
Responsibility	Senior vice president of sales and marketing
Accountability	Employees will be measured on a monthly basis to start
Costs	$1,500 to train each employee and $100,000 to update call center capabilities

In theory, you should have an internal communications plan like this for every functional area within the organization. These functional communication plans should all bubble up into a master internal communications plan that is owned at the very top of the organization.

Determine the Best Internal Communications Vehicles to Leverage

Many effective communications vehicles are available internally. A few of these have already been mentioned, so I will give just a short description of each and a few comments on how effective they are.

A company's intranet site is a great place to communicate immediately with employees. Companies such as Digital Lava, headquartered in southern California, now offer software that allows you to conduct interactive training through your intranet system.

Internal newsletters are fine except that they are a one-way communication rather than a dialogue, may be too infrequent, and often allow misinterpretation. Annual reports are another tool for articulating the power of the brand. Daily reminders like screen savers, start-up screens, and stationery are also worthwhile investments.

BAM training is critical to long-term success. The key to successful training is to tailor it to each audience's specific needs and to do it frequently enough that employees recognize that this is the new norm. Remember to walk the talk: the most effective training tool is seeing others embrace the BAM concept through words and actions.

Roundtables help you get continuous feedback from employees on their progress and garner suggestions for BAM improvements.

Making a few outside hires may be viewed as threatening by some employees, but others will see it as refreshing. The key here is for these new employees to leverage their experiences within the context of your internal culture and environment.

Summary

The most critical element in creating a strong BAM culture is consistency. If the change is a big deal for the first six months and then gradually loses senior management attention, employees will be quick to pick up on this.

Senior management has to take the lead in this area. Communications need to be frequent and consistent. These should include continual reminders of why BAM is important, how the company is or is not improving, and how each employee is making a difference.

In the end, the most important element of Brand Asset Management within your organization is your employees. Without their belief, guidance, ownership, and participation, you might as well put your brand investment dollars in treasury bills. However, with their involvement and support, there is no telling the limits of BAM success.

Brand Asset Management is about shifting mindsets and shifting practices. I do believe that companies that follow a methodical and strategically focused system will ultimately discover that their brand has been massively underleveraged. Managed correctly, however, your brand can be the lead driver for every major revenue- and profit-generating strategy your company undertakes.

Good luck with your future Brand Asset Management efforts!

About the Author

Scott M. Davis is managing partner at the Chicago office of Prophet Brand Strategy. His focus is on helping companies—both brick and mortar, and digital—maximize the strategic potential and asset value of their brands.

His previous work experience includes twelve years with Kucz-marski & Associates—a Chicago-based innovation and branding consulting company, where he was a senior partner and architect of the Brand Asset Management approach described in this book. Prior to that, Davis worked at Procter & Gamble, where he focused on a number of top global brands.

Davis has worked with a diverse client base in a broad array of industries. His project experience includes customer-focused inno-vation and Brand Asset Management strategies for some of the world's top brands. Most recently, he led cross-organization Brand Asset Management projects for a Fortune 500 energy services com-pany, a $5 billion consumer packaged goods company, and one of the leading media organizations in the nation. Each project resulted in a comprehensive, integrated brand strategy that brought about increased awareness, market share, and overall cus-tomer satisfaction.

Davis is an experienced speaker, who has spoken at and chaired a wide variety of top-tier branding and marketing confer-ences and seminars, both nationally and internationally, including ones organized by the American Marketing Association, the Amer-ican Management Association, the Institute for International Research, the Conference Board, the Product Development Man-agement Association, the AQPC, and the IQPC.

In addition, Davis is an adjunct professor at the J. L. Kellogg Graduate School of Management at Northwestern University, where he teaches a class on Brand Asset Management. He is a featured speaker on new products at the J. L. Kellogg's Allen Center, and at the University of Chicago's executive program on marketing services companies. Also, he has guest-lectured at many top-tier graduate school programs throughout the country. In conjunction with the American Management Association, Davis created the curriculum for a three-day corporate branding workshop that has been running several times a year throughout the country since 1998.

A contributing writer for *Brandweek,* Davis has published articles in numerous well-respected marketing publications, including *The Journal of Consumer Marketing, The Journal of Product and Brand Management, Marketing News, Management Review,* and *New Product News.* Also, he has been cited in the *Wall Street Journal, Fortune, USA Today, Business Week, and Crain's.*

He earned a master's degree in marketing, finance, and management strategy from the J. L. Kellogg Graduate School of Management at Northwestern University, and a bachelor's degree in marketing management from the University of Illinois.

Davis resides in Glencoe, Illinois, a suburb of Chicago, with his wife, three children, and their golden retriever. He has traveled around the world several times, is a sports enthusiast, and will argue with anyone that the Chicago Cubs will reach the World Series at some point during his lifetime.

Index